What readers are saying about
Practical Vim

I've learned more about Vim by reading this book than I have from any other resource.

➤ **Robert Evans**
  Software Engineer, Code Wranglers

After reading a couple of chapters of *Practical Vim*, I realized how little I knew. From intermediate to beginner in thirty minutes!

➤ **Henrik Nyh**
  Software Engineer

Practical Vim continues to change what I believe a text editor can do.

➤ **John P. Daigle**
  Developer, ThoughtWorks, Inc.

Drew has continued the wonderful work he has done with Vimcasts in this book, a must-read for anyone serious about Vim.

➤ **Anders Janmyr**
  Developer, Jayway

Practical Vim bridges the gap between the official documentation and how to really use Vim. After reading a few chapters, I switched to using Vim as my default editor. I've never looked back.

➤ **Javier Collado**
  QA Automation Engineer, Canonical Ltd.

Drew Neil does more than show the right tool for the job. He paces the narrative, laying out the philosophy behind each decision. Instead of expecting you to memorize everything, *Practical Vim* teaches you to think with Vim under your fingertips.

➤ **Mislav Marohnic**
  Consultant

I've been using Vim for server maintenance for more than fifteen years now, but I've only recently started using it for software development. I thought I knew Vim, but *Practical Vim* has massively improved my code-wrangling productivity.

➤ **Graeme Mathieson**
  Software Engineer, Rubaidh Ltd.

Practical Vim made me realize how much there is still to learn about Vim. Every single tip can be easily and immediately applied to your workflow and will improve your productivity manifold.

➤ **Mathias Meyer**
  Author, *Riak Handbook*

Practical Vim is the ultimate treasure chest when it comes to Vim knowledge. I've used Vim daily for over two years now, and this book has been nothing short of a revelation for me.

➤ **Felix Geisendörfer**
  Cofounder, Transloadit

Practical Vim, Second Edition

Edit Text at the Speed of Thought

Drew Neil

The Pragmatic Bookshelf

Dallas, Texas • Raleigh, North Carolina

Many of the designations used by manufacturers and sellers to distinguish their products are claimed as trademarks. Where those designations appear in this book, and The Pragmatic Programmers, LLC was aware of a trademark claim, the designations have been printed in initial capital letters or in all capitals. The Pragmatic Starter Kit, The Pragmatic Programmer, Pragmatic Programming, Pragmatic Bookshelf, PragProg and the linking *g* device are trademarks of The Pragmatic Programmers, LLC.

Every precaution was taken in the preparation of this book. However, the publisher assumes no responsibility for errors or omissions, or for damages that may result from the use of information (including program listings) contained herein.

Our Pragmatic courses, workshops, and other products can help you and your team create better software and have more fun. For more information, as well as the latest Pragmatic titles, please visit us at *https://pragprog.com*.

The team that produced this book includes:

Katharine Dvorak (editor)
Potomac Indexing, LLC (index)
Cathleen Small (copyedit)
Dave Thomas (layout)
Janet Furlow (producer)
Ellie Callahan (support)

For international rights, please contact *rights@pragprog.com*.

Printed in the United States of America.
ISBN-13: 978-1-68050-127-8
Printed on acid-free paper.
Book version: P1.0—October 2015

Contents

Part II — Files

Part V — Patterns

Acknowledgments

Thanks to Bram Moolenaar for creating Vim and to all those who have contributed to its development. It's a timeless piece of software, and I look forward to growing with it.

Thanks to everyone at the Pragmatic Bookshelf for working together to make this book the best that it could be. Special thanks to Kay Keppler, my developmental editor, for coaching me as a writer and for helping to shape this book, despite its growing pains and my occasional tantrums. Thanks also to Katharine Dvorak, my development editor for this revised edition. I'd also like to thank David Kelly for his adept handling of my unusual formatting requests.

Practical Vim didn't start out as a recipe book, but Susannah Pfalzer recognized that it would work best in this format. It was painful to have to rewrite so much, but in doing so I produced a draft that I was happy with for the first time. Susannah knows what's best, and I thank her for sharing that insight.

Thanks to Dave Thomas and Andy Hunt for creating the Pragmatic Bookshelf. I wouldn't want to be represented by any other publisher, and I'm honored to be listed alongside the other titles in their catalog.

Practical Vim wouldn't have been possible without my technical reviewers. Each of you contributed something and helped to shape the book. I'd like to thank Adam McCrea, Alan Gardner, Alex Kahn, Ali Alwasity, Anders Janmyr, Andrew Donaldson, Angus Neil, Charlie Tanksley, Ches Martin, Daniel Bretoi, David Morris, Denis Gorin, Elyézer Mendes Rezende, Erik St. Martin, Federico Galassi, Felix Geisendörfer, Florian Vallen, Graeme Mathieson, Hans Hasselberg, Henrik Nyh, Javier Collado, Jeff Holland, Josh Sullivan, Joshua Flanagan, Kana Natsuno, Kent Frazier, Luis Merino, Mathias Meyer, Matt Southerden, Mislav Marohnic, Mitch Guthrie, Morgan Prior, Paul Barry, Peter Aronoff, Peter Rihn, Philip Roberts, Robert Evans, Ryan Stenhouse, Steven! Ragnarök, Tibor Simic, Tim Chase, Tim Pope, Tim Tyrrell, and Tobias Sailer.

Even with all of the feedback from my technical reviewers, some mistakes managed to stay hidden. I'd like to thank everyone who has reported errors in the book, helping me to locate and fix them.

Vim's built-in documentation is a terrific resource, and I make many references to it throughout *Practical Vim*. I'd like to thank Carlo Teubner for publishing Vim's documentation online at vimhelp.appspot.com and for keeping it up to date.

Some of the tips in the first edition of *Practical Vim* were awkward, but I included them anyway because I felt that they were important. For this revised edition, I'm pleased to have been able to rewrite those awkward tips. Thanks to Christian Brabandt for implementing the game-changing gn command, which allowed me to rewrite Tip 84, *Operate on a Complete Search Match*, on page 208. Thanks to Yeggapan Lakshmanan for implementing the cfdo command (and family), which allowed me to rewrite Tip 97, *Find and Replace Across Multiple Files*, on page 236. I'd also like to thank David Bürgin for patch 7.3.850, which fixed my pet bug with the vimgrep command.

As a whole, I'd like to thank the Vim community for sharing their insights across the Internet. I learned many of the tips in this book by reading the Vim tag on StackOverflow and by following the vim_use mailing list.

Tim Pope's rails.vim plugin was instrumental in convincing me to take Vim seriously, and many of his other plugins have become essential parts of my setup. I've also gained insight by using the plugins of Kana Natsuno, whose custom text objects are some of the best extensions to Vim's core functionality that I've come across. Thank you both for sharpening the saw so that the rest of us can benefit.

Thanks to Joe Rozner for providing the wakeup source code that I used to introduce the :make command. Thanks to Oleg Efimov for his quick response to nodelint issues. Thanks to Ben Cormack for illustrating the robots and ninjas.

In January 2012, we moved to Berlin, where the tech community inspired me to complete this book. I'd like to thank Gregor Schmidt for founding the Vim Berlin user group and Jan Schulz-Hofen for hosting our meetups. The opportunity to speak to fellow Vim users really helped me to get my thoughts in order, so I'm grateful to everyone who attended the Vim Berlin meetings. Thank you to Daniel and Nina Holle for subletting your home to us. It was a wonderful place to live and a productive environment in which to work.

In March 2011, when I was living in Egypt, I needed surgery to clear adhesions that were obstructing my bowel. Unlucky for me, I was a long way from home. Luckily, my wife was by my side. Hannah had me admitted to the South Sinai Hospital, where I received excellent care. I want to thank all of the staff there for their kind help, and Dr. Shawket Gerges for successfully operating on me.

When my mum learned that I required surgery, she dropped everything and was on the next flight to Egypt. Considering that the country was in revolution, it took enormous courage to do so. I can't imagine how Hannah and I would have got through that difficult time without the support and experience that my mum brought. I consider myself blessed to have two such wonderful women in my life.

Foreword to the First Edition

Conventional wisdom dictates that Vim has a steep learning curve. I think most Vim users would disagree. Sure, there's an initial hump, but once you run through vimtutor and learn the basics of what to put in your vimrc, you reach a point where you can actually get work done—a sort of hobbled productivity.

What comes next? The Internet's answer to this is the "tip"—a recipe for solving a specific problem. You might search for specific tips when your current solution to a problem feels suboptimal, or you might proactively read some of the more popular tips. This strategy works—it's how I learned, after all—but it's slow. Learning that * searches for the word under the cursor is helpful, but it hardly helps you think like a Vim master.

You can understand my skepticism, then, when I found out *Practical Vim* was using a tips format. How could a couple of hundred tips accomplish what took me thousands? A few pages in I realized my definition of "tip" was narrow-minded. In contrast to the problem/solution pattern I had expected, *Practical Vim* tips teach lessons in thinking like a proficient Vim user. In a sense, they are more like parables than recipes. The first few tips are lessons about the wide applicability of the . command. This is a staple of any proficient Vim user's repertoire, yet without guidance it was years before I came to realize this on my own.

It is for this reason that I am excited about the publication of *Practical Vim*. Because now when Vim novices ask me what's the next step, I know what to tell them. After all, *Practical Vim* even taught me a few things.

Tim Pope
Vim core contributor
April 2012

Read Me

Practical Vim is for programmers who want to raise their game. You've heard it said that in the hands of an expert, Vim shreds text at the speed of thought. Reading this book is your next step toward that end.

Practical Vim is a fast track to Vim mastery. It won't hold you by the hand, but beginners can find the prerequisite knowledge by running through the Vim tutor, an interactive lesson distributed with Vim.[1] *Practical Vim* builds on this foundation by highlighting core concepts and demonstrating idiomatic usage.

Vim is highly configurable. However, customization is a personal thing, so I've tried to avoid recommending what should or should not go into your vimrc file. Instead, *Practical Vim* focuses on the core functionality of the editor—the stuff that's always there, whether you're working over SSH on a remote server or using a local instance of GVim, with plugins installed to add extra functionality. Master Vim's core, and you'll gain portable access to a text editing power tool.

How This Book Is Structured

Practical Vim is a recipe book. It's not designed to be read from start to finish. (I mean it! At the start of the next chapter, I'll advise you to skip it and jump straight to the action.) Each chapter is a collection of tips that are related by a theme, and each tip demonstrates a particular feature in action. Some tips are self-contained. Others depend upon material elsewhere in the book. Those tips are cross-referenced so you can find everything easily.

Practical Vim doesn't progress from novice to advanced level, but each individual chapter does. A less-experienced Vim user might prefer to make a first pass through the book, reading just the early tips in each chapter. A more

---

1. http://vimhelp.appspot.com/usr_01.txt.html#vimtutor

advanced user might choose to focus on the later tips or move around the book as needed.

A Note on the Examples

In Vim, there's always more than one way to complete any given task. For example, in Chapter 1, *The Vim Way*, on page 1, all of the problems are designed to illustrate an application of the dot command, but every one of them could also be solved using the :substitute command.

On seeing my solution, you might think to yourself, "Wouldn't it be quicker to do it *this way?*" And you may well be right! My solutions illustrate a particular technique. Look beyond their simplicity, and try to find a resemblance to the problems that you face daily. That's where these techniques will save you time.

Learn to Touch Type, Then Learn Vim

If you have to look down to find the keys on the keyboard, the benefits of learning Vim won't come fast. Learning to touch type is imperative.

Vim traces its ancestry back to the classic Unix editors, vi and ed (see *On the Etymology of Vim (and Family)*, on page 55). These predate the mouse and all of the point-and-click interfaces that came with it. In Vim, everything can be done with the keyboard. For the touch typist, that means Vim does everything *faster*.

Read the Forgotten Manual

In *Practical Vim*, I demonstrate by showing examples rather than by describing them. That's not easy to do with the written word. To show the steps taken during an interactive editing session, I've adopted a simple notation that illustrates the keystrokes and the contents of a Vim buffer side by side.

If you're keen to jump to the action, you can safely skip this chapter for now. It describes each of the conventions used throughout *Practical Vim*, many of which you'll find to be self-explanatory. At some point, you'll probably come across a symbol and wonder what it stands for. When that happens, turn back and consult this chapter for the answer.

Get to Know Vim's Built-in Documentation

The best way to get to know Vim's documentation is by spending time in it. To help out, I've included "hyperlinks" for entries in Vim's documentation. For example, here's the "hyperlink" for the Vim tutor: :h vimtutor ⓘ.

The icon has a dual function. First, it serves as a signpost, drawing the eye to these helpful references. Second, if you're reading this on an electronic device that's connected to the Internet, you can click the icon and it will take you to the relevant entry in Vim's online documentation. In this sense, it truly is a hyperlink.

But what if you're reading the paper edition of the book? Not to worry. If you have an installation of Vim within reach, simply enter the command as it appears in front of the icon.

For example, type :h vimtutor (:h is an abbreviation for the :help command). Consider this a unique address for the documentation on vimtutor: a URL of sorts. In this sense, the help reference is a kind of hyperlink to Vim's built-in documentation.

Notation for Simulating Vim on the Page

Vim's modal interface sets it apart from most other text editors. To make a musical analogy, let's compare the Qwerty and piano keyboards. A pianist can pick out a melody by playing one note at a time or he or she can hold down several keys at once to sound a chord. In most text editors, keyboard shortcuts are triggered by pressing a key while holding down one or more modifier buttons, such as the control and command keys. This is the Qwerty equivalent of playing a chord on the piano keyboard.

Some of Vim's commands are also triggered by playing chords, but Normal mode commands are designed to be typed as a sequence of keystrokes. It's the Qwerty equivalent of playing a melody on the piano keyboard.

`Ctrl-s` is a common convention for representing chordal key commands. It means "Press the Control key and the `s` key at the same time." But this convention isn't well suited to describing Vim's modal command set. In this section, we'll meet the notation used throughout *Practical Vim* to illustrate Vim usage.

Playing Melodies

In Normal mode, we compose commands by typing one or more keystrokes in sequence. These commands appear as follows:

Notation	Meaning
x	Press x once
dw	In sequence, press d, then w
dap	In sequence, press d, a, then p

Most of these sequences involve two or three keystrokes, but some are longer. Deciphering the meaning of Vim's Normal mode command sequences can be challenging, but you'll get better at it with practice.

Playing Chords

When you see a keystroke such as `<C-p>`, it doesn't mean "Press `<`, then `C`, then `-`, and so on." The `<C-p>` notation is equivalent to `Ctrl-p`, which means "Press the `<Ctrl>` and `p` keys at the same time."

I didn't choose this notation without good reason. Vim's documentation uses it (:h key-notation ⓘ), and we can also use it in defining custom key mappings. Some of Vim's commands are formed by combining chords and keystrokes in sequence, and this notation handles them well. Consider these examples:

Notation	Meaning
`<C-n>`	Press `<Ctrl>` and `n` at the same time
`g<C-]>`	Press `g`, followed by `<Ctrl>` and `]` at the same time
`<C-r>0`	Press `<Ctrl>` and `r` at the same time, then `0`
`<C-w><C-=>`	Press `<Ctrl>` and `w` at the same time, then `<Ctrl>` and `=` at the same time

Placeholders

Many of Vim's commands require two or more keystrokes to be entered in sequence. Some commands must be followed by a particular kind of keystroke, while other commands can be followed by any key on the keyboard. I use curly braces to denote the set of valid keystrokes that can follow a command. Here are some examples:

Notation	Meaning
`f{char}`	Press `f`, followed by any other character
`` `{a-z} ``	Press `` ` ``, followed by any lowercase letter
`m{a-zA-Z}`	Press `m`, followed by any lowercase or uppercase letter
`d{motion}`	Press `d`, followed by any motion command
`<C-r>{register}`	Press `<Ctrl>` and `r` at the same time, followed by the address of a register

Showing Special Keys

Some keys are called by name. This table shows a selection of them:

Notation	Meaning
`<Esc>`	Press the Escape key
`<CR>`	Press the carriage return key (also known as `<Enter>`)
`<Ctrl>`	Press the Control key
`<Tab>`	Press the Tab key
`<Shift>`	Press the Shift key
`<S-Tab>`	Press the `<Shift>` and `<Tab>` keys at the same time
`<Up>`	Press the up arrow key
`<Down>`	Press the down arrow key
`␣`	Press the space bar

Note that the space bar is represented as `␣`. This could be combined with the `f{char}` command to form `f␣`.

Switching Modes Midcommand

When operating Vim, it's common to switch from Normal to Insert mode and back again. Each keystroke could mean something different, depending on which mode is active. I've used an alternative style to represent keystrokes entered in Insert mode, which makes it easy to differentiate them from Normal mode keystrokes.

Consider this example: `cw`replacement`<Esc>`. The Normal mode `cw` command deletes to the end of the current word and switches to Insert mode. Then we type the word "replacement" in Insert mode and press `<Esc>` to switch back to Normal mode again.

The Normal mode styling is also used for Visual mode keystrokes, while the Insert mode styling can indicate keystrokes entered in Command-Line mode and Replace mode. Which mode is active should be clear from context.

Interacting with the Command Line

In some tips we'll execute a command line, either in the shell or from inside Vim. This is what it looks like when we execute the `grep` command in the shell:

⇒ `$ grep -n Waldo *`

And this is how it looks when we execute Vim's built-in `:grep` command:

⇒ `:grep Waldo *`

In *Practical Vim*, the $ symbol indicates that a command line is to be executed in an external shell, whereas the : prompt indicates that the command line is to be executed internally from Command-Line mode. Occasionally we'll see other prompts, including these:

Prompt	Meaning
$	Enter the command line in an external shell
:	Use Command-Line mode to execute an Ex command
/	Use Command-Line mode to perform a forward search
?	Use Command-Line mode to perform a backward search
=	Use Command-Line mode to evaluate a Vim script expression

Any time you see an Ex command listed inline, such as :write, you can assume that the `<CR>` key is pressed to execute the command. Nothing happens otherwise, so you can consider `<CR>` to be implicit.

By contrast, Vim's search command allows us to preview the first match before pressing `<CR>` (see Tip 82, *Preview the First Match Before Execution*, on page 205). When you see a search command listed inline, such as /pattern`<CR>`, the `<CR>` keystroke is listed explicitly. If the `<CR>` is omitted, that's intentional, and it means you shouldn't press the Enter key just yet.

Showing the Cursor Position in a Buffer

When showing the contents of a buffer, it's useful to be able to indicate where the cursor is positioned. In this example, you should see that the cursor is placed on the first letter of the word "One":

`One two three`

When we make a change that involves several steps, the contents of the buffer pass through intermediate states. To illustrate the process, I use a table showing the commands executed in the left column and the contents of the buffer in the right column. Here's a simple example:

Keystrokes	Buffer Contents
{start}	One two three
dw	two three

In row 2 we run the `dw` command to delete the word under the cursor. We can see how the buffer looks immediately after running this command by looking at the contents of the buffer in the same row.

Highlighting Search Matches

When demonstrating Vim's search command, it's helpful to be able to highlight any matches that occur in the buffer. In this example, searching for the string "the" causes four occurrences of the pattern to be highlighted:

Keystrokes	Buffer Contents
{start}	the problem with these new recruits is that they don't keep their boots clean.
/the`<CR>`	the problem with these new recruits is that they don't keep their boots clean.

Skip ahead to Tip 81, *Highlight Search Matches*, on page 204, to find out how to enable search highlighting in Vim.

Selecting Text in Visual Mode

Visual mode lets us select text in the buffer and then operate on the selection. Here, we use the `it` text object to select the contents of the <a> tag:

Keystrokes	Buffer Contents
{start}	<a href="http://pragprog.com/dnvim/">Practical Vim</a>
vit	<a href="http://pragprog.com/dnvim/">Practical Vim</a>

Note that the styling for a Visual selection is the same for highlighted search matches. When you see this style, it should be clear from context whether it represents a search match or a Visual selection.

Downloading the Examples

The examples in *Practical Vim* usually begin by showing the contents of a file *before* we change it. These code listings include the file path:

```
macros/incremental.txt
partridge in a pear tree
turtle doves
French hens
calling birds
golden rings
```

Each time you see a file listed with its file path in this manner, it means that you can download the example. I recommend that you open the file in Vim and try out the exercises for yourself. It's the best way to learn!

To follow along, download all the examples and source code from the Pragmatic Bookshelf.[1] If you're reading on an electronic device that's connected to the Internet, you can also fetch each file one by one by clicking on the filename. Try it with the example above.

Use Vim's Factory Settings

Vim is highly configurable. If you don't like the defaults, then you can change them. That's a good thing, but it could cause confusion if you follow the examples in this book using a customized version of Vim. You may find that some things don't work for you the way that they are described in the text. If you suspect that your customizations are causing interference, here's a quick test. Try quitting Vim and then launching it with these options:

```
$ vim -u NONE -N
```

---

1. http://pragprog.com/titles/dnvim/source_code

The -u NONE flag tells Vim not to source your vimrc on startup. That way, your customizations won't be applied and plugins will be disabled. When Vim starts up without loading a vimrc file, it reverts to vi compatible mode, which causes many useful features to be disabled. The -N flag prevents this by setting the 'nocompatible' option.

For most examples in *Practical Vim*, the vim -u NONE -N trick should guarantee that you get the same experience as described, but there are a couple of exceptions. Some of Vim's built-in features are implemented with Vim script, which means that they will only work when plugins are enabled. This file contains the absolute minimum configuration that is required to activate Vim's built-in plugins:

```
essential.vim
set nocompatible
filetype plugin on
```

When launching Vim, you can use this file instead of your vimrc by running the following:

```
$ vim -u code/essential.vim
```

You'll have to adjust the code/essential.vim path accordingly. With Vim's built-in plugins enabled, you'll be able to use features such as netrw (Tip 44, *Explore the File System with netrw*, on page 104) and omni-completion (Tip 119, *Autocomplete with Context Awareness*, on page 293), as well as many others. I consider Vim's factory settings to mean built-in plugins enabled and vi compatibility disabled.

Look out for subsections titled "Preparation" at the top of a tip. To follow along with the material in these tips, you'll need to configure Vim accordingly. If you start up with Vim's factory settings and then apply the customizations on the fly, you should be able to reproduce the steps from these tips without any problems.

If you're still having problems, see *On Vim Versions*, on page xxvi.

On the Role of Vim Script

Vim script enables us to add new functionality to Vim or to change existing functionality. It's a complete scripting language in itself and a subject worthy of a book of its own. *Practical Vim* is not that book.

But we won't steer clear of the subject entirely. Vim script is always just below the surface, ready to do our bidding. We'll see a few examples of how it can be used for everyday tasks in Tip 16, *Do Back-of-the-Envelope Calculations in*

Place, on page 33; Tip 71, *Evaluate an Iterator to Number Items in a List*, on page 177; Tip 95, *Perform Arithmetic on the Replacement*, on page 233; and Tip 96, *Swap Two or More Words*, on page 234.

Practical Vim shows you how to get by with Vim's core functionality. In other words, no third-party plugins assumed. I've made an exception for Tip 87, *Search for the Current Visual Selection*, on page 216. The visual-star.vim plugin adds a feature that I find indispensable, and it requires very little code—less than ten lines of Vim script. It demonstrates how easily Vim's functionality can be extended. The implementation of visual-star.vim is presented inline without explanation. This should give you an idea of what Vim script looks like and what you can accomplish with it. If it piques your interest, then so much the better.

On Vim Versions

All examples in *Practical Vim* were tested on the latest version of Vim, which was 7.4 at the time of writing. That said, most examples should work fine on any 7.x release, and many of the features discussed are also available in 6.x.

Some of Vim's functionality can be disabled during compilation. For example, when configuring the build, we could provide the --with-features=tiny option, which would disable all but the most fundamental features (there are also feature sets labeled small, normal, big, and huge). You can browse the feature list by looking up :h +feature-list ⓘ.

If you find that you're missing a feature discussed in this book, you might be using a minimal Vim build. Check whether or not the feature is available to you with the :version command:

```
⇒ :version
❮ VIM - Vi IMproved 7.4 (2013 Aug 10, compiled Oct 14 2015 18:41:08)
  Huge version without GUI.  Features included (+) or not (-):
  +arabic +autocmd +balloon_eval +browse +builtin_terms +byte_offset
  +cindent +clientserver +clipboard +cmdline_compl +cmdline_hist
  +cmdline_info +comments
  ...
```

On a modern computer, there's no reason to use anything less than Vim's huge feature set!

Vim in the Terminal or Vim with a GUI? You Choose!

Traditionally, Vim runs inside of the terminal, with no graphical user interface (GUI). We could say instead that Vim has a TUI: a textual user interface. If you spend most of your day at the command line, this will feel natural.

If you're accustomed to using a GUI-based text editor, then GVim (or MacVim on OS X) will provide a helpful bridge into the world of Vim (see :h gui ⓘ). GVim supports more fonts and more colors for syntax highlighting. Also, you can use the mouse. And some of the conventions of the operating system are honored. For example, in MacVim you can interact with the system clipboard using `Cmd-X` and `Cmd-V`, save a document with `Cmd-S`, or close a window with `Cmd-W`. Use these while you find your bearings, but be aware that there's always a better way.

For the purposes of this book, it doesn't matter whether you run Vim in the terminal or as GVim. We'll focus on core commands that work just as well in either. We'll learn how to do things *the Vim way*.

CHAPTER 1

The Vim Way

Our work is repetitive by nature. Whether we're making the same small change in several places or moving around between similar regions of a document, we repeat many actions. Anything that can streamline a repetitive workflow will save our time multifold.

Vim is optimized for repetition. Its efficiency stems from the way it tracks our most recent actions. We can always replay the last change with a single keystroke. Powerful as this sounds, it's useless unless we learn to craft our actions so that they perform a useful unit of work when replayed. Mastering this concept is the key to becoming effective with Vim.

The dot command is our starting point. This seemingly simple command is the most versatile tool in the box, and understanding it is the first step toward Vim mastery. We'll work through a handful of simple editing tasks that can be rapidly completed with the dot command. Although each task looks quite different from the next, their solutions almost converge. We'll identify an ideal editing formula, which requires only one keystroke to move and another to execute.

Tip 1

Meet the Dot Command

The dot command lets us repeat the last change. It is the most powerful and versatile command in Vim.

Vim's documentation simply states that the dot command "repeats the last change" (see :h .⊙). It doesn't sound like much, but in that simple definition we'll find the kernel of what makes Vim's modal editing model so effective. First we have to ask, "What is a change?"

To understand the power of the dot command, we have to realize that the "last change" could be one of many things. A change could act at the level of individual characters, entire lines, or even the whole file.

To demonstrate, we'll use this snippet of text:

the_vim_way/0_mechanics.txt
```
Line one
Line two
Line three
Line four
```

The x command deletes the character under the cursor. When we use the dot command in this context, "repeat last change" tells Vim to delete the character under the cursor:

Keystrokes	Buffer Contents
{start}	Line one Line two Line three Line four
x	ine one Line two Line three Line four
.	ne one Line two Line three Line four
. .	one Line two Line three Line four

We can restore the file to its original state by pressing the u key a few times to undo the changes.

The dd command also performs a deletion, but this one acts on the current line as a whole. If we use the dot command after dd, then "repeat last change" instructs Vim to delete the current line:

Keystrokes	Buffer Contents
{start}	Line one Line two Line three Line four
dd	Line two Line three Line four
.	Line three Line four

Finally, the `>G` command increases the indentation from the current line until the end of the file. If we follow this command with the dot command, then "repeat last change" tells Vim to increase the indentation level from the current position to the end of the file. In this example, we'll start with the cursor on the second line to highlight the difference

Keystrokes	Buffer Contents
{start}	Line one Line two Line three Line four

>G	Line one
	   Line two
	   Line three
	   Line four

j	Line one Line two Line three Line four

.	Line one
	Line two
	      Line three
	   Line four

j.	Line one
	Line two
	   Line three
	      Line four

The `x`, `dd`, and `>` commands are all executed from Normal mode, but we also create a change each time we dip into Insert mode. From the moment we enter Insert mode (by pressing `i`, for example) until we return to Normal mode (by pressing `<Esc>`), Vim records every keystroke. After making a change such as this, the dot command will replay our keystrokes (see *Moving Around in Insert Mode Resets the Change,* on page 17, for a caveat).

The Dot Command Is a Micro Macro

Later, in Chapter 11, *Macros*, on page 161, we'll see that Vim can record any arbitrary number of keystrokes to be played back later. This allows us to capture our most repetitive workflows and replay them at a keystroke. We can think of the dot command as being a miniature macro, or a "micro" if you prefer.

We'll see a few applications of the dot command throughout this chapter. We'll also learn a couple of best practices for working with the dot command in Tip 9, *Compose Repeatable Changes*, on page 18, and Tip 23, *Prefer Operators to Visual Commands Where Possible*, on page 45.

Tip 2

Don't Repeat Yourself

For such a common use case as appending a semicolon at the end of a series of lines, Vim provides a dedicated command that combines two steps into one.

Suppose that we have a snippet of JavaScript code like this:

```
the_vim_way/2_foo_bar.js
var foo = 1
var bar = 'a'
var foobar = foo + bar
```

We need to append a semicolon at the end of each line. Doing so involves moving our cursor to the end of the line and then switching to Insert mode to make the change. The $ command will handle the motion for us, and then we can run a;<Esc> to make the change.

To finish the job, we could run the exact same sequence of keystrokes on the next two lines, but that would be missing a trick. The dot command will repeat that last change, so instead of duplicating our efforts, we could just run j$. twice. One keystroke (.) buys us three (a;<Esc>). It's a small saving, but these efficiencies accumulate when repeated.

But let's take a closer look at this pattern: j$.. The j command moves the cursor down one line, and then the $ command moves it to the end of the line. We've used two keystrokes just to maneuver our cursor into position so that we can use the dot command. Do you sense that there's room for improvement here?

Reduce Extraneous Movement

While the `a` command appends after the current cursor position, the `A` command appends at the end of the current line. It doesn't matter where our cursor is at the time, pressing `A` will switch to Insert mode and move the cursor to the end of the line. In other words, it squashes `$a` into a single keystroke. In *Two for the Price of One,* on page 6, we see that Vim has a handful of compound commands.

Here is a refinement of our previous example:

Keystrokes	Buffer Contents

{start}	`var foo = 1`
	`var bar = 'a'`
	`var foobar = foo + bar`

A;<Esc>	`var foo = 1;`
	`var bar = 'a'`
	`var foobar = foo + bar`

j	`var foo = 1;`
	`var bar = 'a'`
	`var foobar = foo + bar`

.	`var foo = 1;`
	`var bar = 'a';`
	`var foobar = foo + bar`

j.	`var foo = 1;`
	`var bar = 'a';`
	`var foobar = foo + bar;`

By using `A` instead of `$a`, we give the dot command a boost. Instead of having to position the cursor at the *end* of the line we want to change, we just have to make sure it is *somewhere* (anywhere!) on that line. Now we can repeat the change on consecutive lines just by typing `j.` as many times as it takes.

One keystroke to move, another to execute. That's about as good as it gets! Watch for this pattern of usage, because we'll see it popping up in a couple more examples.

Although this formula looks terrific for our short example, it's not a universal solution. Imagine if we had to append a semicolon to fifty consecutive lines. Pressing `j.` for each change starts to look like a lot of work. For an alternative approach, skip ahead to Tip 30, *Run Normal Mode Commands Across a Range,* on page 63.

Two for the Price of One

We could say that the A command compounds two actions ($a) into a single keystroke. It's not alone in doing this. Many of Vim's single-key commands can be seen as a condensed version of two or more other commands. The table below shows an approximation of some examples. Can you identify anything else that they all have in common?

Compound Command	Equivalent in Longhand
C	c$
s	cl
S	^C
I	^i
A	$a
o	A<CR>
O	ko

If you catch yourself running ko (or worse, k$a<CR>), stop! Think about what you're doing. Then recognize that you could have used the O command instead.

Did you identify the other property that these commands share? They all switch from Normal to Insert mode. Think about that and how it might affect the dot command.

Tip 3

Take One Step Back, Then Three Forward

We can pad a single character with two spaces (one in front, the other behind) by using an idiomatic Vim solution. At first it might look slightly odd, but the solution has the benefit of being repeatable, which allows us to complete the task effortlessly.

Suppose that we have a line of code that looks like this:

```
the_vim_way/3_concat.js
var foo = "method("+argument1+","+argument2+")";
```

Concatenating strings in JavaScript never looks pretty, but we could make this a little easier on the eye by padding each + sign with spaces to make it look like this:

```
var foo = "method(" + argument1 + "," + argument2 + ")";
```

Make the Change Repeatable

This idiomatic approach solves the problem:

Keystrokes	Buffer Contents
{start}	`var foo = "method("+argument1+","+argument2+")";`
f+	`var foo = "method("+argument1+","+argument2+")";`
s␣+␣<Esc>	`var foo = "method(" +argument1+","+argument2+")";`
;	`var foo = "method(" + argument1+","+argument2+")";`
.	`var foo = "method(" + argument1 +","+argument2+")";`
;.	`var foo = "method(" + argument1 + "," +argument2+")";`
;.	`var foo = "method(" + argument1 + "," + argument2 +")";`

The `s` command compounds two steps into one: it deletes the character under the cursor and then enters Insert mode. Having deleted the + sign, we then type `␣+␣` and leave Insert mode.

One step back and then three steps forward. It's a strange little dance that might seem unintuitive, but we get a big win by doing it this way: we can repeat the change with the dot command; all we need to do is position our cursor on the next + symbol, and the dot command will repeat that little dance.

Make the Motion Repeatable

There's another trick in this example. The `f{char}` command tells Vim to look ahead for the next occurrence of the specified character and then move the cursor directly to it if a match is found (see :h f⑩). So when we type `f+`, our cursor goes straight to the next + symbol. We'll learn more about the `f{char}` command in Tip 50, *Find by Character*, on page 120.

Having made our first change, we could jump to the next occurrence by repeating the `f+` command, but there's a better way. The `;` command will repeat the last search that the `f` command performed. So instead of typing `f+` four times, we can use that command once and then follow up by using the `;` command three times.

All Together Now

The `;` command takes us to our next target, and the `.` command repeats the last change, so we can complete the changes by typing `;.` three times. Does that look familiar?

Instead of fighting Vim's modal input model, we're working with it, and look how much easier it makes this particular task.

Tip 4

Act, Repeat, Reverse

When facing a repetitive task, we can achieve an optimal editing strategy by making both the motion and the change repeatable. Vim has a knack for this. It remembers our actions and keeps the most common ones within close reach so that we can easily replay them. In this tip, we'll introduce each of the actions that Vim can repeat and learn how to reverse them.

We've seen that the dot command repeats the last *change*. Since lots of operations count as a change, the dot command proves to be versatile. But some commands can be repeated by other means. For example, `@:` can be used to repeat any Ex command (as discussed in Tip 31, *Repeat the Last Ex Command*, on page 65). Or we can repeat the last :substitute command (which itself happens to be an Ex command as well) by pressing `&` (see Tip 93, *Repeat the Previous Substitute Command*, on page 229).

If we know how to repeat our actions without having to spell them out every single time, then we can be more efficient. First we act; then we repeat.

But when so much can be achieved with so few keystrokes, we have to watch our step. It's easy to get trigger-happy. Rapping out `j.j.j.` again and again feels a bit like doing a drum roll. What happens if we accidentally hit the `j` key twice in a row? Or worse, the `.` key?

Whenever Vim makes it easy to repeat an action or a motion, it always provides some way of backing out in case we accidentally go too far. In the case of the dot command, we can always hit the `u` key to undo the last change. If we hit the `;` key too many times after using the `f{char}` command, we'll miss our mark. But we can back up again by pressing the `,` key, which repeats the last `f{char}` search in the reverse direction (see Tip 50, *Find by Character*, on page 120).

It always helps to know where the reverse gear is in case you accidentally go a step too far. Table 1, *Repeatable Actions and How to Reverse Them*, on page 9, summarizes Vim's repeatable commands along with their corresponding reverse action. In most cases, the undo command is the one that we reach for. No wonder the `u` key on my keyboard is so worn out!

Intent	Act	Repeat	Reverse
Make a change	{edit}	.	u
Scan line for next character	f{char} / t{char}	;	,
Scan line for previous character	F{char} / T{char}	;	,
Scan document for next match	/pattern<CR>	n	N
Scan document for previous match	?pattern<CR>	n	N
Perform substitution	:s/target/replacement	&	u
Execute a sequence of changes	qx{changes}q	@x	u

Table 1—Repeatable Actions and How to Reverse Them

Tip 5

Find and Replace by Hand

Vim has a :substitute command for find-and-replace tasks, but with this alternative technique, we'll change the first occurrence by hand and then find and replace every other match one by one. The dot command will save us from labor, but we'll meet another nifty one-key command that makes jumping between matches a snap.

In this excerpt, the word "content" appears on every line:

```
the_vim_way/1_copy_content.txt
...We're waiting for content before the site can go live...
...If you are content with this, let's go ahead with it...
...We'll launch as soon as we have the content...
```

Suppose that we want to use the word "copy" (as in "copywriting") instead of "content." Easy enough, you might think; we can just use the substitute command, like this:

⇒ `:%s/content/copy/g`

But wait a minute! If we run this command, then we're going to create the phrase "If you are 'copy' with this," which is nonsense!

We've run into this problem because the word "content" has two meanings. One is synonymous with "copy" (and pronounced *content*), the other with "happy" (pronounced con*tent*). Technically, we're dealing with heteronyms (words that are spelled the same but differ in both meaning and pronunciation), but that doesn't really matter. The point is, we have to watch our step.

We can't just blindly replace every occurrence of "content" with "copy." We have to eyeball each one and answer "yay" or "nay" to the question, should this occurrence be changed? The substitute command is up to the task, and we'll find out how in Tip 90, *Eyeball Each Substitution*, on page 223. But right now, we'll explore an alternative solution that fits with the theme of this chapter.

Be Lazy: Search Without Typing

You might have guessed by now that the dot command is my favorite single-key Vim trigger. In second place is the `*` command. This executes a search for the word under the cursor at that moment (see :h * ⓘ).

We could search for the word "content" by pulling up the search prompt and spelling out the word in full:

⇒ **/content**

Or we could simply place our cursor on the word and hit the `*` key. Consider the following workflow:

Keystrokes	Buffer Contents
{start}	...We're waiting for content before the site can go live... ...If you are content with this, let's go ahead with it... ...We'll launch as soon as we have the content...
*	...We're waiting for content before the site can go live... ...If you are content with this, let's go ahead with it... ...We'll launch as soon as we have the content...
cwcopy<Esc>	...We're waiting for content before the site can go live... ...If you are content with this, let's go ahead with it... ...We'll launch as soon as we have the copy...
n	...We're waiting for content before the site can go live... ...If you are content with this, let's go ahead with it... ...We'll launch as soon as we have the copy...
.	...We're waiting for copy before the site can go live... ...If you are content with this, let's go ahead with it... ...We'll launch as soon as we have the copy...

We begin with our cursor positioned on the word "content" and then use the `*` command to search for it. Try it for yourself. Two things should happen: the cursor will jump forward to the next match, and all occurrences will be highlighted. If you don't see any highlighting, try running :set hls and then refer to Tip 81, *Highlight Search Matches*, on page 204, for more details.

Having executed a search for the word "content," we can now advance to the next occurrence just by hitting the `n` key. In this case, pressing `*nn` would cycle through all matches, taking us back to where we started.

Make the Change Repeatable

With our cursor positioned at the start of the word "content," we are poised to change it. This involves two steps: deleting the word "content" and then typing its replacement. The `cw` command deletes to the end of the word and then drops us into Insert mode, where we can spell out the word "copy." Vim records our keystrokes until we leave Insert mode, so the full sequence `cwcopy<Esc>` is considered to be a single change. Pressing the `.` command deletes to the end of the current word and changes it to "copy."

All Together Now

We're all set! Each time we press the `n` key, our cursor advances to the next occurrence of the word "content." And when we press the `.` key, it changes the word under the cursor to "copy."

If we wanted to replace all occurrences, we could blindly hammer out `n.n.n.` as many times as it took to complete all the changes (although in that case, we might as well have used the `:%s/content/copy/g` command). But we need to watch out for false matches. So after pressing `n`, we can examine the current match and decide if it should be changed to "copy." If so, we trigger the `.` command. If not, we don't. Whatever our decision, we can then move on to the next occurrence by pressing `n` again. Rinse and repeat until done.

Tip 6
Meet the Dot Formula

We've considered three simple editing tasks so far. Even though each problem was different, we found a solution using the dot command for each one. In this tip, we'll compare each solution and identify a common pattern—an optimal editing strategy that I call the Dot Formula.

Reviewing Three Dot-Command Editing Tasks

In Tip 2, *Don't Repeat Yourself,* on page 4, we wanted to append a semicolon at the end of a sequence of lines. We changed the first line by invoking `A;<Esc>`, which set us up so that we could use the dot command to repeat the change on each subsequent line. We could move between lines using the `j` command, and the remaining changes could be completed simply by pressing `j.` as many times as necessary.

In Tip 3, *Take One Step Back, Then Three Forward*, on page 6, we wanted to pad each occurrence of the + symbol with a space both in front and behind. We used the `f+` command to jump to our target and then the `s` command to substitute one character with three. That set us up so that we could complete the task by pressing `;.` a few times.

In Tip 5, *Find and Replace by Hand*, on page 9, we wanted to substitute every occurrence of the word "content" with the word "copy." We used the `*` command to initiate a search for the target word and then ran the `cw` command to change the first occurrence. This set us up so that the `n` key would take us to the next match and the `.` key would apply the same change. We could complete the task simply by pressing `n.` as many times as it took.

The Ideal: One Keystroke to Move, One Keystroke to Execute

In all of these examples, using the dot command repeats the last change. But that's not the only thing they share. A single keystroke is all that's required to move the cursor to its next target.

We're using one keystroke to move and one keystroke to execute. It can't really get any better than that, can it? It's an ideal solution. We'll see this editing strategy coming up again and again, so for the sake of convenience, we'll refer to this pattern as the Dot Formula.

Part I

Modes

Vim provides a modal user interface. This means that the result of pressing any key on the keyboard may differ depending on which mode is active at the time. It's vital to know which mode is active and how to switch between Vim's modes. In this part of the book, we'll learn how each mode works and what it can be used for.

CHAPTER 2

Normal Mode

Normal mode is Vim's natural resting state. If this chapter seems surprisingly short, then that's because most of this book is about how to use Normal mode! Here, however, is where we cover some core concepts and general tips.

Other text editors spend most of their time in something that resembles Insert mode. So to the Vim newcomer, it can seem strange that Normal mode is the default. In Tip 7, *Pause with Your Brush Off the Page*, on page 16, we'll begin explaining why this is by drawing an analogy with the workspace of a painter.

Many Normal mode commands can be executed with a count, which causes them to be run multiple times. In Tip 10, *Use Counts to Do Simple Arithmetic*, on page 20, we'll meet a pair of commands that increment and decrement numerical values and see how these commands can be combined with a count to do simple arithmetic.

Just because you can save keystrokes by using a count doesn't mean that you should. We'll look at some examples where it's better simply to repeat a command than take the time to count how many times you want to run it.

Much of the power of Normal mode stems from the way that operator commands can be combined with motions. We'll finish by looking at the consequences of this.

Tip 7

Pause with Your Brush Off the Page

For those unused to Vim, Normal mode can seem like an odd default. But experienced Vim users have difficulty imagining it any other way. This tip uses an analogy to illustrate the Vim way.

How much time do you reckon artists spend with their paint brushes in contact with the canvas? No doubt it would vary from artist to artist, but I'd be surprised if it counted for as much as half of the time painters spend at work.

Think of all of the things that painters do besides paint. They study their subject, adjust the lighting, and mix paints into new hues. And when it comes to applying paint to the canvas, who says they have to use brushes? A painter might switch to a palette knife to achieve a different texture or use a cotton swab to touch up the paint that's already been applied.

The painter does not rest with a brush on the canvas. And so it is with Vim. Normal mode is the natural resting state. The clue is in the name, really.

Just as painters spend a fraction of their time applying paint, programmers spend a fraction of their time composing code. More time is spent thinking, reading, and navigating from one part of a codebase to another. And when we do want to make a change, who says we have to switch to Insert mode? We can reformat existing code, duplicate it, move it around, or delete it. From Normal mode, we have many tools at our disposal.

Tip 8

Chunk Your Undos

In other text editors, invoking the undo command after typing a few words might revert the last typed word or character. However, in Vim we can control the granularity of the undo command.

The  u key triggers the undo command, which reverts the most recent change. A change could be anything that modifies the text in the document. That includes commands triggered from Normal, Visual, and Command-Line modes, but a change could also encompass any text entered (or deleted) in Insert mode. So we could also say that `i{insert some text}<Esc>` constitutes a change.

In nonmodal text editors, triggering the undo command after typing a few words could do one of two things. It could undo the last character that was typed. Or, more helpfully, it could chunk a set of characters together so that each undo operation removed a word instead of a character.

In Vim, we can control the granularity of the undo command. From the moment we enter Insert mode until we return to Normal mode, everything we type (or delete) counts as a single change. So we can make the undo command operate on words, sentences, or paragraphs just by moderating our use of the `<Esc>` key.

So how often should you leave Insert mode? It's a matter of preference, but I like to make each "undoable chunk" correspond to a thought. As I write this text (in Vim, of course!), I often pause at the end of a sentence to consider what I'll write next. No matter how brief its duration, each pause forms a natural break point, giving me a cue to leave Insert mode. When I'm ready to continue writing, I press `A` and carry on where I left off.

If I decide that I've taken a wrong turn, I'll switch to Normal mode and press `u`. Each time I undo, my text decomposes in coherent chunks that correspond to my thought process as I was writing the original text. It means that I can easily try out a sentence or two and then throw them away with a couple of keystrokes.

If I'm in Insert mode with my cursor at the end of a line, the quickest way to open a new line is to press `<CR>`. And yet I sometimes prefer to press `<Esc>o` just because I anticipate that I might want that extra granularity from the undo command. If this sounds hard core, don't worry. As you become adept with Vim, switching modes feels more and more lightweight.

As a general rule, if you've paused for long enough to ask the question, "Should I leave Insert mode?" then do it.

Moving Around in Insert Mode Resets the Change

When I said that the undo command would revert all characters entered (or deleted) during a trip into Insert mode and back, I was glossing over a small detail. If we use the `<Up>`, `<Down>`, `<Left>`, or `<Right>` cursor keys while in Insert mode, a new undo chunk is created. It's just as though we had switched back to Normal mode to move around with the `h`, `j`, `k`, or `l` commands, except that we don't have to leave Insert mode. This also has implications on the operation of the dot command.

Tip 9

Compose Repeatable Changes

Vim is optimized for repetition. In order to exploit this, we have to be mindful of how we compose our changes.

In Vim, we always have more than one way of doing something. In evaluating which way is best, the most obvious metric is efficiency: which technique requires the fewest keystrokes (a.k.a. VimGolf[1]). But how should we pick a winner in the event of a tie?

Suppose that our cursor is positioned on the "h" at the end of this line of text, and we want to delete the word "nigh."

normal_mode/the_end.txt
```
The end is nigh
```

Delete Backward

Since our cursor is already at the end of the word, we might begin by deleting backward.

Keystrokes	Buffer Contents
{start}	The end is nigh
db	The end is h
x	The end is

Pressing `db` deletes from the cursor's starting position to the beginning of the word, but it leaves the final "h" intact. We can delete this rogue character by pressing `x`. That gives us a Vim golf score of 3.

Delete Forward

This time, let's try deleting forward instead.

Keystrokes	Buffer Contents
{start}	The end is nigh
b	The end is nigh
dw	The end is

---

1. http://vimgolf.com/

We have to start by maneuvering our cursor into position with the `b` motion. Once it's in place, we can excise the word with a single `dw` command. Once again, our Vim golf score is 3.

Delete an Entire Word

Both of our solutions so far have involved some kind of preparation or clean-up. We can be more surgical by using the `aw` text object instead of a motion (see :h aw ⓘ):

Keystrokes	Buffer Contents
{start}	The end is nigh
daw	The end is

The `daw` command is easily remembered by the mnemonic *delete a word*. We'll go into more detail on text objects in Tip 52, *Trace Your Selection with Precision Text Objects*, on page 126, and Tip 53, *Delete Around, or Change Inside*, on page 129.

Tie-Breaker: Which Is Most Repeatable?

We've tried three techniques for deleting a word: `dbx`, `bdw`, and `daw`. In each case, our Vim golf score is 3. So how can we settle the question of which is best?

Remember, Vim is optimized for repetition. Let's go through these techniques again. This time, we'll finish by invoking the dot command and see what happens. I urge you to try these out for yourself.

The backward deletion technique involves two operations: `db` deletes to the start of the word and then `x` deletes a single character. If we invoke the dot command, it repeats the single character deletion (`.` == `x`). That's not what I would call a big win.

The forward deletion technique also involves two steps. This time, `b` is just a plain motion, while `dw` makes a change. The dot command repeats `dw`, deleting from the cursor position to the beginning of the next word. It so happens that we're already at the end of the line. There is no "next word," so in this context the dot command isn't useful. But at least it's shorthand for something longer (`.` == `dw`).

The final solution only invokes a single operation: `daw`. This technique doesn't just remove the word, it also deletes a whitespace character. As a result, our cursor ends up on the last character of the word "is." If we invoke the dot command, it will repeat the instruction to delete a word. This time, the dot command does something truly useful (`.` == `daw`).

Discussion

The `daw` technique invests the most power into the dot command, so I declare it the winner of this round.

Making effective use of the dot command often requires some forethought. If you notice that you have to make the same small change in a handful of places, you can attempt to compose your changes in such a way that they can be repeated with the dot command. Recognizing those opportunities takes practice. But if you develop a habit of making your changes repeatable wherever possible, then Vim will reward you for it.

Sometimes, I won't see an opportunity to use the dot command. After making a change—and finding that I need to perform an identical edit—I realize that the dot command is primed and ready to do the work for me. It makes me grin every time.

Tip 10

Use Counts to Do Simple Arithmetic

Most Normal mode commands can be executed with a count. We can exploit this feature to do simple arithmetic.

Many of the commands that are available in Normal mode can be prefixed with a count. Instead of executing the command just once, Vim will attempt to execute the command the specified number of times (see :h count ⓘ).

The `<C-a>` and `<C-x>` commands perform addition and subtraction on numbers. When run without a count they increment by one, but if we prefix a number, then we can add or subtract by any whole number. For example, if we positioned our cursor on a 5 character, running `10<C-a>` would modify it to read 15.

But what happens if the cursor is not positioned on a numeric digit? The documentation says that the `<C-a>` command will "add [count] to the number *at or after the cursor*" (see :h ctrl-a ⓘ). So if the cursor is not already positioned on a number, then the `<C-a>` command will look ahead for a digit on the current line. If it finds one, it jumps straight to it. We can use this to our advantage.

Here's a snippet of CSS:

```
normal_mode/sprite.css
.blog, .news { background-image: url(/sprite.png); }
.blog { background-position: 0px 0px }
```

We're going to duplicate the last line and make two small modifications to it: replace the word "blog" with "news," and change "0px" to "-180px." We can duplicate the line by running `yyp` and then using `cW` to change the first word. But how should we deal with that number?

One approach would be to jump to the digit with `f0` and then dip into Insert mode to change the value by hand: `i-18<Esc>`. But it's quicker just to run `180<C-x>`. Since our cursor isn't on a digit to begin with, it jumps forward to the first one that it finds. That saves us the step of moving the cursor by hand. Let's see this work flow in action:

Keystrokes	Buffer Contents
{start}	`.blog, .news { background-image: url(/sprite.png); }` `.blog { background-position: 0px 0px }`

yyp	`.blog, .news { background-image: url(/sprite.png); }`
	`.blog { background-position: 0px 0px }`
	`.blog { background-position: 0px 0px }`

cW.news<Esc>	`.blog, .news { background-image: url(/sprite.png); }`
	`.blog { background-position: 0px 0px }`
	`.news { background-position: 0px 0px }`

180<C-x>	`.blog, .news { background-image: url(/sprite.png); }`
	`.blog { background-position: 0px 0px }`
	`.news { background-position: -180px 0px }`

In this example, we've only duplicated the line once and made changes. But suppose we had to make ten copies, subtracting 180 from the number in each successive copy. If we were to switch to Insert mode to amend each number, we'd have to type something different each time (-180, then -360, and so on). But by using the `180<C-x>` command, our work flow is identical for each successive line. We could even record our keystrokes as a macro (see Chapter 11, *Macros*, on page 161) and then play it back as many times as needed.

> ### Number Formats
>
> What follows 007? No, this isn't a James Bond gag; I'm asking what result would you expect if you added one to 007.
>
> If you answered 008, then you might be in for a surprise when you try using Vim's `<C-a>` command on any number with a leading zero. As is the convention in some programming languages, Vim interprets numerals with a leading zero to be in octal notation rather than in decimal. In the octal numeric system, 007 + 001 = 010, which looks like the decimal ten but is actually an octal eight. Confused?
>
> If you work with octal numbers frequently, Vim's default behavior might suit you. If you don't, you probably want to add the following line to your vimrc:
>
> `set nrformats=`
>
> This will cause Vim to treat all numerals as decimal, regardless of whether they are padded with zeros.

Tip 11

Don't Count If You Can Repeat

We can minimize the keystrokes required to perform certain tasks by providing a count, but that doesn't mean that we should. Consider the pros and cons of counting versus repeating.

Suppose that we had the following text in our buffer:

`Delete more than one word`

We want to do as the text says, changing it to read "Delete one word" instead. That is to say, we're going to delete two words.

We can approach this in a handful of ways. Both `d2w` and `2dw` will work. With `d2w`, we invoke the delete command and then give `2w` as the motion. We could read that as "delete two words." However, `2dw` turns things around. This time the count applies to the delete command, but the motion acts over a single word. We could read this as "delete a word two times." Putting semantics aside, we get the same result either way.

Now let's consider an alternative: `dw.`. This we can read as "Delete a word and then repeat."

To recap, our options are as follows: `d2w`, `2dw`, or `dw.`—three keystrokes each. But which is best?

For our discussion, `d2w` and `2dw` are identical. After running either of these, we can press the `u` key to undo, and the two words that were deleted will appear again. Or, instead of undoing our change, we could repeat it with the dot command, which would delete the next two words.

In the case of `dw.`, the result of pressing `u` or `.` is subtly different. Here, the change was `dw`—"delete word." So if we wanted to restore the two words that were deleted, we'd have to undo twice: pressing `uu` (or `2u` if you prefer). Pressing the dot command would just delete the next word rather than the next two.

Now suppose that instead of deleting two words, our original intent was to delete three words. By a small error in judgment, we run `d2w` instead of `d3w`. What next? We can't use the dot command, because that would cause a total of four words to be deleted. So we could either back up and revise our count (`ud3w`) or continue by deleting the next word (`dw`).

If, on the other hand, we had used the command `dw.` in the first place, we would have to repeat the dot command only one more time. Because our original change was simply `dw`, the `u` and `.` commands have more granularity. Each acts upon one word at a time.

Now suppose that we want to delete seven words. We could either run `d7w`, or `dw......` (that is, `dw` followed by the dot command six times). Counting keystrokes, we have a clear winner. But would you trust yourself to make the right count?

Counting is tedious. I'd rather hit the dot command six times than spend the same time looking ahead in order to reduce the number of keys that I have to press. What if I hit the dot command one too many times? No matter, I just back up by hitting the `u` key once.

Remember our mantra (from Tip 4, *Act, Repeat, Reverse*, on page 8): act, repeat, reverse. Here it is in action.

Use a Count When It Matters

Suppose that we wanted to change the text "I have a couple of questions" to instead read "I have *some more* questions." We could do so as follows:

Keystrokes	Buffer Contents
{start}	I have a couple of questions.
c3wsome more<Esc>	I have some more questions.

In this scenario, it doesn't make much sense to use the dot command. We could delete one word and then another (with the dot command), but then we'd have to switch gears and change to Insert mode (using `i` or `cw`, for example). To me, that feels awkward enough that I'd rather go ahead and use a count.

There's another advantage to using a count: it gives us a clean and coherent undo history. Having made this change, we could undo it with a single press of the `u` key, which ties in with the discussion in Tip 8, *Chunk Your Undos*, on page 16.

That same argument also goes in favor of counting (`d5w`) over repeating (`dw....`), so my preferences may seem inconsistent here. You'll develop your own opinion on this, depending on how much you value keeping your undo history clean and whether or not you find it tiresome to use counts.

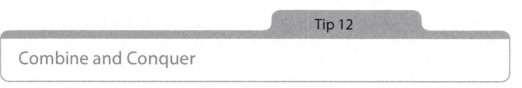

Combine and Conquer

Much of Vim's power stems from the way that operators and motions can be combined. In this tip, we'll look at how this works and consider the implications.

Operator + Motion = Action

The `d{motion}` command can operate on a single character (`dl`), a complete word (`daw`), or an entire paragraph (`dap`). Its reach is defined by the motion. The same goes for `c{motion}`, `y{motion}`, and a handful of others. Collectively, these commands are called *operators*. You can find the complete list by looking up `:h operator` ⓘ, while Table 2, *Vim's Operator Commands*, on page 25, summarizes some of the more common ones.

The `g~`, `gu`, and `gU` commands are invoked by two keystrokes. In each case, we can consider the `g` to be a prefix that modifies the behavior of the subsequent keystroke. See *Meet Operator-Pending Mode*, on page 27, for further discussion.

The combination of operators with motions forms a kind of grammar. The first rule is simple: an action is composed from an operator followed by a motion. Learning new motions and operators is like learning the vocabulary of Vim. If we follow the simple grammar rules, we can express more ideas as our vocabulary grows.

Trigger	Effect
c	Change
d	Delete
y	Yank into register
g~	Swap case
gu	Make lowercase
gU	Make uppercase
>	Shift right
<	Shift left
=	Autoindent
!	Filter {motion} lines through an external program

Table 2—Vim's Operator Commands

Suppose that we already know how to delete a word using `daw`, and then we learn about the `gU` command (see `:h gU` ⓘ). It's an operator too, so we can invoke `gUaw` to convert the current word to SHOUTY case. If we then expand our vocabulary to include the `ap` motion, which acts upon a paragraph, then we find two new operations at our disposal: `dap` to delete, or `gUap` to make the whole paragraph shout.

Vim's grammar has just one more rule: when an operator command is invoked in duplicate, it acts upon the current line. So `dd` deletes the current line, while `>>` indents it. The `gU` command is a special case. We can make it act upon the current line by running either `gUgU` or the shorthand `gUU`.

Extending Vim's Combinatorial Powers

The number of actions that we can perform using Vim's default set of operators and motions is vast. But we can expand these even further by rolling our own custom motions and operators. Let's consider the implications.

Custom Operators Work with Existing Motions

The standard set of operators that ships with Vim is relatively small, but it is possible to define new ones. Tim Pope's commentary.vim plugin provides a good example.[2] This adds a command for commenting and uncommenting lines of code in all languages supported by Vim.

The commentary command is triggered by `gc{motion}`, which toggles commenting for the specified lines. It's an operator command, so we can combine it

---

2. https://github.com/tpope/vim-commentary

with all of the usual motions. `gcap` will toggle commenting for the current paragraph. `gcG` comments from the current line to the end of the file. `gcc` comments the current line.

If you're curious about how to create your own custom operators, start by reading :h :map-operator ⓘ.

Custom Motions Work with Existing Operators

Vim's standard set of motions is fairly comprehensive, but we can augment it further by defining new motions and text objects.

Kana Natsuno's textobj-entire plugin is a good example.[3] It adds two new text objects to Vim: `ie` and `ae`, which act upon the entire file.

If we wanted to autoindent the entire file using the `=` command, we could run `gg=G` (that is, `gg` to jump to the top of the file and then `=G` to autoindent everything from the cursor position to the end of the file). But if we had the textobj-entire plugin installed, we could simply run `=ae`. It wouldn't matter where our cursor was when we ran this command; it would always act upon the entire file.

Note that if we had both the commentary and textobj-entire plugins installed, we could use them together. Running `gcae` would toggle commenting throughout the current file.

If you're curious about how to create your own custom motions, start by reading :h omap-info ⓘ.

---

3. https://github.com/kana/vim-textobj-entire

Meet Operator-Pending Mode

Normal, Insert, and Visual modes are readily identified, but Vim has other modes that are easy to overlook. Operator-Pending mode is a case in point. We use it dozens of times daily, but it usually lasts for just a fraction of a second. For example, we invoke it when we run the command dw. It lasts during the brief interval between pressing d and w keys. Blink and you'll miss it!

If we think of Vim as a finite-state machine, then Operator-Pending mode is a state that accepts only motion commands. It is activated when we invoke an operator command, and then nothing happens until we provide a motion, which completes the operation. While Operator-Pending mode is active, we can return to Normal mode in the usual manner by pressing escape, which aborts the operation.

Many commands are invoked by two or more keystrokes (for examples, look up :h g ⓘ, :h z ⓘ, :h ctrl-w ⓘ, or :h [ⓘ), but in most cases, the first keystroke merely acts as a prefix for the second. These commands don't initiate Operator-Pending mode. Instead, we can think of them as namespaces that expand the number of available command mappings. Only the operator commands initiate Operator-Pending mode.

Why, you might be wondering, is an entire mode dedicated to those brief moments between invoking operator and motion commands, whereas the namespaced commands are merely an extension of Normal mode? Good question! Because we can create custom mappings that initiate or target Operator-Pending mode. In other words, it allows us to create custom operators and motions, which in turn allows us to expand Vim's vocabulary.

CHAPTER 3

Insert Mode

Most of Vim's commands are triggered from other modes, but some functionality is within easy reach from Insert mode. In this chapter, we'll explore these commands. Although delete, yank, and put commands are all triggered from Normal mode, we'll see that there is a convenient shortcut for pasting text from a register without leaving Insert mode. We'll learn that Vim provides two easy ways for inserting unusual characters that are not represented on the keyboard.

Replace mode is a special case of Insert mode, which overwrites existing characters in the document. We'll learn how to invoke this and consider some scenarios where it proves useful. We'll also meet Insert Normal mode, a sub-mode that lets us fire a single Normal mode command before dropping us back into Insert mode.

Autocompletion is the most advanced functionality available to us from Insert mode. We'll cover it in depth in Chapter 19, *Dial X for Autocompletion*, on page 281.

Tip 13

Make Corrections Instantly from Insert Mode

If we make a mistake while composing text in Insert mode, we can fix it immediately. There's no need to change modes. Besides the backspace key, we can use a couple of other Insert mode commands to make quick corrections.

Touch typing is more than just not looking at the keyboard; it means doing it by feel. When touch typists make an error, they know it even before their eyes process the information on the screen in front of them. They feel it in their fingers, like a misplaced step.

When we make a typing error, we can use the backspace key to erase the mistake and then make a correction. As long as the error appears near the end of the word, this may be the quickest strategy for making amends. But what if the mistake was at the start of the word?

Expert typists recommend drastic measures: delete the entire word; then type it out again. If you can type at a rate above sixty words per minute, retyping a word from scratch will only take a second. If you can't type that fast, consider this to be good practice! There are particular words that I consistently mistype. Since I started following this advice, I've become more aware of which words trip me up. As a result, I now make fewer mistakes.

Alternatively, you could switch to Normal mode, navigate to the start of the word, fix the error, then hit A to return to where you left off in Insert mode. That little dance could take longer than a second, and it would do nothing to improve your touch-typing skills. Just because we can switch modes doesn't mean that we should.

In Insert mode, the backspace key works just as you would expect: it deletes the character in front of the cursor. The following chords are also available to us:

Keystrokes	Effect
`<C-h>`	Delete back one character (backspace)
`<C-w>`	Delete back one word
`<C-u>`	Delete back to start of line

These commands are not unique to Insert mode or even to Vim. We can also use them in Vim's command line as well as in the bash shell.

Tip 14

Get Back to Normal Mode

Insert mode is specialized for one task—entering text—whereas Normal mode is where we spend most of our time (as the name suggests). So it's important to be able to switch quickly between them. This tip demonstrates a couple of tricks that reduce the friction of mode switching.

The classic way of getting back to Normal mode is with the `<Esc>` key, but on many keyboards that can seem like a long reach. Alternatively, we can press `<C-[>`, which has exactly the same effect (see :h i_CTRL-[ⓘ).

Keystrokes	Effect
`<Esc>`	Switch to Normal mode
`<C-[>`	Switch to Normal mode
`<C-o>`	Switch to Insert Normal mode

Vim novices frequently become fatigued by the constant need to switch modes, but with practice it starts to feel more natural. Vim's modal nature can feel awkward in one particular scenario: when we're in Insert mode and we want to run only one Normal command and then continue where we left off in Insert mode. Vim has a neat solution to ease the friction caused by switching modes: *Insert Normal mode.*

Meet Insert Normal Mode

Insert Normal mode is a special version of Normal mode, which gives us one bullet. We can fire off a single command, after which we'll be returned to Insert mode immediately. From Insert mode, we can switch to Insert Normal mode by pressing `<C-o>` (:h i_CTRL-O ⓘ).

When the current line is right at the top or bottom of the window, I sometimes want to scroll the screen to see a bit more context. The `zz` command redraws the screen with the current line in the middle of the window, which allows us to read half a screen above and below the line we're working on. I'll often trigger this from Insert Normal mode by tapping out `<C-o>zz`. That puts me straight back into Insert mode so that I can continue typing uninterrupted.

Tip 15

Paste from a Register Without Leaving Insert Mode

Vim's yank and put operations are usually executed from Normal mode, but sometimes we might want to paste text into the document without leaving Insert mode.

Here's an unfinished excerpt of text:

`insert_mode/practical-vim.txt`
```
Practical Vim, by Drew Neil
Read Drew Neil's
```

> ## Remap the Caps Lock Key
>
> For Vim users, the Caps Lock key is a menace. If Caps Lock is engaged and you try using the k and j keys to move the cursor around, you'll instead trigger the K and J commands. Briefly: K looks up the man page for the word under the cursor (:h K ⓘ), and J joins the current and next lines together (:h J ⓘ). It's surprising how quickly you can mangle the text in your buffer by accidentally enabling the Caps Lock key!
>
> Many Vim users remap the Caps Lock button to make it act like another key, such as <Esc> or <Ctrl>. On modern keyboards, the <Esc> key is difficult to reach, whereas the Caps Lock key is handy. Mapping Caps Lock to behave as an <Esc> key can save a lot of effort, especially since the <Esc> key is so heavily used in Vim. I prefer to map the Caps Lock button to behave instead as a <Ctrl> key. The <C-[> mapping is synonymous with <Esc>, and it's easier to type when the <Ctrl> key is within easy reach. Additionally, the <Ctrl> key can be used for many other mappings, both in Vim and in other programs too.
>
> The simplest way to remap the Caps Lock key is to do it at the system level. The methods differ on OS X, Linux, and Windows, so rather than reproducing instructions here for each system, I suggest that you consult Google. Note that this customization won't just affect Vim: it applies system-wide. If you take my advice, you'll throw away the Caps Lock key forever. You won't miss it, I promise.

We want to complete the last line by inserting the title of this book. Since that text is already present at the start of the first line, we'll yank it into a register and then append the text at the end of the next line in Insert mode:

Keystrokes	Buffer Contents
yt,	Practical Vim, by Drew Neil Read Drew Neil's
jA␣	Practical Vim, by Drew Neil Read Drew Neil's █
<C-r>0	Practical Vim, by Drew Neil Read Drew Neil's Practical Vim█
.<Esc>	Practical Vim, by Drew Neil Read Drew Neil's Practical Vim.

The command yt, yanks the words *Practical Vim* into the yank register (we'll meet the t{char} motion in Tip 50, *Find by Character*, on page 120). In Insert mode, we can press <C-r>0 to paste the text that we just yanked at the current cursor position. We'll discuss registers and the yank operation at greater length in Chapter 10, *Copy and Paste*, on page 145.

The general format of the command is <C-r>{register}, where {register} is the address of the register we want to insert (see :h i_CTRL-R ⓘ).

Use <C-r>{register} for Character-wise Registers

The `<C-r>{register}` command is convenient for pasting a few words from Insert mode. If the register contains a lot of text, you might notice a slight delay before the screen updates. That's because Vim inserts the text from the register as if it were being typed one character at a time. If the 'textwidth' or 'autoindent' options are enabled, you might end up with unwanted line breaks or extra indentation.

The `<C-r><C-p>{register}` command is smarter. It inserts text literally and fixes any unintended indentation (see :h i_CTRL-R_CTRL-P ⓘ). But it's a bit of a handful! If I want to paste a register containing multiple lines of text, I prefer to switch to Normal mode and use one of the put commands (see Tip 63, *Paste from a Register*, on page 155).

Tip 16

Do Back-of-the-Envelope Calculations in Place

The expression register allows us to perform calculations and then insert the result directly into our document. In this tip, we'll see one application for this powerful feature.

Most of Vim's registers contain text either as a string of characters or as entire lines of text. The delete and yank commands allow us to set the contents of a register, while the put command allows us to get the contents of a register by inserting it into the document.

The expression register is different. It can evaluate a piece of Vim script code and return the result. Here, we can use it like a calculator. Passing it a simple arithmetic expression, such as 1+1, gives a result of 2. We can use the return value from the expression register just as though it were a piece of text saved in a plain old register.

The expression register is addressed by the = symbol. From Insert mode we can access it by typing `<C-r>=`. This opens a prompt at the bottom of the screen where we can type the expression that we want to evaluate. When done, we hit `<CR>`, and Vim inserts the result at our current position in the document.

Suppose that we've just typed the following:

insert_mode/back-of-envelope.txt
```
6 chairs, each costing $35, totals $
```

There's no need to scribble on the back side of an envelope. Vim can do the math for us, and we don't even have to leave Insert mode. Here's how:

Keystrokes	Buffer Contents
`A`	`6 chairs, each costing $35, totals $`▮
`<C-r>=6*35<CR>`	`6 chairs, each costing $35, totals $210`▮

The expression register is capable of much more than simple arithmetic. We'll meet a slightly more advanced example in Tip 71, *Evaluate an Iterator to Number Items in a List*, on page 177.

Tip 17

Insert Unusual Characters by Character Code

Vim can insert any character by its numeric code. This can be handy for entering symbols that are not found on the keyboard.

We can tell Vim to insert any arbitrary character if we know its numeric code. From Insert mode, we just have to type `<C-v>{code}`, where {code} is the address of the character that we want to insert.

Vim expects the numeric code to consist of three digits. Suppose, for example, that we wanted to insert an uppercase "A" character. The character code is 65, so we would have to enter it as `<C-v>065`.

But what if we wanted to insert a character whose numeric code is longer than three digits? For example, the Unicode Basic Multilingual Plane has an address space for up to 65,535 characters. It turns out that we can enter all of these using a four-digit hexadecimal code if we type `<C-v>u{1234}` (note the *u* preceding the digit this time). Let's say we wanted to insert an inverted question mark symbol ("¿"), which is represented by the character code 00bf. From Insert mode, we would just have to type `<C-v>u00bf`. See `:h i_CTRL-V_digit` ⓘ for more details.

If you want to find out the numeric code for any character in your document, just place the cursor on it and trigger the `ga` command. This outputs a message at the bottom of the screen, revealing the character code in decimal and hexadecimal notations (see `:h ga` ⓘ). Of course, this is of little help if you want to know the code for a character that is not already present in your document. In that case, you might want to look up the unicode tables.

In another scenario, if the `<C-v>` command is followed by any *nondigit* key, it will insert the character represented by that key literally. For example, if the 'expandtab' option is enabled, then pressing the `<Tab>` key will insert space characters instead of a tab character. However, pressing `<C-v><Tab>` will *always* insert a tab character literally, regardless of whether 'expandtab' is enabled or not.

Table 3, *Inserting Unusual Characters*, on page 35, summarizes the commands for entering unusual characters.

Keystrokes	Effect
`<C-v>{123}`	Insert character by decimal code
`<C-v>u{1234}`	Insert character by hexadecimal code
`<C-v>{nondigit}`	Insert nondigit literally
`<C-k>{char1}{char2}`	Insert character represented by `{char1}{char2}` digraph

Table 3—Inserting Unusual Characters

Tip 18

Insert Unusual Characters by Digraph

While Vim allows us to insert any character by its numeric code, these can be hard to remember and awkward to type. We can also insert unusual characters as digraphs: pairs of characters that are easy to remember.

Digraphs are easy to use. From Insert mode, we just type `<C-k>{char1}{char2}`. So if we wanted to insert the "¿" character, which is represented by the digraph ?I, we would simply type `<C-k>?I`.

The character pairs that make up a digraph are chosen to be descriptive, making them easier to remember or even guess. For example, the double-angle quotation marks « and » are represented by the digraphs << and >>; the vulgar (or common) fractions ½, ¼, and ¾ are represented by the digraphs 12, 14, and 34, respectively. The default set of digraphs that ship with Vim follows certain conventions, which are summarized under :h digraphs-default ⓘ.

We can view a list of the available digraphs by running :digraphs, but the output of this command is difficult to digest. A more usable list can be found by looking up :h digraph-table ⓘ.

Tip 19

Overwrite Existing Text with Replace Mode

Replace mode is identical to Insert mode, except that it overwrites existing text in the document.

Suppose that we had an excerpt of text such as this:

insert_mode/replace.txt
```
Typing in Insert mode extends the line. But in Replace mode
the line length doesn't change.
```

Instead of using two separate sentences, we're going to run this together into a single sentence by changing the period to a comma. We also have to down-case the "B" in the word "But." This example shows how we could do this using Replace mode.

Keystrokes	Buffer Contents
{start}	`Typing in Insert mode extends the line. But in Replace mode` `the line length doesn't change.`
`f.`	`Typing in Insert mode extends the line. But in Replace mode` `the line length doesn't change.`
`R,␣b<Esc>`	`Typing in Insert mode extends the line, but in Replace mode` `the line length doesn't change.`

From Normal mode, we can engage Replace mode with the `R` command. As the example demonstrates, typing ", b" overwrites the existing ". B" characters. And when we're finished with Replace mode, we can hit the `<Esc>` key to return to Normal mode. Not all keyboards have an `<Insert>` key, but if yours does, then you can use it to toggle between Insert and Replace modes.

Overwrite Tab Characters with Virtual Replace Mode

Some characters can complicate matters for Replace mode. Consider the tab character. This is represented by a single character in the file, but onscreen it expands to fill several columns, as defined by the 'tabstop' setting (see :h 'tabstop' ⓘ). If we placed our cursor on a tab stop and initiated Replace mode, then the next character we typed would overwrite the tab character. Supposing that the 'tabstop' option was set to 8 (the default), this would appear to replace eight characters with one, causing a drastic reduction in the length of the current line.

Vim has a second variant of Replace mode. *Virtual Replace mode* is triggered with `gR` and treats the tab character as though it consisted of spaces. Suppose that we position the cursor on a tab stop spanning eight columns of screen real estate. If we switch to Virtual Replace mode, we could type up to seven characters, each of which would be inserted in front of the tab character. Finally, if we typed an eighth character, it would replace the tab stop.

In Virtual Replace mode, we overwrite characters of screen real estate rather than dealing with the actual characters that would eventually be saved in a file. This tends to produce fewer surprises, so I would recommend using Virtual Replace mode whenever possible.

Vim also provides a single-shot version of Replace mode and Virtual Replace mode. The `r{char}` and `gr{char}` commands allow us to overwrite a single character before switching straight back to Normal mode (:h r ⓘ).

CHAPTER 4

Visual Mode

Vim's Visual mode allows us to define a selection of text and then operate upon it. This should feel pretty intuitive, since it is the model that most editing software follows. But Vim's take is characteristically different, so we'll start by making sure we grok Visual mode (Tip 20, *Grok Visual Mode*, on page 39).

Vim has three variants of Visual mode involving working with characters, lines, or rectangular blocks of text. We'll explore ways of switching between these modes as well as some useful tricks for modifying the bounds of a selection (Tip 21, *Define a Visual Selection*, on page 41).

We'll see that the dot command can be used to repeat Visual mode commands, but that it's especially effective when operating on line-wise regions. When working with character-wise selections, the dot command can sometimes fall short of our expectations. We'll see that in these scenarios, operator commands may be preferable.

Visual-Block mode is rather special in that it allows us to operate on rectangular columns of text. You'll find many uses for this feature, but we'll focus on three tips that demonstrate some of its capabilities.

Tip 20

Grok Visual Mode

Visual mode allows us to select a range of text and then operate upon it. However intuitive this might seem, Vim's perspective on selecting text is different from other text editors.

Suppose for a minute that we're not working with Vim but instead filling out a text area on a web page. We've written the word "March," but it should read

"April," so using the mouse, we double-click the word to select it. Having highlighted the word, we could hit the backspace key to delete it and then type out the correct month as a replacement.

You probably already know that there's no need to hit the backspace key in this example. With the word "March" selected, we would only have to type the letter "A" and it would replace the selection, preparing the way so that we could type out the rest of the word "April." It's not much, but a keystroke saved is a keystroke earned.

If you expect this behavior to carry over to Vim's Visual mode, you're in for a surprise. The clue is right there in the name: Visual *mode* is just another mode, which means that each key performs a different function.

Many of the commands that you are familiar with from Normal mode work just the same in Visual mode. We can still use `h`, `j`, `k`, and `l` as cursor keys. We can use `f{char}` to jump to a character on the current line and then repeat or reverse the jump with the `;` and `,` commands, respectively. We can even use the search command (and `n`/`N`) to jump to pattern matches. Each time we move our cursor in Visual mode, we change the bounds of the selection.

Some Visual mode commands perform the same basic function as in Normal mode but with a slight twist. For example, the `c` command is consistent in both modes in that it deletes the specified text and then switches to Insert mode. The difference is in how we specify the range on which to act. From Normal mode, we trigger the change command first and then specify the range as a motion. This, if you'll remember from Tip 12, *Combine and Conquer*, on page 24, is called an operator command. Whereas in Visual mode, we start off by making the selection and then trigger the change command. This inversion of control can be generalized for all operator commands (see Table 2, *Vim's Operator Commands*, on page 25). For most people, the Visual mode approach feels more intuitive.

Let's revisit the simple example where we wanted to change the word "March" to "April." This time, suppose that we have left the confines of the text area on a web page and we're comfortably back inside Vim. We place our cursor somewhere on the word "March" and run `viw` to visually select the word. Now, we can't just type the word "April" because that would trigger the `A` command and append the text "pril"! Instead, we'll use the `c` command to *change* the selection, deleting the word and dropping us into Insert mode, where we can type out the word "April" in full. This pattern of usage is similar to our original example, except that we use the `c` key instead of backspace.

> ### Meet Select Mode
>
> In a typical text editing environment, selected text is deleted when we type any printable character. Vim's Visual mode doesn't follow this convention—but Select mode does. According to Vim's built-in documentation, it "resembles the selection mode in Microsoft Windows" (see :h Select-mode ⓘ). Printable characters cause the selection to be deleted, Vim enters Insert mode, and the typed character is inserted.
>
> We can toggle between Visual and Select modes by pressing <C-g>. The only visible difference is the message at the bottom of screen, which switches between -- VISUAL -- and -- SELECT --. But if we type any printable character in Select mode, it will replace the selection and switch to Insert mode. Of course, from Visual mode you could just as well use the c key to change the selection.
>
> If you are happy to embrace the modal nature of Vim, then you should find little use for Select mode, which holds the hand of users who want to make Vim behave more like other text editors. I can think of only one place where I consistently use Select mode: when using a plugin that emulates TextMate's snippet functionality, Select mode highlights the active placeholder.

Tip 21

Define a Visual Selection

Visual mode's three submodes deal with different kinds of text. In this tip, we'll look at the ways of enabling each visual submode, as well as how to switch between them.

Vim has three kinds of Visual mode. In *character-wise Visual mode*, we can select anything from a single character up to a range of characters within a line or spanning multiple lines. This is suitable for working at the level of individual words or phrases. If we want to operate on entire lines, we can use *line-wise* Visual mode instead. Finally, *block-wise* Visual mode allows us to work with columnar regions of the document. Block-wise Visual mode is quite special, so we'll discuss it at greater length in Tip 24, *Edit Tabular Data with Visual-Block Mode*, on page 47, Tip 25, *Change Columns of Text*, on page 49, and Tip 26, *Append After a Ragged Visual Block*, on page 50.

Enabling Visual Modes

The v key is our gateway into Visual mode. From Normal mode, we can press v by itself to enable character-wise Visual mode. Line-wise Visual mode is enabled by pressing V (with the Shift key), and block-wise Visual mode by pressing `<C-v>` (with the Control key). These commands are summarized in the following table:

Command	Effect
v	Enable character-wise Visual mode
V	Enable line-wise Visual mode
`<C-v>`	Enable block-wise Visual mode
gv	Reselect the last visual selection

The gv command is a useful little shortcut. It reselects the range of text that was last selected in Visual mode. No matter whether the previous selection was character-wise, line-wise, or block-wise, the gv command should do the right thing. The only case where it might get confused is if the last selection has since been deleted.

Switching Between Visual Modes

We can switch between the different flavors of Visual mode in the same way that we enable them from Normal mode. If we're in character-wise Visual mode, we can switch to the line-wise variant by pressing V, or to block-wise Visual mode with `<C-v>`. But if we were to press v from character-wise Visual mode, it would switch us back into Normal mode. So you can think of the v key as a toggle between Normal mode and character-wise Visual mode. The V and `<C-v>` keys also toggle between Normal mode and their respective flavors of Visual mode. Of course, you can always switch back to Normal mode by pressing `<Esc>` or `<C-[>` (just like getting out of Insert mode). This table summarizes the commands for switching between Visual modes:

Command	Effect
`<Esc>` / `<C-[>`	Switch to Normal mode
v / V / `<C-v>`	Switch to Normal mode (when used from character-, line- or block-wise Visual mode, respectively)
v	Switch to character-wise Visual mode
V	Switch to line-wise Visual mode
`<C-v>`	Switch to block-wise Visual mode
o	Go to other end of highlighted text

Toggling the Free End of a Selection

The range of a Visual mode selection is marked by two ends: one end is fixed and the other moves freely with our cursor. We can use the `o` key to toggle the free end. This is really handy if halfway through defining a selection we realize that we started in the wrong place. Rather than leaving Visual mode and starting afresh, we can just hit `o` and redefine the bounds of the selection. The following demonstrates how we can use this technique:

Keystrokes	Buffer Contents
{start}	Select from here to here.
vbb	Select from here to here.
o	Select from here to here.
e	Select from here to here.

Tip 22

Repeat Line-Wise Visual Commands

When we use the dot command to repeat a change made to a visual selection, it repeats the change on the same range of text. In this tip, we'll make a change to a line-wise selection and then repeat it with the dot command.

When we execute a command from Visual mode, we are dropped back into Normal mode and the range of text that was marked out in Visual mode is unselected. So what should we do if we want to perform another Visual mode command on the same range of text?

Suppose that we had the following excerpt of malformatted Python:

visual_mode/fibonacci-malformed.py
```
def fib(n):
    a, b = 0, 1
    while a < n:
print a,
a, b = b, a+b
fib(42)
```

This code sample uses four spaces per indentation. First, we'll have to configure Vim to match this style.

Preparation

To make the `<` and `>` commands work properly, we should set the 'shiftwidth' and 'softtabstop' settings to 4 and enable 'expandtab'. If you want to understand how these settings work together, check out the "Tabs and Spaces" episode on Vimcasts.org.[1] This one-liner does the trick:

⇒ `:set shiftwidth=4 softtabstop=4 expandtab`

Indent Once, Then Repeat

In our malformed Python excerpt, the two lines below the while keyword should be indented further by two levels. We could fix it by visually selecting the text and triggering the `>` command to indent it. But that would only increase the indentation by one level before dropping us back into Normal mode.

One solution would be to reselect the same text using the `gv` command and then invoke the indentation command again. But if you're getting a feel for the Vim way, then this should raise alarm bells for you.

When we need to repeat ourselves, the dot command is our friend. Rather than reselecting the same range of text and repeating the same command manually, we can just hit the `.` key from Normal mode. Here it is in action:

Keystrokes	Buffer Contents

{start}	```def fib(n):```
	``` a, b = 0, 1```
	``` while a < n:```
	```print a,```
	```a, b = b, a+b```
	```fib(42)```

Vj	```def fib(n):```
	``` a, b = 0, 1```
	``` while a < n:```
	```print a,```
	```a, b = b, a+b```
	```fib(42)```

>.	```def fib(n):```
	``` a, b = 0, 1```
	``` while a < n:```
	``` print a,```
	``` a, b = b, a+b```
	```fib(42)```

If you're good at counting, you might prefer to hit the target in a single blow by running `2>` from Visual mode. I prefer using the dot command because it

---

1. http://vimcasts.org/e/2

gives me instant visual feedback. If I need to trigger the indentation command again, I just hit `.` another time. Or if I get trigger-happy and overshoot my mark, I press the `u` key to bring it back in line. Tip 11, *Don't Count If You Can Repeat*, on page 22, discusses the differences in a little more detail.

When we use the dot command to repeat a Visual mode command, it acts on the same amount of text as was marked by the most recent visual selection. This behavior tends to work in our favor when we make line-wise visual selections, but it can have surprising results with character-wise selections. Next, we'll look at an example that illustrates this.

Tip 23

Prefer Operators to Visual Commands Where Possible

Visual mode may be more intuitive than Vim's Normal mode of operation, but it has a weakness: it doesn't always play well with the dot command. We can route around this weakness by using Normal mode operators when appropriate.

Suppose that we want to transform the following list of links to make them shout:

```
visual_mode/list-of-links.html
<a href="#">one</a>
<a href="#">two</a>
<a href="#">three</a>
```

We can select the inner contents of a tag by running `vit`, which can be read as: *visually* select *inside* the *tag*. The `it` command is a special kind of motion called a text object, which we'll cover in detail in Tip 52, *Trace Your Selection with Precision Text Objects*, on page 126.

Using a Visual Operator

In Visual mode, we make a selection and then act on it. In this case, we could use the `U` command, which converts the selected characters to uppercase (`:h v_U`). See Table 4, *Uppercasing in Visual Mode*, on page 46.

Having transformed the first line, we now want to perform the same change on the next two lines. How about we try using the Dot Formula?

Running `j.` advances our cursor to the next line and then repeats the last change. It works fine on line two, but if we try it again we end up with this strange-looking result:

Keystrokes	Buffer Contents

{start}	`<a href="#">one</a>`
	`<a href="#">two</a>`
	`<a href="#">three</a>`

vit	`<a href="#">one</a>`
	`<a href="#">two</a>`
	`<a href="#">three</a>`

U	`<a href="#">ONE</a>`
	`<a href="#">two</a>`
	`<a href="#">three</a>`

Table 4—Uppercasing in Visual Mode

```
<a href="#">ONE</a>
<a href="#">TWO</a>
<a href="#">THRee</a>
```

Do you see what's happened? When a Visual mode command is repeated, it affects the same range of text (see :h visual-repeat ⓘ). In this case, the original command affected a word consisting of three letters. This works fine for line two, which happens to also contain a three-letter word, but it falls short when we try to repeat the command on a word containing five letters.

Using a Normal Operator

The Visual mode U command has a Normal mode equivalent: gU{motion} (:h gU ⓘ). If we use this to make the first change, we can complete the subsequent edits using the Dot Formula:

Keystrokes	Buffer Contents

{start}	`<a href="#">one</a>`
	`<a href="#">two</a>`
	`<a href="#">three</a>`

gUit	`<a href="#">ONE</a>`
	`<a href="#">two</a>`
	`<a href="#">three</a>`

j.	`<a href="#">ONE</a>`
	`<a href="#">TWO</a>`
	`<a href="#">three</a>`

j.	`<a href="#">ONE</a>`
	`<a href="#">TWO</a>`
	`<a href="#">THREE</a>`

Discussion

Both of these techniques require only four keystrokes: `vitU` versus `gUit`, but the underlying semantics are quite different. In the Visual mode approach, the four keystrokes can be considered as two separate commands: `vit` to make a selection and `U` to transform the selection. In contrast, `gUit` can be considered as a single command comprised of an operator (`gU`) and a motion (`it`).

If we want to set up the dot command so that it repeats something useful, then we're better off staying out of Visual mode. As a general rule, we should prefer operator commands over their Visual mode equivalents when working through a repetitive set of changes.

That's not to say that Visual mode is out of bounds. It still has a place. Not every editing task needs to be repeated, so Visual mode is perfectly adequate for one-off changes. And even though Vim's motions allow for surgical precision, sometimes we need to modify a range of text whose structure is difficult to trace. In these cases, Visual mode is the right tool for the job.

Tip 24

Edit Tabular Data with Visual-Block Mode

We can work with rows of text in any editor, but manipulating columns of text requires a more specialized tool. Vim provides this capability in the form of its Visual-Block mode, which we'll use to transform a plain-text table.

Suppose that we have a plain-text table such as this one:

```
visual_mode/chapter-table.txt
Chapter          Page
Normal mode        15
Insert mode        31
Visual mode        44
```

We want to draw a vertical line out of pipe characters to separate the two columns of text and make it look more like a table. But first, we'll reduce the spacing between the two columns, which are farther apart than they need be. We can make both of these changes using Visual-Block mode. See how in Table 5, *Adding vertical pipes between columns*, on page 48.

Keystrokes	Buffer Contents	
{start}	Chapter ▊ Page
	Normal mode 15
	Insert mode 31
	Visual mode 44
`<C-v>3j`	Chapter ▊ Page
	Normal mode ▊ 15
	Insert mode ▊ 31
	Visual mode ▊ 44
x...	Chapter ▊ Page
	Normal mode 15
	Insert mode 31
	Visual mode 44
gv	Chapter ▊ Page
	Normal mode ▊ 15
	Insert mode ▊ 31
	Visual mode ▊ 44
r|	Chapter ▊ Page
	Normal mode | 15
	Insert mode | 31
	Visual mode | 44
yyp	Chapter | Page
	▊hapter | Page
	Normal mode | 15
	Insert mode | 31
	Visual mode | 44
Vr-	Chapter | Page
	▊-------------------
	Normal mode | 15
	Insert mode | 31
	Visual mode | 44

Table 5—Adding vertical pipes between columns

To begin, we use `<C-v>` to engage Visual-Block mode; then we define the column selection by moving our cursor down several lines. Pressing the x key deletes that column, and the dot command repeats the deletion for the same range of text. We repeat until the two columns are about the right distance apart.

Instead of using the dot command, we could have expanded our column selection into a box by moving the cursor two or three steps to the right. Then we would have to make only a single deletion. I prefer the instant visual feedback that we get when we delete a single column and repeat it.

Now that we've lined up the two columns of text where we want them, we're ready to draw a line between them. We can reselect our last visual selection using the `gv` command and then press `r|` to replace each character in the selection with a pipe character.

While we're at it, we may as well draw a horizontal line to separate the table headers from the rows beneath. We do a quick line-wise yank-and-put to duplicate the top line (`yyp`) and then replace every character in that line with a dash character (`Vr-`).

Tip 25

Change Columns of Text

We can use Visual-Block mode to insert text into several lines of text simultaneously.

Visual-Block mode is not just useful to us when working with tabular data. Oftentimes, we can benefit from this feature when working with code. For example, take this snippet of (suboptimal) CSS:

```
visual_mode/sprite.css
li.one   a{ background-image: url('/images/sprite.png'); }
li.two   a{ background-image: url('/images/sprite.png'); }
li.three a{ background-image: url('/images/sprite.png'); }
```

Suppose that the sprite.png file has been moved from images/ into a components/ directory. We'll need to change each of these lines to reference the file's new location. We could do this using Visual-Block mode as shown in Table 6, *Inserting into Multiple Lines*, on page 50.

The procedure should look pretty familiar. We begin by defining the selection that we want to operate on, which happens to be a rectangular Visual-Block. When we hit the `c` key, all of the selected text disappears and we are dropped into Insert mode.

As we type the word "components" in Insert mode, it appears on the topmost line only. Nothing happens to the two lines below. We see the text that we typed in those lines only when we press `<Esc>` to return to Normal mode.

The behavior of Vim's Visual-Block change command may be a little surprising. It seems inconsistent that the deletion should affect all marked lines simultaneously, but the insertion affects only the topmost line (at least for the duration of Insert mode). Some text editors provide similar functionality, but they update all selected lines at the same time. If you're used to that kind of behavior (as I was), then you might find Vim's implementation less polished.

Keystrokes	Buffer Contents

{start}
 	
Normal mode
	`li.one   a{ background-image: url('/`**i**`mages/sprite.png'); }`
	`li.two   a{ background-image: url('/images/sprite.png'); }`
	`li.three a{ background-image: url('/images/sprite.png'); }`

`<C-v>jje`
 	
Visual mode
	`li.one   a{ background-image: url('/`images`/sprite.png'); }`
	`li.two   a{ background-image: url('/`images`/sprite.png'); }`
	`li.three a{ background-image: url('/`image**s**`/sprite.png'); }`

`c`
 	
Insert mode
	`li.one   a{ background-image: url('/`**/**`sprite.png'); }`
	`li.two   a{ background-image: url('//sprite.png'); }`
	`li.three a{ background-image: url('//sprite.png'); }`

components
 	
Insert mode
	`li.one   a{ background-image: url('/components`**/**`sprite.png'); }`
	`li.two   a{ background-image: url('//sprite.png'); }`
	`li.three a{ background-image: url('//sprite.png'); }`

`<Esc>`
 	
Normal mode
	`li.one   a{ background-image: url('/component`**s**`/sprite.png'); }`
	`li.two   a{ background-image: url('/components/sprite.png'); }`
	`li.three a{ background-image: url('/components/sprite.png'); }`

Table 6—Inserting into Multiple Lines

But in practice, it makes no difference in the final outcome. So long as you dip into Insert mode only for short bursts, you shouldn't have any surprises.

Tip 26

Append After a Ragged Visual Block

Visual-Block mode is great for operating on rectangular chunks of code such as lines and columns, but it's not confined to rectangular regions of text.

We've already met this snippet of JavaScript:

```
the_vim_way/2_foo_bar.js
var foo = 1
var bar = 'a'
var foobar = foo + bar
```

Three consecutive lines, each of different length. We want to append a semicolon at the end of each. In Tip 2, *Don't Repeat Yourself*, on page 4, we solved this problem using the dot command, but we could just as well use Visual-Block mode:

Keystrokes	Buffer Contents

{start}
 	
Normal mode
	`var foo = `**`1`**
	`var bar = 'a'`
	`var foobar = foo + bar`

`<C-v>jj$` *Visual-Block*	`var foo = `**`1`** `var bar = `**`'a'`** `var foobar`**` = foo + bar`**

`A;`
 	
Insert mode
	`var foo = 1;`
	`var bar = 'a'`
	`var foobar = foo + bar`

`<Esc>`
 	
Normal mode
	`var foo = `**`1`**`;`
	`var bar = 'a';`
	`var foobar = foo + bar;`

After engaging Visual-Block mode, we extend our selection to the end of each line by pressing `$`. At first glance, one might expect this to cause difficulty because each line is a different length. But in this context, Vim understands that we want to extend our selection to the end of all selected lines. This lets us break free from our rectangular constraints, creating a selection that traces the ragged right edge of our text.

Having defined our selection, we can append at the end of each line using the `A` command (see *Vim's Conventions for "i" and "a" Keys*, on page 51). This drops us into Insert mode on the topmost line of our selection. Anything that we type will appear on this line only for the duration of Insert mode, but as soon as we revert to Normal mode, our changes are propagated across the rest of the lines that we selected.

Vim's Conventions for "i" and "a" Keys

Vim has a couple of conventions for switching from Normal to Insert mode. The `i` and `a` commands both do it, positioning the cursor in front of or after the current *character*, respectively. The `I` and `A` commands behave similarly, except that they position the cursor at the start or end of the current *line*.

Vim follows similar conventions for switching from Visual-Block to Insert mode. The `I` and `A` commands both do it, placing the cursor at the start or end of the *selection*, respectively. So what about the `i` and `a` commands; what do they do in Visual mode?

In Visual and Operator-Pending modes the `i` and `a` keys follow a different convention: they form the first half of a *text object*. These are covered in greater depth in Tip 52, *Trace Your Selection with Precision Text Objects*, on page 126. If you've made a selection with Visual-Block mode and you wonder why you're not in Insert mode after pressing `i`, try using `I` instead.

In the beginning, there was ed. ed begat ex, and ex begat vi, and vi begat Vim.

➤ *The Old Testament of Unix*

CHAPTER 5

Command-Line Mode

Vim traces its ancestry back to vi, which is where the modal editing paradigm was conceived. In turn, vi traces its ancestry back to a line editor called ex, which is why we have Ex commands. The DNA of these early Unix text editors is preserved in modern Vim. For some line-oriented tasks, Ex commands are still the best tool for the job. In this chapter, we'll learn how to use Command-Line mode, which exposes us to the vestiges of ex.

Tip 27

Meet Vim's Command Line

Command-Line mode prompts us to enter an Ex command, a search pattern, or an expression. In this tip, we'll meet a selection of Ex commands that operate on the text in a buffer, and we'll learn about some of the special key mappings that can be used in this mode.

When we press the `:` key, Vim switches into Command-Line mode. This mode has some resemblance to the command line that we use in the shell. We can type the name of a command and then execute it by pressing `<CR>`. At any time, we can switch from Command-Line mode back to Normal mode by pressing `<Esc>`.

For historical reasons, the commands that we execute from Command-Line mode are called *Ex commands* (see *On the Etymology of Vim (and Family)*, on page 55). Command-Line mode is also enabled when we press `/` to bring up a search prompt or `<C-r>=` to access the expression register (see Tip 16, *Do Back-of-the-Envelope Calculations in Place*, on page 33). Some of the tricks in this chapter are applicable with each of these different prompts, but for the most part we'll focus on Ex commands.

Command	Effect
:[range]delete [x]	Delete specified lines [into register x]
:[range]yank [x]	Yank specified lines [into register x]
:[line]put [x]	Put the text from register x after the specified line
:[range]copy {address}	Copy the specified lines to below the line specified by {address}
:[range]move {address}	Move the specified lines to below the line specified by {address}
:[range]join	Join the specified lines
:[range]normal {commands}	Execute Normal mode {commands} on each specified line
:[range]substitute/{pattern}/{string}/[flags]	Replace occurrences of {pattern} with {string} on each specified line
:[range]global/{pattern}/[cmd]	Execute the Ex command [cmd] on all specified lines where the {pattern} matches

Table 7—Ex Commands That Operate on the Text in a Buffer

We can use Ex commands to read and write files (:edit and :write), to create tabs (:tabnew) or split windows (:split), or to interact with the argument list (:prev/:next) or the buffer list (:bprev/:bnext). In fact, Vim has an Ex command for just about everything (see :h ex-cmd-index ⓘ for the full list).

In this chapter, we'll focus mainly on the handful of Ex commands we can use to edit text. Table 7, *Ex Commands That Operate on the Text in a Buffer*, on page 54, shows a selection of some of the most useful ones.

Most of these commands can accept a range. We'll find out what this means in Tip 28, *Execute a Command on One or More Consecutive Lines*, on page 56. The :copy command is great for quickly duplicating a line, as we'll see in *Duplicate Lines with the ':t' Command*, on page 61. The :normal command provides a convenient way to make the same change on a range of lines, as we'll see in Tip 30, *Run Normal Mode Commands Across a Range*, on page 63.

We'll learn more about :delete, :yank, and :put commands in Chapter 10, *Copy and Paste*, on page 145. The :substitute and :global commands are very powerful, so they each get a chapter of their own. See Chapter 14, *Substitution*, on page 219, and Chapter 15, *Global Commands*, on page 241.

> ## On the Etymology of Vim (and Family)
>
> ed was the original Unix text editor. It was written at a time when video displays were uncommon. Source code was usually printed onto a roll of paper and edited on a teletype terminal.[a] Commands entered at the terminal would be sent to a mainframe computer for processing, and the output from each command would be printed. In those days, the connection between a terminal and a mainframe was slow, so much so that a quick typist could outpace the network, entering commands faster than they could be sent for processing. In this context, it was vital that ed provide a terse syntax. Consider how p prints the current line, while %p prints the entire file.
>
> ed went through several generations of improvements, including em (dubbed the "editor for mortals"), en, and eventually ex.[b] By this time, video displays were more common. ex added a feature that turned the terminal screen into an interactive window that showed the contents of a file. Now it was possible to see changes as they were made in real time. The screen-editing mode was activated by entering the :visual command, or just :vi for short. And that is where the name vi comes from.
>
> Vim stands for *vi improved*. That's an understatement—I can't stand to use regular vi! Look up :h vi-differences ⓘ for a list of Vim features that are unavailable in vi. Vim's enhancements are essential, but it still owes much to its heritage. The constraints that guided the design of Vim's ancestors have endowed us with a highly efficient command set that's still valuable today.
>
> ---
>
> a.   http://en.wikipedia.org/wiki/Teleprinter
>
> b.   http://www.theregister.co.uk/2003/09/11/bill_joys_greatest_gift/

Special Keys in Vim's Command-Line Mode

Command-Line mode is similar to Insert mode in that most of the buttons on the keyboard simply enter a character. In Insert mode, the text goes into a buffer, whereas in Command-Line mode the text appears at the prompt. In both of these modes, we can use control key chords to trigger commands.

Some of these commands are shared between Insert mode and Command-Line mode. For example, `<C-w>` and `<C-u>` delete backward to the start of the previous word or to the start of the line, respectively. We can use `<C-v>` or `<C-k>` to insert characters that are not found on the keyboard. And we can insert the contents of any register at the command line using the `<C-r>{register}` command, just as we saw in Tip 15, *Paste from a Register Without Leaving Insert Mode*, on page 31. Some Command-Line mode mappings are not found in Insert mode. We'll meet a few of these in Tip 33, *Insert the Current Word at the Command Prompt*, on page 68.

At the command-line prompt, we are limited in the range of motions that we can use. The `<left>` and `<right>` arrow keys move our cursor one character at a time in either direction. Compared to the rich set of motions that we're used to using in Normal mode, this can feel quite limiting. But as we'll see in Tip 34, *Recall Commands from History*, on page 70, Vim's command-line window provides all of the editing power that we could want for composing complex commands at the prompt.

Ex Commands Strike Far and Wide

It can sometimes be quicker to use an Ex command than to get the same job done with Vim's Normal commands. For example, Normal commands tend to act on the current character or the current line, whereas an Ex command can be executed anywhere. This means that we can use Ex commands to make changes without having to move our cursor. But the greatest feature that distinguishes Ex commands is their ability to be executed across many lines at the same time.

As a general rule, we could say that Ex commands are long range and have the capacity to modify many lines in a single move. Or to condense that even further: Ex commands strike far and wide.

Tip 28

Execute a Command on One or More Consecutive Lines

Many Ex commands can be given a [range] of lines to act upon. We can specify the start and end of a range with either a line number, a mark, or a pattern.

One of the strengths of Ex commands is that they can be executed across a range of lines. We'll use this short excerpt of HTML as an example:

cmdline_mode/practical-vim.html

```
Line 1  <!DOCTYPE html>
     2  <html>
     3    <head><title>Practical Vim</title></head>
     4    <body><h1>Practical Vim</h1></body>
     5  </html>
```

To demonstrate, we'll use the :print command, which simply echoes the specified lines below Vim's command line. This command doesn't perform any useful work, but it helps to illustrate which lines make up a range. Try replacing :print in each of the following examples with a command such as :delete, :join, :substitute, or :normal, and you should get a feel for how useful Ex commands can be.

Use Line Numbers as an Address

If we enter an Ex command consisting only of a number, then Vim will interpret that as an address and move our cursor to the specified line. We can jump to the top of the file by running the following:

```
⇒ :1
⇒ :print
❰ 1 <!DOCTYPE html>
```

This file contains only five lines. If we wanted to jump to the end of the file, we could enter :5 or we could use the special $ symbol:

```
⇒ :$
⇒ :p
❰ 5 </html>
```

Here we've used :p, which is the abbreviated form of :print. Instead of splitting up the two commands, we could roll them into a single incantation:

```
⇒ :3p
❰ 3 <head><title>Practical Vim</title></head>
```

That moves the cursor to line 3 and then echoes the contents of that line. Remember, we're just using the :p command for illustrative purposes here. If we had issued the command :3d, then we would have jumped to line 3 and deleted it in a single move. The equivalent Normal mode commands would be 3G followed by dd. So this is one example where an Ex command can be quicker than a Normal mode command.

Specify a Range of Lines by Address

So far, we've specified addresses as a single line number. But we can also specify a range of lines. Here's an example:

```
⇒ :2,5p
❰ 2 <html>
  3   <head><title>Practical Vim</title></head>
  4   <body><h1>Practical Vim</h1></body>
  5 </html>
```

That prints each line from 2 to 5, inclusive. Note that after running this command, the cursor would be left positioned on line 5. In general, we could say that a range takes this form:

```
:{start},{end}
```

Note that both the {start} and {end} are addresses. So far, we've looked at using line numbers for addresses, but we'll soon see that using a pattern or a mark is also possible.

We can use the . symbol as an address to represent the current line. So, we can easily compose a range representing everything from here to the end of the file:

⇒ **:2**
⇒ **:.,$p**
❮ 2 `<html>`
   3   `<head><title>Practical Vim</title></head>`
   4   `<body><h1>Practical Vim</h1></body>`
   5 `</html>`

The % symbol also has a special meaning—it stands for all the lines in the current file:

⇒ **:%p**
❮ 1 `<!DOCTYPE html>`
   2 `<html>`
   3   `<head><title>Practical Vim</title></head>`
   4   `<body><h1>Practical Vim</h1></body>`
   5 `</html>`

This is equivalent to running :1,$p. Using this shorthand in combination with the :substitute command is very common:

⇒ **:%s/Practical/Pragmatic/**

This command tells Vim to replace the first occurrence of "Practical" with "Pragmatic" on each line. We'll learn more about this command in Chapter 14, *Substitution*, on page 219.

Specify a Range of Lines by Visual Selection

Instead of addressing a range of lines by number, we could just make a visual selection. If we ran the command `2G` followed by `VG`, we would make a visual selection that looks like this:

```
<!DOCTYPE html>
<html>
    <head><title>Practical Vim</title></head>
    <body><h1>Practical Vim</h1></body>
</html>
```

If we press the `:` key now, the command-line prompt will be prepopulated with the range :'<,'>. It looks cryptic, but you can think of it simply as a range standing for the visual selection. Then we can specify our Ex command, and it will execute on every selected line:

```
➭ :'<,'>p
❮ 2 <html>
  3   <head><title>Practical Vim</title></head>
  4   <body><h1>Practical Vim</h1></body>
  5 </html>
```

This range can be really handy if we want to run a :substitute command on a subset of the file.

'< is a mark standing for the first line of the visual selection, while '> is the last line of the visual selection (see Tip 54, *Mark Your Place and Snap Back to It*, on page 131, for more about marks). These marks persist even when we leave Visual mode. If you try running :'<,'>p straight from Normal mode, it will always act on the lines that most recently formed a Visual mode selection.

Specify a Range of Lines by Patterns

Vim also accepts a pattern as an address for an Ex command, such as the one shown here:

```
➭ :/<html>/,/<\/html>/p
❮ 2 <html>
  3   <head><title>Practical Vim</title></head>
  4   <body><h1>Practical Vim</h1></body>
  5 </html>
```

This looks quite complex, but it follows the usual form for a range: :{start},{end}. The {start} address in this case is the pattern /<html>/, while the {end} address is /<\/html>/. In other words, the range begins on the line containing an opening <html> tag and ends on the line containing the corresponding closing tag.

In this particular case, we could achieve the same result using the address :2,5, which is shorter but more brittle. If we use patterns to specify the range, then our command will always operate on the entire <html></html> element, no matter how many lines it comprises.

Modify an Address Using an Offset

Suppose that we wanted to run an Ex command on every line inside the <html></html> block but not on the lines that contain the <html> and </html> tags themselves. We could do so using an offset:

```
➭ :/<html>/+1,/<\/html>/-1p
❮ 3   <head><title>Practical Vim</title></head>
  4   <body><h1>Practical Vim</h1></body>
```

The general form for an offset goes like this:

`:{address}+n`

If n is omitted, it defaults to 1. The {address} could be a line number, a mark, or a pattern.

Suppose that we wanted to execute a command on a particular number of lines, starting with the current line. We could use an offset relative to the current line:

⇒   `:2`
⇒   `:.,.+3p`

The . symbol stands for the current line, so :.,.+3 is equivalent to :2,5 in this case.

Discussion

The syntax for defining a range is very flexible. We can mix and match line numbers, marks, and patterns, and we can apply an offset to any of them. This table summarizes a few of the symbols that can be used to create addresses and ranges for Ex commands:

Symbol	Address
1	First line of the file
$	Last line of the file
0	Virtual line above first line of the file
.	Line where the cursor is placed
'm	Line containing mark m
'<	Start of visual selection
'>	End of visual selection
%	The entire file (shorthand for :1,$)

Line 0 doesn't really exist, but it can be useful as an address in certain contexts. In particular, it can be used as the final argument in the :copy {address} and :move {address} commands when we want to copy or move a range of lines to the top of a file. We'll see examples of these commands in the next two tips.

When we specify a [range], it always represents a set of contiguous lines. It's also possible to execute an Ex command on a set of noncontiguous lines using the :global command. We'll learn more about that in Chapter 15, *Global Commands*, on page 241.

Tip 29

Duplicate or Move Lines Using ':t' and ':m' Commands

The :copy command (and its shorthand :t) lets us duplicate one or more lines from one part of the document to another, while the :move command lets us place them somewhere else in the document.

For demonstration purposes, we'll use this shopping list:

cmdline_mode/shopping-list.todo
```
Line 1  Shopping list
     2      Hardware Store
     3          Buy new hammer
     4      Beauty Parlor
     5          Buy nail polish remover
     6          Buy nails
```

Duplicate Lines with the ':t' Command

Our shopping list is incomplete: we also need to buy nails at the hardware store. To fix the list, we'll reuse the last line of the file, creating a copy of it below "Hardware Store." We can easily do so using the :copy Ex command:

Keystrokes	Buffer Contents

{start}	Shopping list
	    Hardware Store
	        Buy new hammer
	    Beauty Parlor
	        Buy nail polish remover
	        Buy nails

:6copy.	Shopping list
	    Hardware Store
	        Buy nails
	        Buy new hammer
	    Beauty Parlor
	        Buy nail polish remover
	        Buy nails

The format of the copy command goes like this (see :h :copy 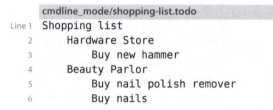):

```
:[range]copy {address}
```

In our example, the [range] was line 6. For our {address}, we used the . symbol, which stands for the current line. So we can read the :6copy. command as "Make a copy of line 6 and put it below the current line."

We could shorten the :copy command to only two letters, as :co. Or we can be even more succinct by using the :t command, which is a synonym for :copy. As a mnemonic, you can think of it as *copy TO*. This table shows a few examples of the :t command in action:

Command	Effect
:6t.	Copy line 6 to just below the current line
:t6	Copy the current line to just below line 6
:t.	Duplicate the current line (similar to Normal mode yyp)
:t$	Copy the current line to the end of the file
:'<,'>t0	Copy the visually selected lines to the start of the file

Note that :t. duplicates the current line. Alternatively, we could achieve the same effect using Normal mode yank and put commands (yyp). The one notable difference between these two techniques for duplicating the current line is that yyp uses a register, whereas :t. doesn't. I'll sometimes use :t. to duplicate a line when I don't want to overwrite the current value in the default register.

In this example, we could have used a variant of yyp to duplicate the line we wanted, but it would require some extra moving around. We would have to jump to the line we wanted to copy (6G), yank it (yy), snap back to where we started (<C-o>), and use the put command (p) to duplicate the line. When duplicating a distant line, the :t command is usually more efficient.

In *Ex Commands Strike Far and Wide*, on page 56, we observed the general rule that Normal commands act locally, whereas Ex commands are long range. This example demonstrates this principle in action.

Move Lines with the ':m' Command

The :move command looks similar to the :copy command (see :h :move ⓘ):

```
:[range]move {address}
```

We can shorten it to a single letter: :m. Suppose that we want to move the Hardware Store section after the Beauty Parlor section. We could do so using the :move command as shown in Table 8, *Moving a Set of Lines with the ':m' Command*, on page 63.

Having made our visual selection, we simply have to run the command :'<,'>m$. Alternatively, we could run dGp. This breaks down like this: d to delete the visual selection, G to jump to the end of the file, and p to paste the text that was deleted.

Keystrokes	Buffer Contents

{start}	Shopping list
	    Hardware Store
	        Buy nails
	        Buy new hammer
	    Beauty Parlor
	        Buy nail polish remover
	        Buy nails

Vjj	Shopping list
	    Hardware Store
	        Buy nails
	        Buy new hammer
	    Beauty Parlor
	        Buy nail polish remover
	        Buy nails

:'<,'>m$	Shopping list
	    Beauty Parlor
	        Buy nail polish remover
	        Buy nails
	    Hardware Store
	        Buy nails
	        Buy new hammer

Table 8—Moving a Set of Lines with the ':m' Command

Remember that the '<,'> range stands for the visual selection. We could easily make another visual selection and then repeat the :'<,'>m$ command to move the selected text to the end of the file. Repeating the last Ex command is as easy as pressing @: (see Tip 31, *Repeat the Last Ex Command*, on page 65, for another example), so this method is more easily reproducible than using Normal mode commands.

Tip 30

Run Normal Mode Commands Across a Range

If we want to run a Normal mode command on a series of consecutive lines, we can do so using the :normal command. When used in combination with the dot command or a macro, we can perform repetitive tasks with very little effort.

Consider the example we met in Tip 2, *Don't Repeat Yourself*, on page 4. We wanted to append a semicolon at the end of a series of lines. Using the Dot Formula allowed us to complete the task rapidly, but in that example we needed to make the change only on three consecutive lines. What if we had to make the same change fifty times? Using the Dot Formula, we would have to press `j.` fifty times. That makes a total of one hundred keystrokes!

There is a better way. To demonstrate, we'll append a semicolon at the end of each line in this file. To save space, I've only included five lines, but if you can imagine instead that there are fifty lines, then this technique will seem more potent:

```
cmdline_mode/foobar.js
var foo = 1
var bar = 'a'
var baz = 'z'
var foobar = foo + bar
var foobarbaz = foo + bar + baz
```

We'll start off as we did before, by changing the first line:

Keystrokes	Buffer Contents
{start}	var foo = 1 var bar = 'a' var baz = 'z' var foobar = foo + bar var foobarbaz = foo + bar + baz
A;<Esc>	var foo = 1; var bar = 'a' var baz = 'z' var foobar = foo + bar var foobarbaz = foo + bar + baz

We want to avoid executing the `.` command on each line one by one. Instead, we can use the `:normal` Ex command to execute the dot command across a range of lines:

Keystrokes	Buffer Contents
jVG	var foo = 1; var bar = 'a' var baz = 'z' var foobar = foo + bar var foobarbaz = foo + bar + baz

:'<,'>normal .	var foo = 1;
	var bar = 'a';
	var baz = 'z';
	var foobar = foo + bar;
	var foobarbaz = foo + bar + baz;

The `:'<,'>normal .` command can be read as follows: "For each line in the visual selection, execute the Normal mode `.` command." This technique works just as well whether we're operating on five lines or fifty lines. The real beauty of it is that we don't even have to count the lines—we can get away with selecting them in Visual mode.

In this case, we've used :normal to execute the dot command, but we can execute any Normal mode commands in the same way. For example, we could have solved the problem above with this single command:

⇒ `:%normal A;`

The % symbol is used as a range representing the entire file. So :%normal A; instructs Vim to append a semicolon at the end of every line of the file. Making this change involves switching into Insert mode, but Vim automatically reverts to Normal mode afterward.

Before executing the specified Normal mode command on each line, Vim moves the cursor to the beginning of the line. So we don't have to worry about where the cursor is positioned when we execute the command. This single command could be used to comment out an entire JavaScript file:

⇒ `:%normal i//`

While it's possible to use :normal with any normal command, I find it most powerful when used in combination with one of Vim's repeat commands: either :normal . for simple repeats or :normal @q for more complex tasks. Skip ahead to Tip 68, *Repeat a Change on Contiguous Lines*, on page 168, and Tip 70, *Act Upon a Collection of Files*, on page 173, for a couple of examples.

In *Ex Commands Strike Far and Wide*, on page 56, we noted that Ex commands can change multiple lines at once. The :normal command allows us to combine the expressive nature of Vim's Normal mode commands with the range of Ex commands. It's a powerful combination!

For yet another alternative solution to the problem covered in this tip, refer to Tip 26, *Append After a Ragged Visual Block*, on page 50.

Tip 31

Repeat the Last Ex Command

While the `.` *command can be used to repeat our most recent Normal mode command, we have to use* `@:` *instead if we want to repeat the last Ex command. Knowing how to reverse the last command is always useful, so we'll consider that, too, in our discussion.*

In Chapter 1, *The Vim Way*, on page 1, we saw how the . command can be used to repeat the last change. But the dot command won't replay changes made from Vim's command line. Instead, we can repeat the last Ex command by pressing @: (see :h @: ⓘ).

For example, this command can be useful when iterating through items in the buffer list. We can step forward through the list with the :bn[ext] command and backward with the :bp[revious] command (Tip 37, *Track Open Files with the Buffer List*, on page 83, discusses the buffer list in more detail). Suppose that we had a dozen or so items in the buffer list, and we wanted to take a look at each one of them. We could type this command once:

⇒ **:bnext**

Then we use @: to repeat the command. Note the similarity between this and the method for executing a macro (*Play Back a Sequence of Commands by Executing a Macro*, on page 163). Also note that the : register always holds the most recently executed command line (see :h quote_: ⓘ). After running @: for the first time, we can subsequently repeat it with the @@ command.

Suppose that we got trigger-happy and fired the @: command too many times, overshooting our mark. How would we change direction then? We could execute the :bprevious command. But think about what would happen if we were to use the @: command again. It would go backward through the buffer list, which is the exact opposite of what it did before. That could be confusing.

In this case, a better option would be to use the <C-o> command (see Tip 56, *Traverse the Jump List*, on page 135). Each time we run :bnext (or repeat it with the @: command), it adds a record to the jump list. The <C-o> command goes back to the previous record in the jump list.

We could run :bnext once and then repeat it as often as we like using the @: command. If we needed to back up, we could do so using the <C-o> command. Then, if we wanted to continue going forward through the buffer list, we could go back to using the @: command. Remember our mantra from Tip 4, *Act, Repeat, Reverse*, on page 8: act, repeat, reverse.

Vim provides an Ex command for just about everything. While it's always possible to *repeat* the last Ex command by pressing @:, it's not always straightforward to *reverse* the effects. The <C-o> trick covered in this tip also works for reversing the effects of :next, :cnext, and :tnext commands (and so on). Whereas, for each of the items in Table 7, *Ex Commands That Operate on the Text in a Buffer*, on page 54, we could undo their effects by pressing u.

Tip 32

Tab-Complete Your Ex Commands

Just like in the shell, we can use the <Tab> key to autocomplete commands at the prompt.

Vim is smart about picking suggestions for tab-completion. It looks at the context of what has already been typed at the command line and builds a list of suitable suggestions. For example, we could type this:

```
⇒ :col<C-d>
‹ colder          colorscheme
```

The <C-d> command asks Vim to reveal a list of possible completions (see :h c_CTRL-D ⓘ). If we hit the <Tab> key, the prompt will cycle through colder, colorscheme, and then the original col again. We can scroll backward through the suggestions by pressing <S-Tab>.

Suppose we want to change the color scheme, but we can't remember the name of the theme we want. We could use the <C-d> command to show all the options:

```
⇒ :colorscheme <C-d>
‹ blackboard    desert       morning      shine
  blue          elflord      murphy       slate
  darkblue      evening      pablo        solarized
  default       koehler      peachpuff    torte
  delek         mac_classic  ron          zellner
```

This time, <C-d> shows a list of suggestions based on the color schemes that are available. If we wanted to enable the solarized theme, we could just type the letters "so" and then hit the Tab key to complete our command.

In many scenarios, Vim's tab-completion does the right thing. If we type a command that expects a filepath as an argument (such as :edit or :write), then <Tab> will complete directories and filenames relative to the current working directory. With the :tag command we can autocomplete tag names. The :set and :help commands know about every configuration option in Vim.

We can even define the tab-completion behavior when creating our own custom Ex commands. To see what's possible, check out :h :command-complete ⓘ.

Choosing from Multiple Matches

When Vim finds only a single suggestion for tab-completion, it uses the entire match. But if Vim finds multiple suggestions, then one of several things could happen. By default, Vim expands the first suggestion when the Tab key is pressed for the first time. With each subsequent press of the Tab key, we can scroll through the remaining suggestions.

We can customize this behavior by tweaking the 'wildmode' option (see :h 'wildmode' ⓘ). If you're used to working with the bash shell, then this setting will match your expectations:

```
set wildmode=longest,list
```

If you're used to the autocomplete menu provided by zsh, you might want to try this instead:

```
set wildmenu
set wildmode=full
```

With the 'wildmenu' option enabled, Vim provides a navigable list of suggestions. We can scroll forward through the items by pressing `<Tab>`, `<C-n>`, or `<Right>`, and we can scroll backward through them with `<S-Tab>`, `<C-p>`, or `<Left>`.

Tip 33

Insert the Current Word at the Command Prompt

Even in Command-Line mode, Vim always knows where the cursor is positioned and which split window is active. To save time, we can insert the current word (or WORD) from the active document onto our command prompt.

At Vim's command line, the `<C-r><C-w>` mapping copies the word under the cursor and inserts it at the command-line prompt. We can use this to save ourselves a bit of typing.

Suppose that we want to rename the tally variable in this excerpt to counter:

```
cmdline_mode/loop.js
var tally;
for (tally=1; tally <= 10; tally++) {
  // do something with tally
};
```

With our cursor positioned on the word tally, we could use the * command to search for each occurrence. (The * command is equivalent to typing the sequence /\< <C-r><C-w>\> <CR>. See Tip 77, *Stake the Boundaries of a Word*, on page 193, for a discussion of how \< and \> items work in a pattern.)

Keystrokes	Buffer Contents

{start}	var tally;
	for (tally=1; tally <= 10; tally++) {
	  // do something with tally
	};

*	var tally;
	for (tally=1; tally <= 10; tally++) {
	  // do something with tally
	};

cwcounter<Esc>	var tally;
	for (counter=1; tally <= 10; tally++) {
	  // do something with tally
	};

When we press the * key, our cursor jumps forward to the next match, but the cursor ends up on the same word anyway. Typing cwcounter<Esc> makes the change.

We'll carry out the remaining changes using a :substitute command. Since our cursor is on the word "counter," we don't need to type it out again. We can just use the <C-r><C-w> mapping to populate the replacement field:

⇒ :%s//<C-r><C-w>/g

That command doesn't look very succinct when written down, but two keystrokes to insert a word ain't bad. We didn't have to type the search pattern either, thanks to the * command. Refer to Tip 91, *Reuse the Last Search Pattern*, on page 225, to see why we can leave the search field blank like that.

While <C-r><C-w> gets the *word* under the cursor, we can instead use <C-r><C-a> if we want to get the WORD (for an explanation, see Tip 49, *Move Word-Wise*, on page 118). See :h c_CTRL-R_CTRL-W ⓘ for more details. We've used the :substitute command in this example, but these mappings can be used with any Ex command.

For another application, try opening your vimrc file, place your cursor on a setting, and then type :help <C-r><C-w> to look up the documentation for that setting.

Tip 34

Recall Commands from History

Vim records the commands that we enter in Command-Line mode and provides two ways of recalling them: scrolling through past command-lines with the cursor keys or dialing up the command-line window.

Vim keeps a history of our activity in Command-Line mode. We can easily recall previous commands, so there's no need to type out a long Ex command at the prompt more than once.

To begin with, let's switch to Command-Line mode by pressing the `:` key. Leave the prompt empty; then press the `<Up>` arrow key. The command line should be populated with the most recent Ex command that we executed. We can use the `<Up>` key again to go further back through our Ex command history or use the `<Down>` key to go in the opposite direction.

Now try typing :help, followed by the `<Up>` key. Again, this should scroll through previous Ex commands, but instead of showing everything, the list will be filtered to only include Ex commands that started with the word "help."

By default, Vim records the last twenty commands. With memory becoming ever cheaper in today's computers, we can probably afford to up this limit by changing the 'history' option. Try adding this line to your vimrc:

```
set history=200
```

Note that history is not recorded just for the current editing session. It persists even when we quit and relaunch Vim (see :h viminfo ⓘ). Increasing the number of items recorded in history can be really useful.

As well as recording a history of Ex commands, Vim keeps a separate record of our search history. If we press `/` to bring up the search prompt, we can also scroll backward and forward through previous searches with the `<Up>` and `<Down>` keys. The search prompt is, after all, just another form of Command-Line mode.

Meet the Command-Line Window

Like Insert mode, Command-Line mode is fine for composing something from scratch, but it's not a comfortable place to edit text.

Suppose we're working on a simple Ruby script. Each time we make a change, we find ourselves running the following two commands:

⇒ `:write`
⇒ `:!ruby %`

After running these two commands in quick succession a couple of times, we realize that we could streamline our workflow by folding them into a single command line. This way we can dial up one complete command from our history and replay it:

⇒ `:write | !ruby %`

Each of these commands is already in our history, so we shouldn't have to type the entire command line from scratch. But how can we merge two records from our history into one? Press `q:` and meet the command-line window (see :h cmdwin ⓘ).

The command-line window is like a regular Vim buffer, where each line contains an item from our history. With the `k` and `j` keys, we can move backward and forward through our history. Or we can use Vim's search feature to find the line that we're looking for. When we press the `<CR>` key, the contents of the current line are executed as an Ex command.

The beauty of the command-line window is that it allows us to change historical commands using the full modal editing power of Vim. We can navigate with any of the motions we're accustomed to using in Normal mode. We can operate on visual selections or switch to Insert mode. We can even run Ex commands on the contents of the command-line window!

Having summoned the command-line window by pressing `q:`, we could solve our problem as follows:

Keystrokes	Buffer Contents
{start}	⬚write !ruby %
A␣|<Esc>	write ⬚ !ruby %
J	write | ⬚!ruby %
:s/write/update	⬚update | ⬚!ruby %

Pressing `<CR>` would then execute the :update | !ruby % command as though we had typed it into the command line.

When the command-line window is open, it always gets the focus. That means we can't switch to other windows except by dismissing the command-line window. We can close the command-line window by running the :q command (just like any ordinary Vim window) or by pressing <CR>.

Note that when we press <CR> in the command-line window, the command is executed in the context of the active window: that is, the window that was active before the command-line window was summoned. Vim doesn't indicate which is the active window when the command-line window is open, so pay attention if you're using split windows!

What if halfway through composing an Ex command at the prompt, we realize that we need more editing power? In Command-Line mode, we can use the <C-f> mapping to switch to the command-line window, preserving a copy of the command that was typed at the prompt. This table summarizes a few of the methods for summoning the command-line window:

Command	Action
q/	Open the command-line window with history of searches
q:	Open the command-line window with history of Ex commands
ctrl-f	Switch from Command-Line mode to the command-line window

It's easy to mix up the q: and :q commands. I'm sure that we've all opened the command-line window by accident when we actually meant to quit Vim! It's a shame, because this feature is really useful, but many people are frustrated by their first (accidental) encounter with it. Skip ahead to Tip 85, *Create Complex Patterns by Iterating upon Search History*, on page 211, for another example of the command-line window in action.

Tip 35

Run Commands in the Shell

We can easily invoke external programs without leaving Vim. Best of all, we can send the contents of a buffer as standard input to a command or use the standard output from an external command to populate our buffer.

The commands discussed in this tip work best when used from Vim inside a terminal. If you're using GVim (or MacVim), then things may not work quite as smoothly. That shouldn't come as a great surprise. It's much easier for Vim to delegate work to the shell if Vim itself is already running inside a shell. GVim does some things better, but this is one area where terminal Vim has the edge.

Executing Programs in the Shell

From Vim's Command-Line mode, we can invoke external programs in the shell by prefixing them with a bang symbol (see :h :! ⓘ). For example, if we want to examine the contents of the current directory, we could run the following:

```
⇒ :!ls
❬ duplicate.todo          loop.js
  emails.csv              practical-vim.html
  foobar.js               shopping-list.todo
  history-scrollers.vim

  Press ENTER or type command to continue
```

Note the difference between :!ls and :ls—the former calls the ls command in the shell, whereas :ls calls Vim's built-in command, which shows the contents of the buffer list.

On Vim's command line, the % symbol is shorthand for the current file name (see :h cmdline-special ⓘ). We can exploit this to run external commands that do something with the current file. For example, if we're working on a Ruby file, we could execute it by running this:

```
⇒ :!ruby %
```

Vim also provides a set of filename modifiers, which allow us to extract information from the current filename, such as its path or extension (see :h filename-modifiers ⓘ). Skip ahead to Tip 45, *Save Files to Nonexistent Directories*, on page 107, for an example of how these can be used.

The :!{cmd} syntax is great for firing one-off commands, but what if we want to run several commands in the shell? In that case, we can use Vim's :shell command to start an interactive shell session (see :h :shell ⓘ):

```
⇒ :shell
⇒ $ pwd
❬ /Users/drew/books/PracticalVim/code/cmdline_mode
⇒ $ ls
❬ duplicate.todo          loop.js
  emails.csv              practical-vim.html
  foobar.js               shopping-list.todo
  history-scrollers.vim
⇒ $ exit
```

The exit command kills the shell and returns us to Vim.

Putting Vim in the Background

The :shell command is a feature provided by Vim, which lets us switch to an interactive shell. But if we're already running Vim in a terminal, then we also have access to built-in shell commands. For example, the bash shell supports job control, which allows us to suspend a job by putting it into the background and then lets us resume it later by bringing it back into the foreground.

Suppose that we're running Vim inside a bash shell and we want to execute a series of shell commands. Pressing Ctrl-z suspends the process that's running Vim and returns control to bash. The Vim process sits idle in the background, allowing us to interact with our bash session as normal. We can inspect the list of jobs by running this command:

```
$ jobs
[1]+  Stopped                 vim
```

In bash, we can use the fg command to resume a suspended job, bringing it back into the foreground. That brings Vim back to life exactly as we left it. The Ctrl-z and fg commands are quicker and easier to use than Vim's equivalent :shell and exit commands. For more information, run man bash and read the section on job control.

Using the Contents of a Buffer for Standard Input or Output

When we use the :!{cmd} syntax, Vim echoes output from the {cmd}. This works fine if the command produces little or no output, but it's not very helpful if the command produces many lines of output. As an alternative, we can use the :read !{cmd} command, which puts the output from the {cmd} into our current buffer (see :h :read! ⓘ).

The :read !{cmd} command lets us direct standard output into a buffer. As you might expect, the :write !{cmd} does the inverse: it uses the contents of the buffer as standard input for the specified {cmd} (see :h :write_c ⓘ). Skip ahead to Tip 46, *Save a File as the Super User*, on page 108, to see an example of this feature in use.

The bang symbol can take on different meanings depending on where it is placed within the command line. Compare these commands:

```
:write !sh
:write ! sh
:write! sh
```

The first two commands pass the contents of the buffer as standard input to the external sh command. The last command writes the contents of the buffer to a file called sh by calling the :write! command. In this case, the bang tells

Vim to overwrite any existing sh file. As you can see, the placement of the bang symbol can drastically alter the outcome. Take care when composing this sort of command!

The effect of the :write !sh command is that each line of the current buffer is executed in the shell. Refer to :h rename-files ⓘ for a nice example of this command in use.

Filtering the Contents of a Buffer Through an External Command

The :!{cmd} command takes on a different meaning when it's given a range. The lines specified by [range] are passed as standard input for the {cmd}, and then the output from {cmd} overwrites the original contents of [range]. Or to put it another way, the [range] is filtered through the specified {cmd} (see :h :range! ⓘ). Vim defines a filter as "a program that accepts text as standard input, changes it some way, and sends it to standard output."

As a demonstration, let's use the external sort command to rearrange the records in this CSV file:

cmdline_mode/emails.csv
```
first name,last name,email
john,smith,john@example.com
drew,neil,drew@vimcasts.org
jane,doe,jane@example.com
```

We'll sort the records by the second field: last name. We can use the -t',' option to tell the sort command that fields are separated with commas, and we can use the -k2 flag to indicate that the second field is to be used for the sort.

The first line of the file contains header information. We want to leave it at the top of the file, so we'll exclude it from the sort operation by using a range of :2,$. This command line does what we want:

⇒ `:2,$!sort -t',' -k2`

The records in our CSV file should now be sorted by last name:

```
first name,last name,email
jane,doe,jane@example.com
drew,neil,drew@vimcasts.org
john,smith,john@example.com
```

Vim provides a convenient shortcut for setting the range of a :[range]!{filter} command such as this. The !{motion} operator command drops us into Command-Line mode and prepopulates the [range] with the lines covered by the specified {motion} (see :h ! ⓘ). For example, if we place our cursor on line 2 and then invoke , Vim opens a prompt with the :.,$! range set up for us. We still have to type out the rest of the {filter} command, but it saves a little work.

Discussion

When operating Vim, we're never more than a couple of keystrokes away from the shell. This table summarizes a selection of the most useful methods for calling external commands:

Command	Effect
:shell	Start a shell (return to Vim by typing exit)
:!{cmd}	Execute {cmd} with the shell
:read !{cmd}	Execute {cmd} in the shell and insert its standard output below the cursor
:[range]write !{cmd}	Execute {cmd} in the shell with [range] lines as standard input
:[range]!{filter}	Filter the specified [range] through external program {filter}

Vim gives special treatment to some commands. For example, both make and grep have wrapper commands. Not only are they easy to execute from inside Vim, but their output is parsed and used to populate the quickfix list. These commands are covered in greater depth in both Chapter 17, *Compile Code and Navigate Errors with the Quickfix List*, on page 263, and Chapter 18, *Search Project-Wide with grep, vimgrep, and Others*, on page 273.

Tip 36

Run Multiple Ex Commands as a Batch

If we need to execute a sequence of Ex commands, we can save ourselves work by putting those commands in a script. Next time we want to run those commands, we can source the script rather than typing the commands one by one.

This file contains links to the first couple of episodes from the Vimcasts archive:

cmdline_mode/vimcasts/episodes-1.html
```
<ol>
  <li>
    <a href="/episodes/show-invisibles/">
      Show invisibles
    </a>
  </li>
```

```
<li>
  <a href="/episodes/tabs-and-spaces/">
    Tabs and Spaces
  </a>
</li>
</ol>
```

We need to modify this into a plain-text format showing the title followed by the URL:

cmdline_mode/vimcasts-episodes-1.txt
```
Show invisibles: http://vimcasts.org/episodes/show-invisibles/
Tabs and Spaces: http://vimcasts.org/episodes/tabs-and-spaces/
```

Let's suppose we anticipate having to make these same transformations across a series of files that follow a similar format. We'll look at a couple of different ways we could approach this.

Run Ex Commands One by One

It might be possible to make this transformation using a single :substitute command, but my preference would be to break this up into several small tasks. This sequence of Ex commands is one possible solution:

```
⇒ :g/href/j
⇒ :v/href/d
‹ 8 fewer lines
⇒ :%norm A: http://vimcasts.org
⇒ :%norm yi"$p
⇒ :%s/\v^[^\>]+\>\s//g
```

You don't have to understand what each of these commands does to follow the rest of this tip, but if you're curious, here's a brief outline. The :global and :vglobal commands work together to collapse the file down into two lines that contain the information we need, albeit in the wrong order (Tip 99, *Delete Lines Containing a Pattern*, on page 242). The :normal commands append the URL at the end of the line (Tip 30, *Run Normal Mode Commands Across a Range*, on page 63). And the :substitute command removes the opening <a href=""> tag. As always, the best way to understand these commands is to try them out for yourself.

Write Ex Commands to a Script and Source It

Instead of executing these commands one by one, we could put them all into a file and save it to disk. Let's call it batch.vim. (Using the .vim extension will make Vim use the correct syntax highlighting.) Each line of this file corresponds to a command line from the workflow outlined earlier. In this context we don't need to prefix each line with a : character. Personally, I prefer to use the longhand names for Ex commands when putting them in a script. Saving keystrokes is less of a concern than making the script easy to read.

```
cmdline_mode/batch.vim
global/href/join
vglobal/href/delete
%normal A: http://vimcasts.org
%normal yi"$p
%substitute/\v^[^\>]+\>\s//g
```

We can use the :source command to execute the batch.vim script (see :h source ⓘ). Each line of the script is executed as an Ex command, just as though we had typed it at Vim's command line. You've probably come across the :source command before in another context: it's commonly used to load configuration settings from a vimrc file at runtime. (See *Save Your Configuration in a vimrc File*, on page 304, for more details.)

I suggest you try this out for yourself. You can download the source code from *Practical Vim*'s book page on the Pragmatic Bookshelf site. Before opening Vim, change to the cmdline_mode directory, where you'll find both the batch.vim and episodes-1.html files.

⇒ **$ pwd**
‹ ~/dnvim2/code/cmdline_mode
⇒ **$ ls *.vim**
‹ batch.vim   history-scrollers.vim
⇒ **$ vim vimcasts/episodes-1.html**

Now we can execute our script:

⇒ **:source batch.vim**

With that single command line, we've executed each of the Ex commands from batch.vim. If you change your mind, you can undo those changes by pressing the u key once.

Source the Script to Change Multiple Files

There's little point in saving our Ex commands to a file if we're only going to execute the script one time. This trick comes into its own if we want to run that same sequence of Ex commands several times.

The code samples provided with this book include a few files with the same format as the episodes-1.html file. Make sure that you're in the cmdline_mode directory and launch Vim:

```
⇒   $ pwd
«   ~/dnvim2/code/cmdline_mode
⇒   $ ls vimcasts
«   episodes-1.html episodes-2.html episodes-3.html
⇒   $ vim vimcasts/*.html
```

Launching Vim with a wildcard will populate the argument list with all of the files that match that pattern. We could step through those files one by one, sourcing our batch.vim for each one:

```
⇒   :args
«   [vimcasts/episodes-1.html] vimcasts/episodes-2.html vimcasts/episodes-3.html
⇒   :first
⇒   :source batch.vim
⇒   :next
⇒   :source batch.vim
«   etc.
```

Or better still, we could use the :argdo command (:h :argdo ⓘ):

```
⇒   :argdo source batch.vim
```

Boom! With a single command we've executed each of the Ex commands in batch.vim across each of the files in the argument list.

I've chosen to illustrate this technique using a varied selection of Ex commands to demonstrate what's possible. In practice, I most commonly use this technique to execute one or more :substitute commands if I find myself using them again and again. I'll often discard the batch.vim file after use, but I might put it under source control if I think it could be useful in the future.

Part II

Files

In this part of the book, we'll learn how to work with files and buffers. Vim lets us work on multiple files in a single editing session. We can view them one at a time or divide our workspace into split windows or tabs, each containing a separate buffer. We'll look at several different ways of opening files from inside Vim. We'll also learn a couple of workarounds for common gotchas that may prevent us from saving our buffers to a file.

CHAPTER 6

Manage Multiple Files

Vim lets us work on multiple files at the same time. The buffer list lets us keep track of the set of files that we've opened in the course of an editing session. In Tip 37, *Track Open Files with the Buffer List*, on page 83, we'll learn how to interact with this list as well as learn the distinction between a file and a buffer.

The argument list is a great complement to the buffer list. In Tip 38, *Group Buffers into a Collection with the Argument List*, on page 86, we'll see how to use the :args command to group files from the buffer list into a collection. We can then traverse the list or execute an Ex command on each member of the set using the :argdo command.

Vim allows us to divide our workspace into split windows. We'll learn how in Tip 40, *Divide Your Workspace into Split Windows*, on page 92. Then in Tip 41, *Organize Your Window Layouts with Tab Pages*, on page 95, we'll see how Vim's tabbed interface can be used to organize split windows into a collection.

Tip 37

Track Open Files with the Buffer List

We can load multiple files during an editing session. Vim lets us manage them using the buffer list.

Understand the Distinction Between Files and Buffers

Just like any other text editor, Vim allows us to read files, edit them, and save our changes. When we discuss our workflow, it's tempting to say that we're editing a file, but that's not what we're actually doing. Instead, we're editing an in-memory representation of a file, which is called a *buffer* in Vim's terminology.

Files are stored on the disk, whereas buffers exist in memory. When we open a file in Vim, its contents are read into a buffer, which takes the same name as the file. Initially, the contents of the buffer will be identical to those of the file, but the two will diverge as we make changes to the buffer. If we decide that we want to keep our changes, we can write the contents of the buffer back into the file. Most Vim commands operate on buffers, but a few operate on files, including the :write, :update, and :saveas commands.

Meet the Buffer List

Vim allows us to work with multiple buffers simultaneously. Let's open a few files by running these commands in the shell:

```
⇒ $ cd code/files
⇒ $ vim *.txt
❮ 2 files to edit
```

The *.txt wildcard matches two files in the current directory: a.txt and b.txt. This command tells Vim to open both of those files. When Vim starts up, it shows a single window with a buffer representing the first of the two files. The other file isn't visible, but it has been loaded into a buffer in the background, as we can see by running the following:

```
⇒ :ls
❮ 1 %a    "a.txt"                    line 1
  2        "b.txt"                    line 0
```

The :ls command gives us a listing of all the buffers that have been loaded into memory (:h :ls ⓘ). We can switch to the next buffer in the list by running the :bnext command:

```
⇒ :bnext
⇒ :ls
❮ 1 #     "a.txt"                    line 1
  2 %a    "b.txt"                    line 1
```

The % symbol indicates which of the buffers is visible in the current window, while the # symbol represents the alternate file. We can quickly toggle between the current and alternate files by pressing `<C-^>`. Press it once, and we'll switch to a.txt; press it a second time, and we'll get back to b.txt.

Use the Buffer List

We can traverse the buffer list using four commands—:bprev and :bnext to move backward and forward one at a time, and :bfirst and :blast to jump to the start or end of the list. It's a good idea to map them to something easier to reach. I use these mappings from Tim Pope's unimpaired.vim plugin:[1]

```
nnoremap <silent> [b :bprevious<CR>
nnoremap <silent> ]b :bnext<CR>
nnoremap <silent> [B :bfirst<CR>
nnoremap <silent> ]B :blast<CR>
```

(Vim already uses the [and] keys as prefixes for a series of related commands (see :h [①), so these mappings have a consistent feel to them. The unimpaired.vim plugin provides similar mappings for scrolling through the argument ([a and]a), quickfix ([q and]q), location ([l and]l), and tag lists ([t and]t). Check it out.)

The :ls listing starts with a digit, which is assigned to each buffer automatically on creation. We can jump directly to a buffer by number, using the :buffer N command (see :h :b ①). Alternatively, we can use the more intuitive form, :buffer {bufname}. The {bufname} need only contain enough characters from the filepath to uniquely identify the buffer. If we enter a string that matches more than one of the items in the buffer list, we can use tab-completion to choose between the options (see Tip 32, *Tab-Complete Your Ex Commands*, on page 67).

The :bufdo command allows us to execute an Ex command in all of the buffers listed by :ls (:h :bufdo ①). In practice, I usually find that it's more practical to use :argdo instead, which we'll meet in Tip 38, *Group Buffers into a Collection with the Argument List*, on page 86.

Deleting Buffers

Vim creates a new buffer any time we open a file, and we'll learn a few ways of doing that in Chapter 7, *Open Files and Save Them to Disk*, on page 99. If we want to delete a buffer, we can do so using the :bdelete command. This can take one of these forms:

```
:bdelete N1 N2 N3
:N,M bdelete
```

Note that deleting a buffer has no effect on its associated file; it simply removes the in-memory representation. If we wanted to delete buffers numbered 5

---

1.   https://github.com/tpope/vim-unimpaired

through 10 inclusive, we could do so by running :5,10bd. But if we wanted to keep buffer number 8, then we'd instead have to run :bd 5 6 7 9 10.

Buffer numbers are automatically assigned by Vim, and we have no means of changing them by hand. So if we want to delete one or more buffers, we first have to look them up to find out their numbers. This procedure is relatively time-consuming. Unless I have a good reason to delete a buffer, I usually don't bother. As a result, the :ls listing comes to represent all of the files that I have opened in the course of an editing session.

Vim's built-in controls for managing the buffer list lack flexibility. If we want to arrange buffers in a way that makes sense for our workflow, attempting to organize the buffer list is not the way to go. Instead, we're better off dividing our workspace using split windows, tab pages, or the argument list. The next few tips will show how.

Tip 38

Group Buffers into a Collection with the Argument List

The argument list is easily managed and can be useful for grouping together a collection of files for easy navigation. We can run an Ex command on each item in the argument list using the :argdo command.

Let's start by opening a handful of files in Vim:

```
⇒ $ cd code/files/letters
⇒ $ vim *.txt
❮ 5 files to edit
```

In Tip 37, *Track Open Files with the Buffer List*, on page 83, we saw that the :ls command provides a listing of buffers. Now let's examine the argument list:

```
⇒ :args
❮ [a.txt] b.txt c.txt. d.txt e.txt
```

The argument list represents the list of files that was passed as an argument when we ran the vim command. In our case, we provided a single argument, *.txt, but our shell expanded the * wildcard, matching the five files that we see in our argument list. The [] characters indicate which of the files in the argument list is active.

Compared to the listing provided by the :ls command, the output from running :args looks crude. It should come as no surprise to learn that the argument list was a feature of vi, whereas the buffer list is an enhancement introduced by Vim. But give the argument list a chance, and you'll see that it makes a fine complement to the buffer list.

Like many features in Vim, the functionality of the argument list has been enhanced, while the original name has stuck. We can change the contents of the argument list at any time, which means that the :args listing doesn't necessarily reflect the values that were passed to the vim command when we launched the editor. Don't take the name literally! (Also, see *':compiler' and ':make' Are Not Just for Compiled Languages*, on page 272.)

Populate the Argument List

When the :args Ex command is run without arguments, it prints the contents of the argument list. We can also set the contents of the argument list using this form (:h :args_f ⓘ):

```
:args {arglist}
```

The {arglist} can include filenames, wildcards, or even the output from a shell command. To demonstrate, we'll use the files/mvc directory, which you can find in the source files that come distributed with this book. If you want to follow along, switch to that directory and launch Vim:

```
$ cd code/files/mvc
$ vim
```

For an overview of the directory tree, refer to the code listing on page 100.

Specify Files by Name

The simplest way of populating the argument list is by specifying filenames one by one:

```
:args index.html app.js
:args
[index.html] app.js
```

This technique works fine if we only want to add a handful of buffers to our set. It has the advantage that we can specify the order, but doing it by hand can be laborious. If we want to add a lot of files to the argument list, we can get the job done faster by using wildcards.

Specify Files by Glob

Wildcards are placeholders that can stand in for characters in the name of a file or directory. The * symbol will match zero or more characters, but only in the scope of the specified directory (:h wildcard ⓘ). The ** wildcard also matches zero or more characters, but it can recurse downward into directories below the specified directory (:h starstar-wildcard ⓘ).

We can combine these wildcards and use partial filenames or directories to form patterns, also known as *globs*, that match the set of files we're interested in. This table shows a representative summary of some (but not all) of the files in the files/mvc directory that are matched by the specified globs.

Glob	Files Matching the Expansion
:args *.*	index.html app.js
:args **/*.js	app.js lib/framework.js app/controllers/Mailer.js ...etc
:args **/*.*	app.js index.js lib/framework.js lib/theme.css app/controllers/Mailer.js ...etc

Just as we can use more than one filename in the {arglist}, we can also supply more than one glob. If we wanted to build an argument list containing all .js and .css files but not other file types, we could use these globs:

⇒ `:args **/*.js **/*.css`

Specify Files by Backtick Expansion

As I wrote this book, I sometimes wanted to populate the argument list with the chapters in the same order that they appear in the table of contents. For this purpose, I maintained a plain-text file that contains one filename per line. Here's an excerpt from it:

```
files/.chapters
the_vim_way.pml
normal_mode.pml
insert_mode.pml
visual_mode.pml
```

I can populate the argument list from this file by running this:

⇒ `:args `cat .chapters``

Vim executes the text inside the backtick characters in the shell, using the output from the cat command as the argument for the :args command. Here, we've used the cat command to get the contents of the .chapters file, but we could use any command that's available in the shell. This feature is not available on all systems. See :h backtick-expansion ⓘ for more details.

Use the Argument List

The argument list is simpler to manage than the buffer list, making it the ideal place to group our buffers into a collection. With the :args {arglist} command, we can clear the argument list and then repopulate it from scratch with a single command. We can traverse the files in the argument list using :next and :prev commands. Or we can use :argdo to execute the same command on each buffer in the set.

The way I see it, the buffer list is like my desktop: it's always messy. The argument list is like a separate workspace that I always keep tidy, just in case I need space to stretch out. We'll see a few examples of how the argument list can be used in other tips, such as Tip 36, *Run Multiple Ex Commands as a Batch*, on page 76, and Tip 70, *Act Upon a Collection of Files*, on page 173.

Tip 39

Manage Hidden Files

When a buffer has been modified, Vim gives it special treatment to ensure that we don't accidentally quit the editor without saving our changes. Find out how to hide a modified buffer and how to handle hidden buffers when quitting Vim.

Run these commands in the shell to launch Vim:

```
⇒ $ cd code/files
⇒ $ ls
❮ a.txt      b.txt
⇒ $ vim *.txt
❮ 2 files to edit
```

Let's make a change to a.txt. We'll just press `Go` to append a blank line at the end of the buffer. Without saving the changes, let's examine the buffer list:

```
⇒ :ls
❮ 1 %a + "a.txt"                       line 1
  2      "b.txt"                       line 0
```

The buffer representing a.txt is annotated with a + sign, which indicates that it has been modified. If we were to save the file now, the contents of the buffer would be written to disk and the + annotation would go away. But let's not save the buffer just yet. Instead, we'll try to switch to the next buffer:

⇒ `:bnext`
⟨ `E37: No write since last change (add ! to override)`

Vim raises an error message, reporting that the current buffer contains unsaved changes. Let's try following the advice in parentheses and add a trailing bang symbol:

⇒ `:bnext!`
⇒ `:ls`
⟨
```
1 #h + "a.txt"                      line 1
2 %a   "b.txt"                      line 1
```

The bang symbol forces Vim to switch buffers, even if our current buffer has unsaved changes. When we run the :ls command now, b.txt is marked with the letter a for *active*, while a.txt is marked with the letter h for *hidden*.

Handle Hidden Buffers on Quit

When a buffer is hidden, Vim lets us go about our business as usual. We can open other buffers, change them, save them, and so on, all without consequences—that is, right up until we attempt to close our editing session. That's when Vim reminds us that we have unsaved changes in one of our buffers:

⇒ `:quit`
⟨
```
E37: No write since last change (add ! to override)
E162: No write since last change for buffer "a.txt"
```

Vim loads the first hidden buffer with modifications into the current window so that we can decide what to do with it. If we want to keep the changes, we can run :write to save the buffer to a file. Or if we want to discard the changes, we can instead run :edit!, which rereads the file from disk, overwriting the contents of the buffer. Having reconciled the contents of the buffer with the file on disk, we can try the :quit command again.

If we have more than one hidden buffer with modifications, then Vim activates the next unsaved buffer each time we enter the :quit command. Again, we could :write or :edit! to keep or discard the changes. This cycle continues until we make a decision for each of the hidden buffers with modifications. When there are no more windows and no more hidden modified buffers, the :q command closes Vim.

If we want to quit Vim without reviewing our unsaved changes, we can issue the :qall! command. Or, if we want to write all modified buffers without reviewing them one by one, we can use the :wall command. Table 9, *Options for Hidden Buffers on Quit*, on page 91 summarizes our options.

Command	Effect
:w[rite]	Write the contents of the buffer to disk
:e[dit]!	Read the file from disk back into the buffer (that is, revert changes)
:qa[ll]!	Close all windows, discarding changes without warning
:wa[ll]	Write all modified buffers to disk

Table 9—Options for Hidden Buffers on Quit

Enable the 'hidden' Setting Before Running ':*do' Commands

By default, Vim prevents us from abandoning a modified buffer. Whether we use the :next!, :bnext!, :cnext!, or any similar command, if we omit the trailing bang symbol, Vim will nag us with the "No write since last change" error message. In most cases, this message is a useful reminder. But in one scenario it becomes a nuisance.

Consider the commands :argdo, :bufdo, and :cfdo commands. The :argdo {cmd} command works like this:

```
:first
:{cmd}
:next
:{cmd}
etc.
```

If our chosen {cmd} modifies the first buffer, the :next command will fail. Vim won't permit us to advance to the second item in the argument list until we save the changes to the first item in the list. That's not much use!

If we enable the 'hidden' setting (see :h 'hidden' ⓘ), then we can use the :next, :bnext, :cnext (and so on) commands without a trailing bang. If the active buffer is modified, Vim will automatically hide it when we navigate away from it. The 'hidden' setting makes it possible to use :argdo, :bufdo, and :cfdo to change a collection of buffers with a single command.

After running :argdo {cmd}, we'll want to save the changes that were made to each item in the argument list. We could do it one at a time by running :first and then :wn, which would give us the opportunity to eyeball each file. Or if we're confident that everything is in order, we could run :argdo write (or :wall) to save all buffers.

Tip 40

Divide Your Workspace into Split Windows

Vim allows us to view multiple buffers side by side by dividing our workspace into split windows.

In Vim's terminology, a *window* is a viewport onto a buffer (:h window ⓘ). We can open multiple windows, each containing the same buffer, or we can load different buffers into each window. Vim's window management system is flexible, allowing us to build a workspace tailored to the demands of our workflow.

Creating Split Windows

When Vim starts up, it contains a single window. We can divide this window horizontally with the `<C-w>s` command, which creates two windows of equal height. Or we can use the `<C-w>v` command to split the window vertically, producing two windows of equal width. We can repeat these commands as often as we like, splitting our workspace again and again in a process that resembles cell division.

The following figure illustrates a few of the possible results. In each case, the shaded rectangle represents the active window.

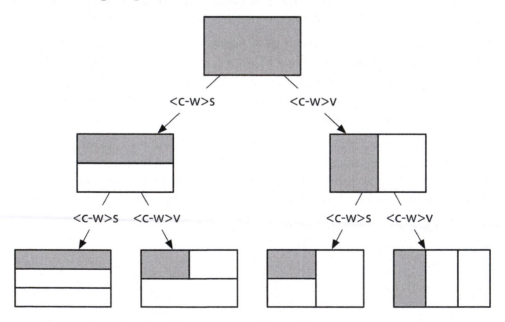

Each time we use the `<C-w>s` and `<C-w>v` commands, the two resulting split windows will contain the same buffer as the original window that was divided. Having the same buffer displayed in separate windows can be useful, especially if we're working on a long file. For example, we could scroll in one of the windows to show a part of the buffer that we want to refer to while making changes to another part of the buffer in the other window.

We can use the :edit command to load another buffer into the active window. If we run `<C-w>s` followed by :edit {filename}, we can divide our workspace and then open another buffer in one split window while keeping the existing buffer visible in the other split. Alternatively, we could use the command :split {filename}, which combines those two steps into one. This table summarizes the ways of dividing our workspace into split windows:

Command	Effect
`<C-w>s`	Split the current window horizontally, reusing the current buffer in the new window
`<C-w>v`	Split the current window vertically, reusing the current buffer in the new window
:sp[lit] {file}	Split the current window horizontally, loading {file} into the new window
:vsp[lit] {file}	Split the current window vertically, loading {file} into the new window

Changing the Focus Between Windows

Vim provides a handful of commands for switching the focus between split windows. This table summarizes some of the highlights (for the complete list, see :h window-move-cursor ⓘ):

Command	Effect
`<C-w>w`	Cycle between open windows
`<C-w>h`	Focus the window to the left
`<C-w>j`	Focus the window below
`<C-w>k`	Focus the window above
`<C-w>l`	Focus the window to the right

In fact, `<C-w><C-w>` does the same thing as `<C-w>w`. That means we can press the `<Ctrl>` key and hold it while typing `ww` (or `wj` or any of the others from the table) to change the active window. It's easier to type `<C-w><C-w>` than `<C-w>w`, even though it looks nastier when written down. Still, if you use split windows heavily, you might want to consider mapping these commands to something even more convenient.

If your terminal supports mouse interactions or if you're using GVim, then you can also activate a window by clicking it with the mouse. If it doesn't work for you, check that the 'mouse' option is set appropriately (:h 'mouse' ⓘ).

Closing Windows

If we want to reduce the number of windows in our workspace, we can take one of two strategies. We could use the :close command to close the active window, or if we want to close all windows *except* the active one, we can instead use the :only command. This table summarizes the options and shows the normal mode equivalents:

Ex Command	Normal Command	Effect
:clo[se]	<C-w>c	Close the active window
:on[ly]	<C-w>o	Keep only the active window, closing all others

Resizing and Rearranging Windows

Vim provides several key mappings for resizing windows. For the full list, look up :h window-resize ⓘ. This table summarizes a handful of the most useful commands:

Keystrokes	Buffer Contents
<C-w>=	Equalize width and height of all windows
<C-w>_	Maximize height of the active window
<C-w>|	Maximize width of the active window
[N]<C-w>_	Set active window height to [N] rows
[N]<C-w>|	Set active window width to [N] columns

Resizing windows is one of the few tasks I prefer to do with the mouse. It's simple: click on the line that separates two windows, drag the mouse until each window is the desired size, and then let go of the mouse. This works only if your terminal supports the mouse or if you're using GVim.

Vim includes commands for rearranging windows, but rather than describing them here, I'd like to point you toward a screencast on Vimcasts.org that demonstrates the possibilities.[2] You can also find more details by looking up :h window-moving ⓘ.

---

2.   http://vimcasts.org/e/7

Tip 41

Organize Your Window Layouts with Tab Pages

Vim's tabbed interface is different from that of many other text editors. We can use tab pages to organize split windows into a collection of workspaces.

In Vim, a *tab page* is a container that can hold a collection of windows (:h tabpage ⓘ). If you're accustomed to using another text editor, then Vim's tabbed interface might seem strange at first. Let's begin by considering how tabs work in many other text editors and IDEs.

The classic graphical user interface (GUI) for a text editor features a main workspace for editing files and a sidebar that shows the directory tree of the current project. If we click on a file in the sidebar, it opens a new tab in the main workspace for the specified file. A new tab is created for each file that we open. In this model, we could say that the tabs represent the set of files that are currently open.

When we open a file using the :edit command, Vim doesn't automatically create a new tab. Instead, it creates a new buffer and loads it into the current window. Vim keeps track of the set of files that are open using the buffer list, as we saw in Tip 37, *Track Open Files with the Buffer List*, on page 83.

Vim's tab pages are not mapped to buffers in a one-to-one relationship. Instead, think of a tab page as a container that can hold a collection of windows. The following figure illustrates a workspace with three tab pages, each containing one or more windows. In each scenario, the shaded rectangles represent the active windows and tabs.

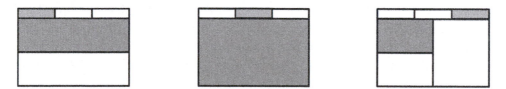

Tab pages are available to us whether we're using GVim or running Vim inside a terminal. GVim draws a tab bar as part of the GUI, giving it an appearance much like that of a web browser or any other tabbed interface. When Vim runs inside a terminal, it draws a tab bar as a textual user interface (TUI). Apart from the differences in appearance, tab pages are functionally identical whether rendered as a GUI or a TUI.

How to Use Tabs

Vim's tab pages can be used to partition work into different workspaces. They have more in common with the virtual desktops in Linux than they do with the tabbed interface of most other text editors.

Suppose that we're at work on a project, with our workspace divided into a few split windows. Out of the blue, something urgent comes up and we have to switch contexts. Rather than opening new files in our current tab page, which would mess up our carefully assembled workspace, we can create a new tab page and do the work there. When we're ready to resume our previous work, we just have to switch back to the original tab page where all of our windows will have been preserved as we left them.

The :lcd {path} command lets us set the working directory locally for the current window. If we create a new tab page and then use the :lcd command to switch to another directory, we can then comfortably scope each tab page to a different project. Note that :lcd applies locally to the current *window*, not to the current *tab page*. If we have a tab page containing two or more split windows, we could set the local working directory for all of them by running :windo lcd {path}. Check out episode 9 of Vimcasts for more information.[3]

Opening and Closing Tabs

We can open a new tab page with the :tabedit {filename} command. If we omit the {filename} argument, then Vim creates a new tab page containing an empty buffer.

Alternatively, if the current tab page contains more than one window, we can use the <C-w>T command, which moves the current window into a new tab page (see :h CTRL-W_T ⓘ).

If the active tab page contains only a single window, the :close command will close the window and the tab page with it. Or we can use the :tabclose command, which closes the current tab page no matter how many windows it contains. Finally, if we want to close all tab pages except for the current one, we can use the :tabonly command.

Command	Effect
:tabe[dit] {filename}	Open {filename} in a new tab
<C-w>T	Move the current window into its own tab

Command	Effect
:tabc[lose]	Close the current tab page and all of its windows
:tabo[nly]	Keep the active tab page, closing all others

Switching Between Tabs

Tabs are numbered starting from 1. We can switch between tabs with the {N}gt command, which can be remembered as *goto tab {N}*. When this command is prefixed with a number, Vim jumps to the specified tab, but if the number is omitted, Vim advances to the next tab. The gT command does the same but in reverse.

Ex Command	Normal Command	Effect
:tabn[ext] {N}	{N}gt	Switch to tab page number {N}
:tabn[ext]	gt	Switch to the next tab page
:tabp[revious]	gT	Switch to the previous tab page

Rearranging Tabs

We can use the :tabmove [N] Ex command to rearrange tab pages. When [N] is 0, the current tab page is moved to the beginning, and if we omit [N], the current tab page is moved to the end. If your terminal supports the mouse or if you're using GVim, reordering tab pages by drag and drop is also possible.

CHAPTER 7

Open Files and Save Them to Disk

Vim has a few ways of opening files. In Tip 42, *Open a File by Its Filepath Using ':edit'*, on page 99, we'll look at the :edit command, which can be used to open any file by providing a filepath.

If we're working on files that are two or more directories beneath our project root, having to specify a complete filepath for every file we want to open can be awkward. In Tip 43, *Open a File by Its Filename Using ':find'*, on page 102, we'll learn how to configure the 'path' option, which makes it possible to use the :find command. This saves us from having to specify fully qualified filepaths and allows us to simply enter the filename.

The netrw plugin, which ships with Vim, makes it possible to explore the contents of a directory tree. We'll find out how to use it in Tip 44, *Explore the File System with netrw*, on page 104.

The :write command lets us save the contents of a buffer to disk. Its usage is generally straightforward, but it can become complicated if we attempt to save to a nonexistent directory or if we don't have the permissions required to write a file. We'll find out how to cope with these scenarios in Tip 45, *Save Files to Nonexistent Directories*, on page 107, and Tip 46, *Save a File as the Super User*, on page 108.

Tip 42

Open a File by Its Filepath Using ':edit'

The :edit command allows us to open files from within Vim, either by specifying an absolute or a relative filepath. We'll also learn how to specify a path relative to the active buffer.

As a demonstration, we'll use the files/mvc directory, which you can find in the source files that come distributed with this book. It contains the following directory tree:

```
app.js
index.html
app/
  controllers/
    Mailer.js
    Main.js
    Navigation.js
  models/
    User.js
  views/
    Home.js
    Main.js
    Settings.js
lib/
  framework.js
  theme.css
```

In the shell, we'll start by changing to the files/mvc directory and then launching Vim:

⇒ **$ cd code/files/mvc**
⇒ **$ vim index.html**

Open a File Relative to the Current Working Directory

In Vim, just as in bash and other shells, we have the notion of a working directory. When Vim is launched, it adopts the same working directory that was active in the shell. We can confirm this by running the :pwd Ex command, which (just as in bash) stands for "print working directory":

⇒ **:pwd**
❮ /Users/drew/practical-vim/code/files/mvc

The :edit {file} command can accept a filepath relative to the working directory. If we wanted to open the lib/framework.js file, we could do so by running this command:

⇒ **:edit lib/framework.js**

Or we could open the app/controllers/Navigation.js file by running this:

⇒ **:edit app/controllers/Navigation.js**

We can use the tab key to autocomplete these filepaths (see Tip 32, *Tab-Complete Your Ex Commands*, on page 67, for more details). So if we wanted to open the Navigation.js file, we could simply press :edit a<Tab>c<Tab>N<Tab>.

Open a File Relative to the Active File Directory

Suppose that we're editing the app/controllers/Navigation.js file, and we decide that we want to edit the Main.js file in the same directory. We could drill down to it from our working directory, but that feels like unnecessary work. The file we want to open is in the same directory as our active buffer. It would be ideal if we could use the context of the active buffer as a reference point. Try this:

⇒ `:edit %<Tab>`

The % symbol is a shorthand for the filepath of the active buffer (see :h cmdline-special ⓘ). Pressing the `<Tab>` key expands the filepath, revealing the absolute path of the active buffer. That's not quite what we want, but it's getting close. Now try this instead:

⇒ `:edit %:h <Tab>`

The :h modifier removes the filename while preserving the rest of the path (see :h ::h ⓘ). In our case, typing %:h `<Tab>` is expanded to the full path of the current file's directory:

⇒ `:edit app/controllers/`

From there, we can type Main.js (or have the tab key autocomplete it for us), and Vim will open the file. In total, we have to enter only the following keystrokes:

⇒ `:edit %:h <Tab> M <Tab><Tab>`

The %:h expansion is so useful that you might want to consider creating a mapping for it. Check out *Easy Expansion of the Active File Directory*, on page 101, for a suggestion.

Easy Expansion of the Active File Directory

Try sourcing this line in your vimrc file:

```
cnoremap <expr> %%  getcmdtype() == ':' ? expand('%:h').'/' : '%%'
```

Now when we type %% on Vim's : command-line prompt, it automatically expands to the path of the active buffer, just as though we had typed %:h`<Tab>`. Besides working nicely with :edit, this can come in handy with other Ex commands such as :write, :saveas, and :read.

For more ideas on how to use this mapping, see the Vimcasts episode on the :edit command.[a]

---

a. http://vimcasts.org/episodes/the-edit-command/

Tip 43

Open a File by Its Filename Using ':find'

The :find command allows us to open a file by its name without having to provide a fully qualified path. To exploit this feature, we first have to configure the 'path' setting.

We can always use the :edit command to open a file by providing its full path. But what if we're working on a project where the files are nested a few directories deep? Entering the full path every time we want to open a file can get tiresome. That's where the :find command comes in.

Preparation

We'll use the files/mvc directory to demonstrate. The source files are distributed with this book. In the shell, we'll launch Vim from the files/mvc directory:

```
⇒ $ cd code/files/mvc
⇒ $ vim index.html
```

Let's see what happens if we attempt to use the :find command right now:

```
⇒ :find Main.js
❮ E345: Can't find file "Main.js" in path
```

The error message tells us that no Main.js file can be found in the path. So let's do something about it.

Configure the 'path'

The 'path' option allows us to specify a set of directories inside of which Vim will search when the :find command is invoked (see :h 'path' ⓘ). In our case, we want to make it easier to look up files in the app/controllers and app/views directories. We can add these to our path simply by running this:

```
⇒ :set path+=app/**
```

The ** wildcard matches all subdirectories beneath the app/ directory. We discussed wildcards in *Populate the Argument List*, on page 87, but the treatment of * and ** is slightly different in the context of the 'path' setting (see :h file-searching ⓘ). The wildcards are handled by Vim rather than by the shell.

> ## Smart Path Management with rails.vim
>
> Tim Pope's rails.vim plugin does some clever things to make navigating around a Rails project easier.[a] The plugin automatically configures the 'path' setting to include all the directories found in a conventional Rails project. This means that we can use the :find command without having to worry about setting up the 'path'.
>
> But rails.vim doesn't stop there. It also provides convenience commands, such as :Rcontroller, :Rmodel, :Rview, and others. Each of these acts as a specialized version of the :find command, scoping its search to the corresponding directory.
>
> _____
>
> a.   https://github.com/tpope/vim-rails

Use ':find' to Look up Files by Name

Now that we've configured our 'path', we can open files in the directories we specified by providing just their filename. For example, if we wanted to open the app/controllers/Navigation.js file, we could enter this command:

⇒ `:find Navigation.js`

We can use the `<Tab>` key to autocomplete filenames, so in fact we can get what we want by typing as little as :find nav`<Tab>` followed by the Enter key.

You might be wondering what happens if the specified filename is not unique. Let's find out. In our demo codebase, we have two files named Main.js: one is in the app/controllers directory and the other is in app/views.

⇒ `:find Main.js``<Tab>`

If we type out the Main.js filename and then hit `<Tab>`, Vim expands the entire path of the first full match: ./app/controllers/Main.js. Press `<Tab>` a second time, and the next matching filepath takes its place, in this case ./app/views/Main.js. When we press the Enter key, Vim will use the entire filepath if it has been expanded or the first full match if no `<Tab>` expansion has been performed.

You may observe slightly different tab-completion behavior if you have changed the 'wildmode' setting from its default value of full. Refer to Tip 32, *Tab-Complete Your Ex Commands*, on page 67, for more details.

Explore the File System with netrw

In addition to letting us view (and edit) the contents of a file, Vim also lets us view the contents of a directory. The netrw plugin, included in the Vim distribution, allows us to explore the file system.

Preparation

The functionality described in this tip is not implemented in Vim's core source code but in a plugin called netrw. This plugin comes as standard with the Vim distribution, so we don't have to install anything, but we do need to make sure that Vim is configured to load plugins. These lines of configuration are the minimum requirement for your vimrc file:

```
essential.vim
set nocompatible
filetype plugin on
```

Meet netrw—Vim's Native File Explorer

If we launch Vim with the path to a directory rather than a file, it will start up with a file explorer window:

```
⇒ $ cd code/file/mvc
⇒ $ ls
❮ app     app.js index.html     lib
⇒ $ vim .
```

The screenshot on page 105 shows how the file explorer looks. It's a regular Vim buffer, but instead of showing the contents of a file, it represents the contents of a directory.

We can move the cursor up and down using the `k` and `j` keys. When we press the `<CR>` key, it opens the item under the cursor. If the cursor is positioned on a directory, the explorer window is redrawn to show the contents of that directory. If the cursor is positioned on a filename, the file is loaded into a buffer in the current window, replacing the file explorer. We can open the parent directory by pressing the `-` key or by positioning the cursor on the `..` item and pressing `<CR>`.

We're not limited to navigating the directory listing with `j` and `k` keys. We can use all of the motions that are available to us in a regular Vim buffer.

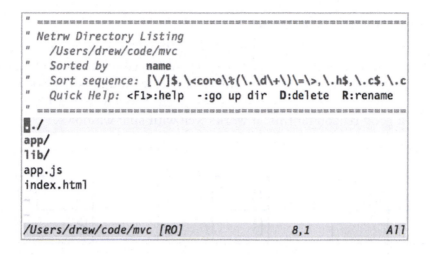

For example, if we wanted to open the index.html file, we could search for /html<CR>, putting our cursor right where we need it.

Opening the File Explorer

We can open the file explorer window with the :edit {path} command by supplying a directory name (instead of a filename) as the {path} argument. The dot symbol stands for the current working directory, so if we run the :edit . command, we can bring up a file explorer for the project root.

If we wanted to open a file explorer for the directory of the current file, we could do so by typing :edit %:h (see *Open a File Relative to the Active File Directory*, on page 101, for an explanation). But the netrw plugin provides a more convenient way with the :Explore command (see :h :Explore ⓘ).

Both of these commands can be abbreviated. Instead of typing out :edit ., we can get away with just :e.—we don't even need the space before the dot. And :Explore can be truncated right down to :E. This table summarizes the long- and shorthand forms of these commands:

Ex Command	Shorthand	Effect
:edit .	:e.	Open file explorer for current working directory
:Explore	:E	Open file explorer for the directory of the active buffer

In addition to :Explore, netrw also provides :Sexplore and :Vexplore commands, which open the file explorer in a horizontal split window or vertical split window, respectively.

Working with Split Windows

The classic GUI for a text editor presents the file explorer in a sidebar, sometimes known as the *project drawer*. If you're used to this kind of interface, then it might seem strange that Vim's :E and :e. commands behave the way they do by *replacing* the contents of the current window with a file explorer. There's a good reason for this: it works well with split windows.

Consider the layout in the first frame of this image:

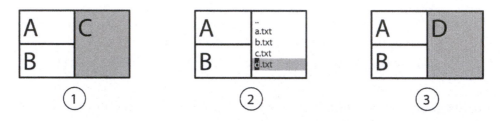

Here we see three split windows, each displaying a different buffer. Let's imagine for a moment that a project drawer containing a file explorer was bolted to the side of Vim's interface. If we want to open a file by clicking its name in the project drawer, where would it open?

The window labeled *C* is active (as indicated by the shading), so that would seem to be the natural target. But the relationship between the project drawer and the active window is not immediately apparent. It would be easy to lose track of which window was active, leading to a surprise result when, on selecting a file from the project drawer, it didn't open where you expected it to.

Now let's remove our imaginary project drawer from this scenario and consider the way it actually works in Vim. If we run the :Explore command, the active window is replaced with a file explorer, as illustrated by frame 2 of the figure. There can be no doubt that when a file is selected it will load in the same window.

Think of each window as a playing card. One side of the card shows the contents of a file, and the other side shows the file explorer. When we run the :Explore command, the card for the active window flips over to show the side with the file explorer (frame 2 of the figure). After choosing the file we want to edit, we press `<CR>` and the card flips over again, this time showing the contents of the file that we just selected (frame 3 of the figure). After summoning the file explorer view, if we decide that we want to switch back to the buffer we were already editing, we can do so using the `<C-^>` command.

In a sense, we could say that Vim's windows have two modes: one for working with files and one for working with directories. This model works together with Vim's split window interface perfectly, whereas the notion of a project drawer doesn't really fit.

Doing More with netrw

The netrw plugin doesn't just let us explore the file system. We can create new files (:h netrw-% ⓘ) or directories (:h netrw-d ⓘ), rename existing ones (:h netrw-rename ⓘ), or delete them (:h netrw-del ⓘ). For a demonstration, watch episode 15 of Vimcasts.[1]

We haven't even touched on the killer feature that gives the plugin its name: netrw makes it possible to read and write files across a network. The plugin can use many protocols, including scp, ftp, curl, and wget, depending on what's available on your system. To find out more, look up :h netrw-ref ⓘ.

> Tip 45

Save Files to Nonexistent Directories

Vim is happy to let us edit a buffer whose path includes directories that don't exist. It's only when we attempt to write the buffer to a file that Vim objects. Here's a quick tip on how to deal with this situation.

The :edit {file} command is most commonly used to open a file that already exists. But if we specify a filepath that doesn't correspond to an existing file, then Vim will create a new empty buffer. If we press <C-g>, we'll see that the buffer is labeled as "new file" (the <C-g> command echoes the name and status of the current file; see :h ctrl-G ⓘ). When we run the :write command, Vim will attempt to write the contents of that buffer to a new file using the filepath that was specified when the buffer was created.

If we run :edit {file} and specify a filepath that contains nonexistent directories, things can get a little awkward:

```
:edit madeup/dir/doesnotexist.yet
:write
"madeup/dir/doesnotexist.yet" E212: Can't open file for writing
```

In this case, the madeup/dir directories do not exist. Vim creates a new buffer anyway, but this time it's labeled as "new DIRECTORY." It's only when we

---

1. http://vimcasts.org/e/15

attempt to write the buffer to disk that Vim raises an error. We can remedy this situation by calling the external mkdir program:

⇒ `:!mkdir -p %:h`
⇒ `:write`

The -p flag tells mkdir to create intermediate directories. See *Open a File Relative to the Active File Directory*, on page 101, for an explanation of what the %:h characters stand for.

Tip 46

Save a File as the Super User

Running Vim as the super user isn't normal, but sometimes we have to save changes to a file that requires sudo permission. We can do so without restarting Vim by delegating the task to a shell process and running that with sudo.

This tip may not work in GVim and certainly won't work on Windows. It does work on Unix systems when you run Vim inside a terminal, which is a common enough scenario to make this tip worthy of inclusion.

Let's use the /etc/hosts file to demonstrate. The file is owned by root, but we're logged in with username "drew," so we have permission only to read this file:

⇒ `$ ls -al /etc/ | grep hosts`
❮ `-rw-r--r--    1 root  wheel         634  6 Apr 15:59 hosts`
⇒ `$ whoami`
❮ `drew`

We'll open up the file in Vim as user drew:

⇒ `$ vim /etc/hosts`

The first thing to note is that if we press `<C-g>` to view the file status, Vim labels it as [readonly].

Let's try to make a change and see what happens. We'll run the `Go` commands to add a blank line at the end of the file. Vim echoes a message that reads "W10: Warning: Changing a readonly file." Consider this a friendly reminder rather than an absolute rule. After showing the message, Vim proceeds by making the change anyway.

Vim won't prevent us from making changes to a readonly buffer, but it will prevent us from saving the changes to disk in the usual manner:

⇒ `:write`
‹ `E45: 'readonly' option is set (add ! to override)`

Let's follow the advice in the message and repeat the command with a trailing bang symbol (which can be read as "This time I mean it!"):

⇒ `:write!`
‹ `"/etc/hosts" E212: Can't open file for writing`

The problem here is that we don't have permission to write the /etc/hosts file. Remember: it's owned by root, and we're running Vim as user drew. The remedy is this strange-looking command:

⇒ `:w !sudo tee % > /dev/null`
‹ `Password:`
  `W12: Warning: File "hosts" has changed and the buffer was`
  `changed in Vim as well`
  `[O]k, (L)oad File, Load (A)ll, (I)gnore All:`

Vim requires interaction from us in two ways: first we have to enter the password for user drew (look away while I type it); then Vim warns us that the file has changed and prompts us with a menu of options. I recommend pressing `l` to load the file back into the buffer.

How does it work? The :write !{cmd} command sends the contents of the buffer as standard input to the specified {cmd}, which can be any external program (see :h :write_c ⓘ). Vim is still running as user drew, but we can tell our external process to operate as the superuser. In this case, the tee utility is executed with sudo permissions, which means that it can write to the /etc/hosts file.

The % symbol has special meaning on Vim's command line: it expands to represent the path of the current buffer (see :h :_% ⓘ), in this case /etc/hosts. So we can expand the final part of this command to read as follows: tee /etc/hosts > /dev/null. This command receives the contents of the buffer as standard input, using it to overwrite the contents of the /etc/hosts file.

Vim detects that the file has been modified by an external program. Usually that would mean that the contents of the buffer and the file were out of sync, which is why Vim prompts us to choose whether we want to keep the version in the buffer or load the version on disk. In this case, the file and buffer happen to have the same contents.

Part III

Getting Around Faster

Motions are some of the most important commands for operating Vim. Not only do they let us move our cursor around, but when used in Operator-Pending mode, they also allow us to specify the range of text on which an operation will act. We'll meet some of the most useful motions in this part of the book. We'll also learn about Vim's jump commands, which allow us to quickly navigate between files.

CHAPTER 8

Navigate Inside Files with Motions

Vim provides many ways of moving around within a document as well as commands for jumping between buffers. In this chapter we'll focus on motions, which allow us to move around within a document.

Perhaps the simplest way of moving around is using the cursor keys. Vim allows us to navigate up, down, left, and right without moving our hands from the home row, as we'll see in Tip 47, *Keep Your Fingers on the Home Row*, on page 114. That's a start, but there are quicker ways of moving around: Tip 49, *Move Word-Wise*, on page 118, shows how to move a word at a time; Tip 50, *Find by Character*, on page 120, shows how to move with precision to any character within the current line; and Tip 51, *Search to Navigate*, on page 124, shows how to use the search command for getting around.

Motions are not just for navigating around a document. They can also be used in Operator-Pending mode to perform real work, as discussed in Tip 12, *Combine and Conquer*, on page 24. Throughout this chapter, we'll study examples of how motions can be used in combination with operator commands. The stars of Operator-Pending mode are text objects, which we'll cover in Tip 52, *Trace Your Selection with Precision Text Objects*, on page 126, and Tip 53, *Delete Around, or Change Inside*, on page 129.

Vim has a vast number of motions. We can't cover them all in this chapter, so I recommend that you look up the :h motion.txt ⓘ section of Vim's documentation for a complete reference. Set yourself the goal of adding a couple of motions to your repertoire each week.

Tip 47

Keep Your Fingers on the Home Row

Vim is optimized for the touch typist. Learn to move around without removing your hands from the home row, and you'll be able to operate Vim quicker.

The first thing you learn as a touch typist is that your fingers should rest on the home row. On a Qwerty keyboard, that means the left-hand fingers rest on `a`, `s`, `d`, and `f`, while the right-hand fingers rest on `j`, `k`, `l`, and `;` keys. When poised in this position, we can reach for any other key on the keyboard without having to move our hands or look at our fingers. It's the ideal posture for touch typing.

Just as with any other text editor, Vim lets us use the arrow keys to move the cursor around, but it also provides an alternative by way of the `h`, `j`, `k`, and `l` keys. They work as follows:

Command	Move cursor
h	One column left
l	One column right
j	One line down
k	One line up

Admittedly, these cursor motions are not as intuitive to use as the arrow keys. The `j` and `k` keys are side by side, making it difficult to remember which goes up and which goes down. And the `l` key doesn't move left, it moves right! The keys are assigned this way for historical reasons, so don't go looking hard for a logical pattern.[1]

Here are a few pointers that might help if you're struggling to remember which key does what. The letter `j` sort of looks like an arrow pointing downward. On a Qwerty keyboard, the `h` and `l` keys are positioned to the left and right of each other, mirroring the direction in which they move the cursor.

Although `h`, `j`, `k`, and `l` may seem unintuitive at first, learning to use them is worth your while. To reach for the arrow keys, you have to move your hand away from its resting place on the home row. Because the `h`, `j`, `k`, and `l` keys are all within easy reach, you can move Vim's cursor without having to move your hand.

---

1. http://www.catonmat.net/blog/why-vim-uses-hjkl-as-arrow-keys/

That might sound like a trivial saving, but it adds up. Once you've acquired the habit of using h, j, k, and l to move around, using any other editor that depends on the arrow keys will feel strange. You'll wonder how you put up with it for so long!

Leave Your Right Hand Where It Belongs

On a Qwerty keyboard, the j, k, and l keys fall directly beneath the index, middle, and ring fingers of the right hand. We use the index finger to press the h key, but we have to reach for it. Some people see this as a problem, and as a solution they recommend shifting your entire right hand one step to the left so that h, j, k, and l are each covered by a finger. Please don't do that.

As we'll see throughout the rest of this chapter, Vim provides much quicker ways of moving around. You're wasting keystrokes if you press the h key more than two times in a row. When it comes to moving horizontally, you can get around quicker using word-wise or character search motions (see Tip 49, *Move Word-Wise*, on page 118, and Tip 50, *Find by Character*, on page 120).

I use the h and l keys for off-by-one errors, when I narrowly miss my target. Apart from that, I hardly touch them. Given how little I use the h key, I'm happy to have to stretch for it on a Qwerty keyboard. On the flip side, I use the character search commands often (see Tip 50, *Find by Character*, on page 120), so I'm pleased that the ; key rests comfortably beneath my little finger.

Break the Habit of Reaching for the Arrow Keys

If you're finding it difficult to break the habit of using the arrow keys, try putting this in your vimrc file:

motions/disable-arrowkeys.vim
```
noremap <Up> <Nop>
noremap <Down> <Nop>
noremap <Left> <Nop>
noremap <Right> <Nop>
```

This maps each of the arrow keys to do nothing. Each time you reach for the arrow keys, you'll be reminded that you should have left your hand on the home row. It won't take long to get the hang of using h, j, k, and l instead.

I don't recommend keeping those mappings in your vimrc forever, just long enough to get into the habit of using h, j, k, and l. After that, you could always consider mapping the arrow keys to something more useful.

Tip 48

Distinguish Between Real Lines and Display Lines

Avoid frustration by learning the difference between real lines and display lines. Vim lets us operate on both.

Unlike many text editors, Vim makes a distinction between *real lines* and *display lines*. When the 'wrap' setting is enabled (and it's on by default), each line of text that exceeds the width of the window will display as wrapped, ensuring that no text is truncated from view. As a result, a single line in the file may be represented by multiple lines on the display.

The easiest way to tell the difference between real lines and display lines is by enabling the 'number' setting. Lines that begin with a number correspond to the real lines, which may span one or more display lines. Each time a line is wrapped to fit inside the window, it begins without a line number. This screenshot shows a Vim buffer containing three real lines (numbered) and nine display lines:

```
 1 Lorem ipsum dolor sit amet, consectetur adipiscing elit. Pra
   esent ut sapien nulla, ac bibendum diam. Suspendisse rutrum
   euismod tincidunt.
 2 Duis leo eros, cursus a vehicula accumsan, venenatis nec mas
   sa. Maecenas porttitor, nulla vel congue euismod, neque puru
   s lobortis nisi, id placerat enim sapien nec enim.
 3 Vestibulum ante ipsum primis in faucibus orci luctus et ultr
   ices posuere cubilia Curae. Nullam pulvinar tempor mollis. M
   auris ac blandit turpis.
:set number                                     2,85          All
```

Understanding the difference between real and display lines is important because Vim provides motions for interacting with both kinds. The j and k commands move down and up by real lines, whereas the gj and gk commands move down and up by display lines.

Consider our screenshot. Suppose that we wanted to move the cursor upward to position it on the word "vehicula." Our target is one display line above the cursor, so we could get where we want to go by pressing gk. The k key would move up by a real line, placing our cursor on the word "ac," which is not what we want in this case.

Vim also provides commands for jumping directly to the first or last character of a line. This table summarizes the commands for interacting with real and display lines:

Command	Move Cursor
`j`	Down one real line
`gj`	Down one display line
`k`	Up one real line
`gk`	Up one display line
`0`	To first character of real line
`g0`	To first character of display line
`^`	To first nonblank character of real line
`g^`	To first nonblank character of display line
`$`	To end of real line
`g$`	To end of display line

Note the pattern: `j`, `k`, `0`, and `$` all interact with real lines, while prefixing any of these with `g` tells Vim to act on display lines instead.

Most other text editors have no notion of the concept of real lines, and they provide the means to interact with display lines only. When you start out, it can be frustrating to discover that Vim seems to treat lines differently. When you learn to use the `gj` and `gk` commands, you'll appreciate that `j` and `k` may let you cover more distance with fewer keystrokes.

Remap Line Motion Commands

If you would prefer to have the `j` and `k` keys operate on display lines rather than on real lines, you can always remap them. Try putting these lines into your vimrc file:

motions/cursor-maps.vim
```
nnoremap k gk
nnoremap gk k
nnoremap j gj
nnoremap gj j
```

These mappings make `j` and `k` move down and up by display lines, while `gj` and `gk` would move down and up by real lines (the opposite of Vim's default behavior). I wouldn't recommend using these mappings if you have to work with Vim on many different machines. In that case, getting used to Vim's default behavior would be better.

Tip 49

Move Word-Wise

Vim has two speeds for moving backward and forward word-wise. Both allow for a more rapid traversal than moving by one column at a time.

Vim provides a handful of motions that let us move the cursor forward and backward by one word at a time (see :h word-motions ⓘ). They're summarized in this table:

Command	Move Cursor
w	Forward to start of next word
b	Backward to start of current/previous word
e	Forward to end of current/next word
ge	Backward to end of previous word

We can think of these motions as coming in pairs: the w and b commands both target the start of a word, while the e and ge commands target the end of a word. w and e both advance the cursor forward, while b and ge move the cursor backward. This matrix of word-wise motions is illustrated here:

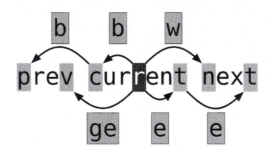

Trying to memorize all four of these commands isn't easy, and I wouldn't recommend it. Start off by using the w and b commands (think of them as (for-)*word* and *back*-word if you need a mnemonic). You should find that moving back and forward a word at a time is considerably faster than using h and l to move a column at a time.

The e and ge commands complete the set, but you can get by without them at first. Eventually you'll notice that sometimes it would be useful to go directly to the end of the current word in a single move. For example, suppose that we want to turn the word "fast" into "faster" in this excerpt:

Keystrokes	Buffer Contents
{start}	Go `f`ast.
ea er<Esc>	Go faste`r`.

Taken together, the `ea` commands can be read as "Append at the end of the current word." I use `ea` often enough that it feels to me like a single command. Occasionally useful, the `gea` command can be read as "append at the end of the previous word."

Know Your Words from Your WORDS

We've been talking a lot about words, but so far we haven't pinned down what a word actually is. Vim provides two definitions and distinguishes between them by calling one a "word" and the other a "WORD." Each word-wise motion we met earlier has a WORD-wise equivalent, including `W`, `B`, `E`, and `gE`.

A word consists of a sequence of letters, digits, and underscores, or as a sequence of other nonblank characters separated with whitespace (see :h word ⓘ). The definition of a WORD is simpler: it consists of a sequence of nonblank characters separated with whitespace (see :h WORD ⓘ).

Ok, but what does that actually mean? The details we can leave to Vim's implementors. As users, we can think of them in simpler terms: WORDS are bigger than words! Look at this text and quickly count the number of words:

```
e.g. we're going too slow
```

Did you count five or ten (or something in between)? That example contains five WORDS and ten words. The periods and apostrophes count as words, so if we try to advance through this text with the `w` command, it'll be slow going:

Keystrokes	Buffer Contents
{start}	`e`.g. we're going too slow
wwww	e.g. `w`e're going too slow
www	e.g. we're `g`oing too slow

If we move WORD-wise instead, we make progress with fewer keystrokes:

Keystrokes	Buffer Contents
{start}	`e`.g. we're going too slow
W	e.g. `w`e're going too slow
W	e.g. we're `g`oing too slow

In this example, the WORD-wise motions appear to be the better choice, but that won't be true every time. Sometimes we'll want to act on "we" as a word. For example, if we wanted it to read "you" instead, we would do this:

Keystrokes	Buffer Contents
{start}	e.g. we're going too slow
cwyou<Esc>	e.g. you're going too slow

Other times, we might prefer to treat "we're" as a WORD. For example, if we wanted to change it to read "it's" instead, we would do this:

Keystrokes	Buffer Contents
{start}	e.g. we're going too slow
cWit's<Esc>	e.g. it's going too slow

Use WORD-wise motions if you want to move faster, and use word-wise motions if you want a more fine-grained traversal. Play around with them, and you'll get a feel for when to use words and when to use WORDS. You can develop an intuition for these things without fully understanding the implementation details.

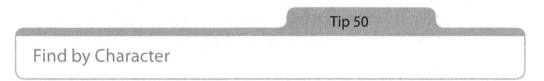

Tip 50

Find by Character

Vim's character search commands allow us to move quickly within a line, and they work beautifully in Operator-Pending mode.

The f{char} command is one of the quickest methods of moving around in Vim. It searches for the specified character, starting with the cursor position and continuing to the end of the current line. If a match is found, then the cursor advances to the specified character. If no match is found, then the cursor stays put (see :h fⓘ).

That may sound complex, but it's quite simple in practice. Observe:

Keystrokes	Buffer Contents
{start}	Find the first occurrence of {char} and move to it.
fx	Find the first occurrence of {char} and move to it.
fo	Find the first occurrence of {char} and move to it.

In this case, the fx command does nothing. Vim searches forward for an occurrence of the "x" character, but no matches are found, so the cursor doesn't move. The `fo` command finds an occurrence of the "o" character, so the cursor is positioned on top of the first match.

If we need to position our cursor at the start of the word "occurrence," there's no way we can do it with fewer than two keystrokes. The `f{char}` command is efficient, and when it works as well as it does in this example, it feels as though Vim is reading our minds.

But the `f{char}` command doesn't always work out so well. Suppose that we wanted to position our cursor on the "c" at the start of the word {char}. Watch what happens when we use the `fc` command:

Keystrokes	Buffer Contents
{start}	Find the first occurrence of {char} and move to it.
fc	Find the first occurrence of {char} and move to it.
;	Find the first occurrence of {char} and move to it.
;	Find the first occurrence of {char} and move to it.
;	Find the first occurrence of {char} and move to it.

The "c" character occurs several times on this line, so this time we don't make a direct hit on our target. It takes a few attempts to move the cursor to the position where we want it. Luckily we don't have to explicitly repeat the `fc` command. Vim keeps track of the most recent `f{char}` search, and we can repeat it using the `;` command (see :h ;ⓘ). In this example, we have to press `;` three times to maneuver the cursor into position.

The `f{char}` and `;` commands make a powerful combination, and we can cover a lot of distance with very few keystrokes. But where the cursor will end up isn't always obvious. As a result, it's easy to get trigger-happy with the `;` key, and occasionally we'll miss our target. For example, suppose that we want to place the cursor at the start of the word "of":

Keystrokes	Buffer Contents
{start}	Find the first occurrence of {char} and move to it.
fo	Find the first occurrence of {char} and move to it.
;;	Find the first occurrence of {char} and move to it.
,	Find the first occurrence of {char} and move to it.

Having accidentally overshot our mark, we can back up using the `,` command. This repeats the last `f{char}` search but in the opposite direction (see :h ,ⓘ). Remember our mantra from Tip 4, *Act, Repeat, Reverse*, on page 8: act, repeat, reverse. I think of `,` as a safety net for those times when I get overzealous with the `;` key.

> ### Don't Throw Away the Reverse Character Search Command
>
> Vim assigns a function to almost every key on the keyboard. If we want to create our own custom mappings, which keys should we bind them to? Vim provides the `<Leader>` key as a namespace for our own user-defined commands. Here is how we can create our own custom mappings using `<Leader>`:
>
> ```
> noremap <Leader>n nzz
> noremap <Leader>N Nzz
> ```
>
> The default leader key is `\`, so we could trigger these custom mappings by pressing `\n` and `\N`. If you want to know what these mappings do, look up `:h zz` ⓘ.
>
> On some keyboards, the `\` command is inconvenient to reach, so Vim makes it easy to set the leader key to something else (see `:h mapleader` ⓘ). A common choice is to set the comma key as leader. If you take this route, I strongly recommend mapping the reverse character search command to another key. Here's an example:
>
> ```
> let mapleader=","
> noremap \ ,
> ```
>
> The `;` and `,` commands complement each other. If you take one of them away, then the whole family of character search commands becomes much less useful.

Character Searches Can Include or Exclude the Target

The `f{char}`, `;`, and `,` commands are part of a set of character-search commands. This table lists them all:

Command	Effect
`f{char}`	Forward to the next occurrence of {char}
`F{char}`	Backward to the previous occurrence of {char}
`t{char}`	Forward to the character before the next occurrence of {char}
`T{char}`	Backward to the character after the previous occurrence of {char}
`;`	Repeat the last character-search command
`,`	Reverse the last character-search command

Think of the `t{char}` and `T{char}` commands as searching *till* the specified character. The cursor stops *one character before* {char}, whereas the `f{char}` and `F{char}` commands position the cursor *on top of* the specified character.

It's not immediately obvious why you would want both kinds of character search. This example demonstrates them in action:

Keystrokes	Buffer Contents
{start}	`I've been expecting you, Mister Bond.`
`f,`	`I've been expecting you, Mister Bond.`
`dt.`	`I've been expecting you.`

To begin with, we want to position our cursor directly on top of the comma symbol. For this we can use the `f,` command. Next we want to delete all of the text until the end of the sentence, but not including the period symbol itself. This time, the `dt.` command does the job.

Alternatively, we could have used `dfd`, which would delete everything from the cursor position to the last letter of the word "Bond." The end result is the same either way, but I find that `dt.` requires less concentration. Deleting through the letter "d" is not a common pattern, whereas deleting the last clause of a sentence is something we do often enough that we can treat `f,dt.` as a finger macro.

In general, I tend to use `f{char}` and `F{char}` in Normal mode when I want to move the cursor quickly within the current line, whereas I tend to use the `t{char}` and `T{char}` character search commands in combination with `d{motion}` or `c{motion}`. To put it another way, I use `f` and `F` in Normal mode, and `t` and `T` in Operator-Pending mode. Refer to Tip 12, *Combine and Conquer*, on page 24 (and *Meet Operator-Pending Mode*, on page 27), for more details.

Think Like a Scrabble® Player

The character search commands can be highly economical with keystrokes, but their efficiency varies depending on our choice of target. As any Scrabble player can tell you, some letters appear more frequently than others. If we can make a habit of choosing less common characters for use with the `f{char}` command, then we'll be more likely to strike our target with a single move.

Suppose that we wanted to delete the only adjective from this sentence:

`Improve your writing by deleting excellent adjectives.`

What motion should we use to position our cursor on the word "excellent"? If we target the first letter by pressing `fe`, then we have to follow up by pressing `;;;` to skip all of the obstacles in between. A better choice would be `fx`, which gets us where we want to go with a single move. From there, we can delete the word with the `daw` command (for more details about `aw`, see Tip 53, *Delete Around, or Change Inside*, on page 129).

Take a look at the text that you're reading. It's composed almost entirely of lowercase letters. Capital letters are much rarer, and so too are punctuation marks. When using the character search commands, it's better to choose target characters with a low frequency of occurrences. With practice you'll learn to spot them.

Tip 51

Search to Navigate

The search command allows us to rapidly cover distances both large and small with very few keystrokes.

The character search commands (`f{char}`, `t{char}`, and so on) are fast and lightweight, but they have limitations. They can only search for a single character at a time, and they can only operate within the current line. If we need to search for more than one character or move beyond the current line, then we can use the search command instead.

Suppose that we want to position our cursor on the word "takes" in this sample:

```
motions/search-haiku.txt
search for your target
it only takes a moment
to get where you want
```

We could do so by searching for the word: /takes`<CR>`. It only occurs once in this short sample, so that would be sure to get us where we want to go in a single move. But let's see if we can we do it with even fewer keystrokes:

Keystrokes	Buffer Contents
{start}	search for your target it only takes a moment to get where you want
/ta`<CR>`	search for your target it only takes a moment to get where you want
/tak`<CR>`	search for your target it only takes a moment to get where you want

Searching for the two-letter string "ta" gets two hits, but the three-letter string "tak" has one unique hit. In this example, the search motion makes a short hop, but in a large document we can use this technique to cover great distances with few keystrokes. The search command is a very economical way to move around.

Even if we had searched for the two-letter "ta" fragment and ended up in the wrong place, we could jump to the next occurrence by repeating the previous search with the `n` command. Also, if we pressed the `n` key too many times, we could back up again with the `N` command. The mantra from Tip 4, *Act, Repeat, Reverse*, on page 8, should be becoming familiar by now: act, repeat, reverse.

In the previous tip, we saw that the `fe` command was rarely useful because the letter *e* is so common. We can get around this shortcoming by searching for a string of two or more letters in sequence. Although *e* may appear many times in the English language, only a fraction of those occurrences are succeeded immediately by the letter *r*. It's surprising how often we can jump to any word of our choice just by searching for the first few characters.

In our "takes" example, I enabled the 'hlsearch' feature to highlight the search matches. When searching for a short string, we'll often find multiple matches scattered across the document. Results can get unsightly when the 'hlsearch' option is enabled, so you might want to disable this feature if you make a habit of using the search command to navigate (it's off by default). However, the 'incsearch' option is very useful in this use case. Refer to Tip 82, *Preview the First Match Before Execution*, on page 205, for more details.

Operate with a Search Motion

We're not limited to using the search command in Normal mode. We can use it from Visual and Operator-Pending modes just as well to do real work. For example, suppose that we wanted to delete the text "takes time but eventually" from this phrase:

Keystrokes	Buffer Contents
`v`	This phrase takes time but eventually gets to the point.
`/ge<CR>`	This phrase takes time but eventually gets to the point.
`h`	This phrase takes time but eventually gets to the point.
`d`	This phrase gets to the point.

To begin with, we press `v` to switch to Visual mode. Then we can extend the selection by searching for the short "ge" string, which puts the cursor where we want it in a single bound. Well, almost—we have an off-by-one error. The selection includes the "g" at the start of the word, but we don't want to delete that. We'll use `h` to back up one character. Then, having defined our selection, we'll delete it with the `d` command.

Here's an even quicker way of doing the same thing:

Keystrokes	Buffer Contents
{start}	This phrase takes time but eventually gets to the point.
d/ge<CR>	This phrase gets to the point.

Here, we use the `/ge<CR>` search motion to tell the `d{motion}` command what to delete. The search command is an *exclusive* motion. That means that even though our cursor ends up on the "g" at the start of the word "gets," that character is excluded from the delete operation (see :h exclusive ⓘ).

By staying out of Visual mode, we've cut out two unnecessary keystrokes (see also Tip 23, *Prefer Operators to Visual Commands Where Possible*, on page 45). It takes a bit of getting used to, but combining the `d{motion}` operator with the search motion is a power move. Use it to amaze your friends and coworkers.

Tip 52

Trace Your Selection with Precision Text Objects

Text objects allow us to interact with parentheses, quotes, XML tags, and other common patterns that appear in text.

Take a look at this code sample:

```
motions/template.js
var tpl = [
  '<a href="{url}">{title}</a>'
]
```

Each opening { character is balanced by a closing } character. The same is true of [and], < and >, and the opening and closing HTML tags, <a> and </a>. This sample also contains single and double quotation marks, which come in pairs.

Vim understands the structure of these well-formed patterns, and it allows us to operate on the regions of text that they delimit. *Text objects* define regions of text by structure (see :h text-objects ⓘ). With only a couple of keystrokes, we can use these to select or operate on a chunk of text.

Suppose that our cursor was positioned inside a set of curly braces and we wanted to visually select the text inside the {}. Press `vi}`:

Keystrokes	Buffer Contents

{start}	```var tpl = [```
	 ``` '<a href="{url}">{title}</a>'```
	 ```]```

vi}	```var tpl = [```
	 ``` '<a href="{url}">{title}</a>'```
	 ```]```

a"	```var tpl = [```
	 ``` '<a href="{url}">{title}</a>'```
	 ```]```

i>	```var tpl = [```
	 ``` '<a href="{url}">{title}</a>'```
	 ```]```

it	```var tpl = [```
	 ``` '<a href="{url}">{title}</a>'```
	 ```]```

at	```var tpl = [```
	 ``` '<a href="{url}">{title}</a>'```
	 ```]```

a]	```var tpl = [```
	 ``` '<a href="{url}">{title}</a>'```
	 ```]```

Normally when we use Visual mode, one end of the selection is anchored to a particular character, while the other end of the selection is free to move. When we use motions such as `l`, `w`, and `f{char}`, we can expand or contract the selection by moving the free end of the visual range.

What's happening here is different. When we press `vi}`, Vim initiates Visual mode and then selects all of the characters contained by the {} braces. Where the cursor is positioned to begin with doesn't matter so long as it's located somewhere inside a block of curly braces when the `i}` text object is invoked.

We can expand the selection again using another text object. For example, `a"` selects a range of characters delimited by double quotes. `i>` selects everything inside a pair of angle brackets.

Vim's text objects consist of two characters, the first of which is always either `i` or `a`. In general, we can say that the text objects prefixed with `i` select inside the delimiters, whereas those that are prefixed with `a` select everything including the delimiters. As a mnemonic, think of `i` as *inside* and `a` as *around* (or *all*).

In the previous example, check whether the text object leads with `i` or `a`. In particular, note the difference between `it` and `at`. Note, too, that in this example `a]` expands the selection to span multiple lines.

A partial list of Vim's built-in text objects is summarized in the following table. In the interests of neatness, some duplicates have been omitted. For example, `i(` and `i)` are equivalent to each other, and so too are `a[` and `a]`. Use whichever style you find most comfortable.

Text Object	Selection	Text Object	Selection
`a)` or `ab`	A pair of (parentheses)	`i)` or `ib`	Inside of (parentheses)
`a}` or `aB`	A pair of {braces}	`i}` or `iB`	Inside of {braces}
`a]`	A pair of [brackets]	`i]`	Inside of [brackets]
`a>`	A pair of \<angle brackets\>	`i>`	Inside of \<angle brackets\>
`a'`	A pair of 'single quotes'	`i'`	Inside of 'single quotes'
`a"`	A pair of "double quotes"	`i"`	Inside of "double quotes"
`` a` ``	A pair of `backticks`	`` i` ``	Inside of `backticks`
`at`	A pair of \<xml\>tags\</xml\>	`it`	Inside of \<xml\>tags\</xml\>

Performing Operations with Text Objects

Visual mode makes for a nice introduction to text objects because it's easy to see what's happening. But text objects reveal their true power when we use them in Operator-Pending mode.

Text objects are not motions themselves: we can't use them to navigate around the document. But we can use text objects in Visual mode and in Operator-Pending mode. Remember this: whenever you see {motion} as part of the syntax for a command, you can also use a text object. Common examples include `d{motion}`, `c{motion}`, and `y{motion}` (see Table 2, *Vim's Operator Commands*, on page 25, for more).

Let's demonstrate using the `c{motion}` command, which deletes the specified text and then switches to Insert mode (:h c ⓘ). We'll use it to replace {url} with a # symbol, and then again to replace {title} with a placeholder:

Keystrokes	Buffer Contents
`{start}`	`'<a href="{u`r`l}">{title}</a>'`
`ci"` #\<Esc\>	`'<a href="`#`">{title}</a>'`
`cit` click here\<Esc\>	`'<a href="#">click her`e`</a>'`

We can read the `ci"` command as "change inside the double quotes." The `cit` command can be read as "change inside the tag." We could just as easily use the `yit` command to yank the text from inside the tag, or `dit` to delete it.

Discussion

Each of these commands requires only three keystrokes, and yet they're elegant in spite of this terseness. I would almost go so far as to say that they are self-documenting. That's because these commands follow the rules of Vim's simple grammar, which is covered in Tip 12, *Combine and Conquer*, on page 24.

In Tip 50, *Find by Character*, on page 120, and Tip 51, *Search to Navigate*, on page 124, we learned a couple of tricks that allow us to move the cursor with precision. Whether we're using `f{char}` to search for a single character or `/target<CR>` to search for several characters, the pattern of usage is the same: we look for a suitable target, take aim, and then fire. If we're good, we'll hit our target with a single move. These power moves allow us to cover a lot of ground with little effort.

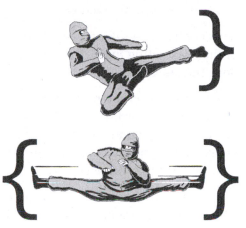

Text objects are the next level up. If the `f{char}` and `/pattern<CR>` commands are like a flying kick to the head, then text objects are like a scissors kick that strikes two targets with a single move:

Tip 53

Delete Around, or Change Inside

Text objects usually come in pairs: one that acts inside the object and another that acts around the object. In this tip, we'll examine a typical use case for each kind of text object.

Vim's text objects fall into two categories: those that interact with pairs of delimiters, such as `i)`, `i"`, and `it`, and those that interact with chunks of text, such as words, sentences, and paragraphs. Here's a summary of the latter.

Keystrokes	Current...	Keystrokes	Current...
`iw`	word	`aw`	word plus space(s)
`iW`	WORD	`aW`	WORD plus space(s)
`is`	sentence	`as`	sentence plus space(s)
`ip`	paragraph	`ap`	paragraph plus blank line(s)

I've labeled the first category as *delimited text objects* because they begin and end with matching symbols. Words, sentences, and paragraphs are defined by boundaries, so I've labeled this category as *bounded text objects* (Vim's documentation calls them "block" and "non-block" objects, but I find that to be an unhelpful distinction).

Let's compare the `iw` and `aw` text objects. Using our mnemonic, we can think of these as acting *inside* the word or *around* the word, respectively. But what does that mean?

The `iw` text object interacts with everything from the first to the last character of the current word. The `aw` text object does the same, but it extends the range to include any whitespace characters after or before the word, if whitespace is present. To see how Vim defines the boundaries of a word, refer to Tip 49, *Move Word-Wise*, on page 118.

The distinction between `iw` and `aw` is subtle, and it's not immediately obvious why we need them both, so let's look at a typical use case for each of them.

Suppose that we want to delete the word "excellent" from the following sentence. We can do it using the `daw` command:

Keystrokes	Buffer Contents
{start}	Improve your writing by deleting e`x`cellent adjectives.
`daw`	Improve your writing by deleting `a`djectives.

This deletes the word plus one space, giving a clean result. If we used `diw` instead, then we'd end up with two adjacent spaces, which is probably not what we want.

Now let's suppose that we want to change the word to something else. This time we'll use the `ciw` command:

Keystrokes	Buffer Contents
{start}	Improve your writing by deleting e`x`cellent adjectives.
`ciw`most<Esc>	Improve your writing by deleting mos`t` adjectives.

The `ciw` command deletes the word without trimming any whitespace and then puts us into Insert mode. That's just what we want. If we had used `caw` instead, then we'd end up running words together to read "mostadjectives." That would be easy enough to mend, but it's better still if we can avoid the problem altogether.

As a general rule, we could say that the `d{motion}` command tends to work well with `aw`, `as`, and `ap`, whereas the `c{motion}` command works better with `iw` and similar.

Tip 54

Mark Your Place and Snap Back to It

Vim's marks allow us to jump quickly to locations of interest within a document. We can set marks manually, but Vim also keeps track of certain points of interest for us automatically.

The `m{a-zA-Z}` command marks the current cursor location with the designated letter (:h m ⓘ). Lowercase marks are local to each individual buffer, whereas uppercase marks are globally accessible. We'll learn more about them in Tip 59, *Snap Between Files Using Global Marks*, on page 141. Vim does nothing to indicate that a mark has been set, but if you've done it right, then you should be able to jump directly to your mark with only two keystrokes from anywhere in the file.

Vim provides two Normal mode commands for jumping to a mark. (Pay attention—they look similar!) `'{mark}` moves to the line where a mark was set, positioning the cursor on the first non-whitespace character. The `` `{mark} `` command moves the cursor to the exact position where a mark was set, restoring the line *and* the column at once (see :h mark-motions ⓘ).

If you commit only one of these commands to memory, go with `` `{mark} ``. Whether you care about restoring the exact position or just getting to the right line, this command will get you there. The only time you have to use the `'{mark}` form is in the context of an Ex command (see Tip 28, *Execute a Command on One or More Consecutive Lines*, on page 56).

The `mm` and `` `m `` commands make a handy pair. Respectively, they set the mark m and jump to it. *Swap Two Words*, on page 154, shows one example of how they can be used for a quick mark-then-snap-back maneuver.

Automatic Marks

We can set up to twenty-six lowercase marks per buffer. That's one mark for each letter of the alphabet, and it's way more than you're ever likely to need! In Vim's predecessor, vi, there was no such thing as Visual mode. Back then, marks would have been a much more important feature than they are now. Many of the tasks that would have required a mark in vi can be done in Vim using Visual mode.

But marks have not become obsolete in Vim; they still have their uses. In particular, the marks that Vim sets for us automatically can be really handy. They include the marks shown in Table 10, *Vim's Automatic Marks*, on page 132.

Keystrokes	Buffer Contents
`` ` `` `` ` ``	Position before the last jump within current file
`` ` ``.	Location of last change
`` ` ``^	Location of last insertion
`` ` ``[	Start of last change or yank
`` ` ``]	End of last change or yank
`` ` ``<	Start of last visual selection
`` ` ``>	End of last visual selection

Table 10—Vim's Automatic Marks

The `` ` `` `` ` `` mark complements the jump list (Tip 56, *Traverse the Jump List*, on page 135), and we'll see a use for it in the next tip. The `` ` ``. complements the change list, which is covered by Tip 57, *Traverse the Change List*, on page 137.

The start and end of the last visual selection are both recorded automatically as marks, so we might even consider Visual mode to be a fancy interface to the underlying marks feature.

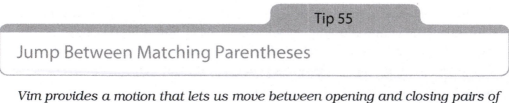

Tip 55

Jump Between Matching Parentheses

Vim provides a motion that lets us move between opening and closing pairs of parentheses. By enabling the matchit.vim plugin, we can extend this behavior to work on pairs of XML tags as well as on keywords in some programming languages.

The `%` command lets us jump between opening and closing sets of parentheses (see `:h %` ⓘ). It works with (), {}, and [], as this example demonstrates:

Keystrokes	Buffer Contents
{start}	`console.log([{'a':1},{'b':2}])`
`%`	`console.log([{'a':1},{'b':2}])`
`h`	`console.log([{'a':1},{'b':2}])`
`%`	`console.log([{'a':1},{'b':2}])`
`l`	`console.log([{'a':1},{'b':2}])`
`%`	`console.log([{'a':1},{'b':2}])`

To see how we might use `%` in practice, let's use this short extract of Ruby:

motions/parentheses.rb
```
cities = %w{London Berlin New\ York}
```

Suppose that we want to switch from the %w{London Berlin New\ York} syntax to a regular list definition: ["London", "Berlin", "New York"]. We'll have to switch opening and closing curly braces to square brackets. You might think that this would be a perfect occasion to use the `%` motion. You'd be right, but there's a gotcha!

Let's say that we start off by positioning our cursor on the opening curly brace and then we press `r[` to change it to an opening square bracket. Now we've got this strange-looking construct: [London Berlin New\ York}. The `%` command only works on well-formed matching parentheses, so we can't use it to jump to the closing } character.

The trick here is to use the `%` command *before* making any changes. When we use the `%` command, Vim automatically sets a mark for the location from which we jumped. We can snap back to it by pressing `` `` ``. Here's a partial solution for our example refactoring:

Keystrokes	Buffer Contents
{start}	`cities = %w{London Berlin New\ York}`
`dt{`	`cities = {London Berlin New\ York}`
`%`	`cities = {London Berlin New\ York}`
`r]`	`cities = {London Berlin New\ York]`
`` `` ``	`cities = {London Berlin New\ York]`
`r[`	`cities = [London Berlin New\ York]`

Note that in this case, the `<C-o>` command would work just as well as the `` `` `` motion (see Tip 56, *Traverse the Jump List*, on page 135). The surround.vim plugin provides commands that would make this task even easier. Find out more in *Surround.vim,* on page 134.

Jump Between Matching Keywords

Vim ships with a plugin called matchit, which enhances the functionality of the % command. When this plugin is enabled, the % command can jump between matching pairs of keywords. For example, in an HTML file, the % command would jump between opening and closing tags. In a Ruby file, it would jump between class/end, def/end, and if/end pairs.

Even though matchit ships with the Vim distribution, it's not enabled by default. This minimal vimrc would make Vim autoload the matchit plugin on startup:

```
set nocompatible
filetype plugin on
runtime macros/matchit.vim
```

The enhancements provided by this plugin are very useful, so I'd recommend enabling it. Consult :h matchit-install ⓘ for more details.

Surround.vim

One of my favorite plugins is surround.vim by Tim Pope,[a] which makes wrapping a selection with a pair of delimiters easy. For example, we could put the words *New York* in quote marks:

Keystrokes	Buffer Contents
{start}	cities = ["London", "Berlin", New York]
vee	cities = ["London", "Berlin", New York]
S"	cities = ["London", "Berlin", "New York"]

The S" command is provided by surround.vim, and it can be read as "Surround the selection with a pair of double quote marks." We could just as easily use S) or S} if we wanted to wrap the selection with opening and closing parentheses or braces.

We can also use surround.vim to *change* existing delimiters. For example, we could change {London} to [London] with the cs}] command, which can be read as "Change surrounding {} braces to [] brackets." Or we could go the other way with the cs]} command. It's a powerful plugin—check it out.

---

a.   http://github.com/tpope/vim-surround

CHAPTER 9

Navigate Between Files with Jumps

As we learned in the previous chapter, motions allow us to move around within a file. Jumps are similar, except that they can also move us between different files. Vim provides a couple of commands that turn keywords in the document into a wormhole, allowing us to jump quickly from one part of our codebase to another. That might seem disorienting at first, but Vim always traces our path by leaving a trail that we can easily follow to get back to where we came from.

Tip 56

Traverse the Jump List

Vim records our location before and after making a jump and provides a couple of commands for retracing our steps.

In web browsers, we're used to using the back button to return to pages that we visited earlier. Vim provides a similar feature by way of the *jump list*: the `<C-o>` command is like the back button, while the complementary `<C-i>` command is like the forward button. These commands allow us to traverse Vim's jump list, but what exactly is a jump?

Let's start by making this distinction: motions move around *within a file*, whereas jumps can move *between files* (although we'll soon see that some motions are also classified as jumps). We can inspect the contents of the jump list by running this command:

```
⇒ :jumps
❮  jump line  col file/text
       4    12    2 <recipe id="sec.jump.list">
       3   114    2 <recipe id="sec.change.list">
```

```
   2    169     2 <recipe id="sec.gf">
   1    290     2 <recipe id="sec.global.marks">
>
Press Enter or type command to continue
```

Any command that changes the active file for the current window can be described as a jump. In the jump list, Vim records the cursor location before and after running such a command. For example, if we run the :edit command to open a new file (see Tip 42, *Open a File by Its Filepath Using ':edit'*, on page 99), then we can use the `<C-o>` and `<C-i>` commands to jump back and forth between the two files.

Moving directly to a line number with `[count]G` counts as a jump, but moving up or down one line at a time does not. The sentence-wise and paragraph-wise motions are jumps, but the character-wise and word-wise motions are not. As a rule of thumb, we could say that long-range motions may be classi-fied as a jump, but short-range motions are just motions.

This table summarizes a selection of jumps:

Command	Effect
`[count]G`	Jump to line number
`/pattern<CR>` / `?pattern<CR>` / `n` / `N`	Jump to next/previous occurrence of pattern
`%`	Jump to matching parenthesis
`(` / `)`	Jump to start of previous/next sentence
`{` / `}`	Jump to start of previous/next paragraph
`H` / `M` / `L`	Jump to top/middle/bottom of screen
`gf`	Jump to file name under the cursor
`<C-]>`	Jump to definition of keyword under the cursor
`'{mark}` / `` `{mark} ``	Jump to a mark

The `<C-o>` and `<C-i>` commands themselves are never treated as a motion. This means that we can't use them to extend the reach of a Visual mode selection, nor can we use them in Operator-Pending mode. I tend to think of the jump list as a breadcrumb trail that makes it easy to retrace my steps through the files that I've visited during the course of an editing session.

Vim can maintain multiple jump lists at the same time. In fact, each separate window has its own jump list. If we're using split windows or multiple tab pages, then the `<C-o>` and `<C-i>` commands will always be scoped to the jump list of the active window.

Beware of Mapping the Tab Key

Try pressing `<C-i>` in Insert mode, and you should find that it has the same effect as pressing the `<Tab>` key. That's because Vim sees `<C-i>` and `<Tab>` as the same thing.

Beware that if you attempt to create a mapping for the `<Tab>` key, it will also be triggered when you press `<C-i>` (and vice versa). That may not seem like a problem, but consider this: if you map the `<Tab>` key to something else, it will *overwrite* the default behavior of the `<C-i>` command. Think carefully about whether that's a worthwhile trade-off. The jump list is much less useful if you can only traverse it in one direction.

Tip 57

Traverse the Change List

Vim records the location of our cursor after each change we make to a document. Traversing this change list is simple and can be the quickest way to get where we want to go.

Have you ever used the undo command followed immediately by redo? The two commands cancel each other out, but they have the side effect of placing the cursor on the most recent change. That could be useful if we wanted to jump back to the part of the document that we edited most recently. It's a hack, but `u<C-r>` gets us there.

It turns out that Vim maintains a list of the modifications we make to each buffer during the course of an editing session. It's called the *change list* (see `:h changelist` ⓘ), and we can inspect its contents by running the following:

⇒ `:changes`
❮
```
change line  col text
      3    1    8 Line one
      2    2    7 Line two
      1    3    9 Line three
>
Press ENTER or type command to continue
```

This example output shows that Vim records the line and column number for each change. Using the `g;` and `g,` commands, we can traverse backward and forward through the change list. As a memory aid for `g;` and `g,`, it may help to remember that the `;` and `,` commands can be used to repeat or reverse the `f{char}` command (see Tip 50, *Find by Character*, on page 120).

To jump back to the most recent modification in the document, we press `g;`. That places the cursor back on the line and column where it ended up after the previous edit. The result is the same as if we had pressed `u<C-r>`, except that we don't make any transitory changes to the document.

Marks for the Last Change

Vim automatically creates a couple of marks that complement the change list. The `` `. `` mark always references the position of the last change (`:h `.` ⓘ), while the `` `^ `` mark tracks the position of the cursor the last time that Insert mode was stopped (`:h `^` ⓘ).

In most scenarios, jumping to the `` `. `` mark has the same effect as the `g;` command. Whereas the mark can only refer to the position of the most recent change, the change list stores multiple locations. We can press `g;` again and again, and each time it takes us to a location that was recorded earlier in the change list. The `` `. ``, on the other hand, will always take us to the last item in the change list.

The `` `^ `` mark references the last *insertion*, which is slightly more specific than the last *change*. If we leave Insert mode and then scroll around the document, we can quickly carry on where we left off by pressing `gi` (`:h gi` ⓘ). In a single move, that uses the `` `^ `` mark to restore the cursor position and then switches back into Insert mode. It's a great little time saver!

Vim maintains a change list for each individual buffer in an editing session. By contrast, a separate jump list is created for each window.

Tip 58

Jump to the Filename Under the Cursor

Vim treats filenames in our document as a kind of hyperlink. When configured properly, we can use the `gf` command to go to the filename under the cursor.

Let's demonstrate with the `jumps` directory, from the source files distributed with this book. It contains the following directory tree:

```
practical_vim.rb
practical_vim/
  core.rb
  jumps.rb
  more.rb
  motions.rb
```

In the shell, we'll start by changing to the jumps directory and then launching Vim. For this demonstration, I recommend using the -u NONE -N flags to ensure that Vim starts up without loading any plugins:

⇒ `$ cd code/jumps`
⇒ `$ vim -u NONE -N practical_vim.rb`

The practical_vim.rb file does nothing more than load the contents of the core.rb and more.rb files:

jumps/practical_vim.rb
```
require 'practical_vim/core'
require 'practical_vim/more'
```

Wouldn't it be useful if we could quickly inspect the contents of the file specified by the require directive? That's what Vim's gf command is for. Think of it as *go to file* (:h gf ⓘ).

Let's try it out. We'll start by placing our cursor somewhere inside the 'practical_vim/core' string (for example, pressing fp would get us there quickly). If we try using the gf command now, we get this error: "E447: Can't find file 'practical_vim/core' in path."

Vim tries to open a file called practical_vim/core and reports that it doesn't exist, but there is a file called practical_vim/core.rb (note the file extension). Somehow we need to instruct Vim to modify the filepath under the cursor by appending the .rb file extension before attempting to open it. We can do this with the 'suffixesadd' option.

Specify a File Extension

The 'suffixesadd' option allows us to specify one or more file extensions, which Vim will attempt to use when looking up a filename with the gf command (:h 'suffixesadd' ⓘ). We can set it up by running this command:

⇒ `:set suffixesadd+=.rb`

Now when we use the gf command, Vim jumps directly to the filepath under the cursor. Try using it to open more.rb. In that file, you'll find a couple of other require declarations. Pick one, and open it up using the gf command.

Each time we use the gf command, Vim adds a record to the jump list, so we can always go back to where we came from using the <C-o> command (see Tip 56, *Traverse the Jump List*, on page 135). In this case, pressing <C-o> the first time would take us back to more.rb, and pressing it a second time would take us back to practical_vim.rb.

Specify the Directories to Look Inside

In this example, each of the files referenced with the require statement was located relative to the working directory. But what if we referenced functionality that was provided by a third-party library, such as a rubygem?

That's where the 'path' option comes in (:h 'path' ⓘ). We can configure this to reference a comma-separated list of directories. When we use the gf command, Vim checks each of the directories listed in 'path' to see if it contains a filename that matches the text under the cursor. The 'path' setting is also used by the :find command, which we covered in Tip 43, *Open a File by Its Filename Using ':find'*, on page 102.

We can inspect the value of the path by running this command:

⇒ `:set path?`
❮ `path=.,/usr/include,,`

In this context, the . stands for the directory of the current file, whereas the empty string (delimited by two adjacent commas) stands for the working directory. The default settings work fine for this simple example, but for a larger project we would want to configure the 'path' setting to include a few more directories.

For example, it would be useful if the 'path' included the directories for all rubygems used in a Ruby project. Then we could use the gf command to open up the modules referenced by any require statements. For an automated solution, check out Tim Pope's bundler.vim plugin,[1] which uses the project Gemfile to populate the 'path' setting.

Discussion

In the setup for this tip, I recommended launching Vim with plugins disabled. That's because Vim is usually distributed with a Ruby file-type plugin, which handles the setup of 'suffixesadd' and 'path' options for us. If you do a lot of work with Ruby, I recommend getting the latest version of the file-type plugin from github because it's actively maintained.[2]

The 'suffixesadd' and 'path' options can be set locally for each buffer, so they can be configured in different ways for different file types. Vim is distributed with file-type plugins for many languages besides Ruby, so in practice you won't often have to set these options yourself. Even so, it's worth understanding

---

1. https://github.com/tpope/vim-bundler
2. https://github.com/vim-ruby/vim-ruby

how the `gf` command works. It makes each filepath in our document behave like a hyperlink, which makes it easier to navigate through a codebase.

The `<C-]>` command has a similar role. It also requires a bit of setup (as discussed in Tip 103, *Configure Vim to Work with ctags*, on page 256), but when it's correctly configured, it allows us to jump from any method invocation directly to the place where it was defined. Skip ahead to Tip 104, *Navigate Keyword Definitions with Vim's Tag Navigation Commands*, on page 258, for a demonstration.

While the jump list and change list are like breadcrumb trails that allow us to retrace our steps, the `gf` and `<C-]>` commands provide wormholes that transport us from one part of our codebase to another.

Tip 59

Snap Between Files Using Global Marks

A global mark is a kind of bookmark that allows us to jump between files. Marks can be especially useful for snapping back to a file after exploring a codebase.

The `m{letter}` command allows us to create a mark at the current cursor position (`:h m`ⓘ). Lowercase letters create marks that are local to a buffer, whereas uppercase letters create global marks. Having set a mark, we can snap our cursor back to it with the `` `{letter} `` command (`:h ` `ⓘ).

Try this: open up your `vimrc` file and press `mV` to set a global mark (mnemonic: *V* for vimrc). Switch to another file and then press `` `V ``, and you should snap back to the global mark you set in the vimrc file. By default, global marks are persisted between editing sessions (although this behavior can be configured; see `:h 'viminfo'`ⓘ). Now you can always open up your `vimrc` file with two keystrokes—that is, unless you set the global *V* mark to another location.

Set a Global Mark Before Going Code Diving

Global marks can be especially useful when we need to browse through a set of files and then quickly snap back to where we started. Suppose that we're working on some code, and we want to find all occurrences of a method called `fooBar()` in our codebase. We could use the `:vimgrep` command (covered in Tip 111, *Grep with Vim's Internal Search Engine*, on page 277):

⇒ `:vimgrep /fooBar/ **`

By default, :vimgrep jumps directly to the first match that it finds, which could mean switching to another file. At this point, we can use the `<C-o>` command to get back to where we were prior to running :vimgrep.

Let's say that our codebase contains dozens of matches for the pattern fooBar. For each match :vimgrep finds, it creates a record in the quickfix list. Now suppose that we spend a minute or two traversing that list until eventually we find what we are looking for. Now we want to get back to where we were before we ran the :vimgrep command. How do we do it?

We could get there using the `<C-o>` command to reverse through the jump list, but it might take a while. This is a scenario where a global mark would come in handy. If we had run the `mM` command before invoking :vimgrep, then we could snap back in one move with the `` `M `` command.

Advice is rarely welcome when it goes "You should have started by doing *X*." Global marks are only useful if we have the forethought to set them up correctly in advance. With practice, you'll learn to recognize the scenarios where it would be useful to set a global mark.

Try to get into a habit of setting a global mark before using any commands that interact with the quickfix list, such as :grep, :vimgrep, and :make. The same goes for the commands that interact with the buffer and argument lists, such as :args {arglist} and :argdo (see Tip 38, *Group Buffers into a Collection with the Argument List*, on page 86).

Remember, you can set up to twenty-six global marks, which is more than you'll ever need. Use them liberally; set a global mark any time you see something that you might want to snap back to later.

Part IV

Registers

Vim's registers are simply containers that hold text. They can be used in the manner of a clipboard for cutting, copying, and pasting text, or they can be used to record a macro by saving a sequence of keystrokes. In this part of the book, we'll master this core feature.

CHAPTER 10

Copy and Paste

Vim's cut, copy, and paste functionality differs from what you may be used to. For a start, the terminology is different, as we'll see in *Vim's Terminology Versus the World*, on page 149. In Tip 60, *Delete, Yank, and Put with Vim's Unnamed Register*, on page 145, we'll learn how to use Vim's delete, yank, and put commands for a handful of common cases.

Instead of dealing with a single system-wide clipboard, Vim provides a couple of dozen registers where we can store regions of text. We'll learn more about Vim's registers in Tip 61, *Grok Vim's Registers*, on page 148. Vim's put command is smart about how it treats line-wise and character-wise text, as we'll see in Tip 63, *Paste from a Register*, on page 155. The put command has some interesting quirks when used from Visual mode, as we'll discover in Tip 62, *Replace a Visual Selection with a Register*, on page 153.

Finally, in Tip 64, *Interact with the System Clipboard*, on page 158, we'll learn about how to use the system paste command inside Vim without producing strange effects.

Tip 60

Delete, Yank, and Put with Vim's Unnamed Register

Vim's delete, yank, and put commands are designed to make common tasks easy by default. We'll study a few problems that can easily be solved using Vim's unnamed register, and then we'll finish by looking at a task that requires a better understanding of how Vim's registers work.

Normally when we discuss cut, copy, and paste, we talk about putting text on a clipboard. In Vim's terminology, we don't deal with a clipboard but instead with *registers*. In Tip 61, *Grok Vim's Registers*, on page 148, we'll see that Vim has multiple registers, and we can specify which ones we want to use. But let's start off by looking at what can be done using the *unnamed register*.

Transposing Characters

I consistently misspell some words. Over time, I may notice that I habitually mistype a certain word, and then I can train myself out of it. But some spelling mistakes are more haphazard. The most common typing error that I make is to get two characters in the wrong order. Vim makes it easy to fix such mistakes.

Suppose that we're typing out the title of this book when we make such a transposition error:

Keystrokes	Buffer Contents
{start}	Practica lvim
F␣	Practica lvim
x	Practicalvim
p	Practical vim

Here we've typed the space too soon, but it's easily mended. The F␣ command places our cursor on the first of the two characters that we want to swap (see Tip 50, *Find by Character*, on page 120). The x command cuts the character under the cursor, placing a copy of it in the unnamed register. Then the p command pastes the contents of the unnamed register after the cursor position. Taken together, the xp commands can be considered as "Transpose the next two characters."

Transposing Lines

We can just as easily transpose the order of two lines of text. Instead of using the x command to cut the current character, we can use the dd command, which cuts the current line, placing it into the unnamed register:

Keystrokes	Buffer Contents
{start}	2) line two 1) line one 3) line three
dd	1) line one 3) line three
p	1) line one 2) line two 3) line three

The `p` command knows that this time we're dealing with a line-wise chunk of text, so it does the thing we would expect: it pastes the contents of the unnamed register after the current *line*. Remember, when we pressed `xp` in the previous example, the `p` command pasted after the current *character*.

The `ddp` sequence could be considered to stand for "Transpose the order of this line and its successor."

Duplicating Lines

If we want to create a new line of text that's broadly similar to another line but with one or two small differences, we can give ourselves a head start by duplicating a line and using it as a template. In Vim, a line-wise yank followed by a put operation does the trick:

Keystrokes	Buffer Contents
{start}	1) line one 2) line two
yyp	1) line one 2) line two 2) line two

Note the similarities between these two sequences, `ddp` and `yyp`. The first does a line-wise cut and paste, which effectively transposes the order of two lines. The second sequence does a line-wise copy and paste, which effectively duplicates a line.

Oops! I Clobbered My Yank

So far, Vim's delete, yank, and put operations are looking quite intuitive. They make common tasks trivially easy to perform. Now let's look at a scenario where things don't work out quite so smoothly. Start off with this sample:

```
copy_and_paste/collection.js
collection = getCollection();
process(somethingInTheWay, target);
```

We're going to copy collection into the unnamed register and then replace somethingInTheWay with the word that we've just copied. Table 11, *Copy and Paste—First Attempt*, on page 148 shows a first attempt.

To begin with, our cursor is already on the word we want to copy, so we can get it into the unnamed register by typing `yiw`.

Next we move our cursor to the place where we want to paste our collection, but before we can put it there we'll have to clear a space for it. So we run `diw` to delete the word somethingInTheWay.

Keystrokes	Buffer Contents
yiw	collection = getCollection(); process(somethingInTheWay, target);
jww	collection = getCollection(); process(somethingInTheWay, target);
diw	collection = getCollection(); process(, target);
P	collection = getCollection(); process(somethingInTheWay, target);

Table 11—Copy and Paste—First Attempt

Now we can hit the P key to paste the contents of our unnamed register in front of the cursor. But instead of pasting the word collection, which we yanked earlier, we get the word somethingInTheWay. What's going on?

The diw command doesn't just delete the word: it also copies it into the unnamed register. Or to rephrase that using more familiar terminology—diw *cuts* the word. (See *Vim's Terminology Versus the World*, on page 149, for a discussion).

It's obvious now what we did wrong. When we ran the diw command, it overwrote the contents of the unnamed register. That's why when we pressed P, we got back the word we just deleted rather than the word we yanked earlier.

To solve this problem, we'll have to get a deeper understanding of how Vim's registers work.

Tip 61

Grok Vim's Registers

Rather than using a single clipboard for all cut, copy, and paste operations, Vim provides multiple registers. When we use the delete, yank, and put commands, we can specify which register we want to interact with.

Addressing a Register

The delete, yank, and put commands all interact with one of Vim's registers. We can specify which register we want to use by prefixing the command with "{register}. If we don't specify a register, then Vim will use the unnamed register.

Vim's Terminology Versus the World

The cut, copy, and paste terminology is universally understood, and these operations are available across most desktop software programs and operating systems. Vim provides these features too, but it uses different terminology: delete, yank, and put.

Vim's put command is effectively identical to the paste operation. Fortunately, both words begin with the letter *p*, so the mnemonic for the key command works whichever terminology we use.

Vim's yank command is equivalent to the copy operation. Historically, the c command was already assigned to the *change* operation, so vi's authors were pushed to come up with an alternative name. The y key was available, so the copy operation became the yank command.

Vim's delete command is equivalent to the standard cut operation. That is, it copies the specified text into a register and then removes it from the document. Understanding this is key to avoiding the common pitfall outlined in *Oops! I Clobbered My Yank*, on page 147.

You might be wondering what Vim's equivalent is for really deleting text—that is, how can you remove text from the document and not copy it into any registers? Vim's answer is a special register called the black hole, from which nothing returns. The black hole register is addressed by the _ symbol (see :h quote_ⓘ), so "_d{motion} performs a true deletion.

For example, if we wanted to yank the current word into register a, we could run "ayiw. Or if we wanted to cut the current line into register b, we could run "bdd. Then we could paste the word from register a by typing "ap, or we could paste the line from register b by typing "bp.

In addition to the Normal mode commands, Vim also provides Ex commands for delete, yank, and put operations. We could cut the current line into register c by running :delete c, and then we could paste it below the current line with the :put c command. These may seem verbose in comparison with the Normal mode commands, but they're useful in combination with other Ex commands and in Vim scripts. For example, Tip 100, *Collect TODO Items in a Register*, on page 244, shows how :yank can be used with the :global command.

The Unnamed Register ("")

If we don't specify which register we want to interact with, then Vim will use the unnamed register, which is addressed by the " symbol (see :h quote_quote ⓘ). To address this register explicitly, we have to use two double quote marks: for example, ""p, which is effectively equivalent to p by itself.

The `x`, `s`, `d{motion}`, `c{motion}`, and `y{motion}` commands (and their uppercase equivalents) all set the contents of the unnamed register. In each case, we can prefix `"{register}` to specify another register, but the unnamed register is the default. The fact that it's so easy to overwrite the contents of the unnamed register can cause problems if we're not careful.

Consider again the example in *Oops! I Clobbered My Yank*, on page 147. We start off by yanking some text (the word "collection") with the intention of pasting it elsewhere. Before we can paste it, we have to clear a space by deleting some text that is in our way, which overwrites the contents of the unnamed register. When we use the `p` command, we get back the text that we just *deleted*, rather than getting the text that we *yanked* previously.

Vim's choice of terminology is unfortunate. The `x` and `d{motion}` commands are usually referred to as "delete" commands. This is a misnomer. It's better to think of them as "cut" commands. The unnamed register often doesn't contain the text that I expected to find there, but luckily, the yank register (which we'll meet next) is more dependable.

The Yank Register ("0)

When we use the `y{motion}` command, the specified text is copied not only into the unnamed register but also into the yank register, which is addressed by the 0 symbol (see :h quote0 ⓘ).

As the name suggests, the yank register is set only when we use the `y{motion}` command. To put it another way: it's not set by the `x`, `s`, `c{motion}`, and `d{motion}` commands. If we yank some text, we can be sure that it will stick around in register 0 until we explicitly overwrite it by yanking something else. The yank register is reliable, whereas the unnamed register is volatile.

We can use the yank register to solve our problem from *Oops! I Clobbered My Yank*, on page 147:

Keystrokes	Buffer Contents
`yiw`	`collection = getCollection();` `process(somethingInTheWay, target);`
`jww`	`collection = getCollection();` `process(somethingInTheWay, target);`
`diw`	`collection = getCollection();` `process(, target);`
`"0P`	`collection = getCollection();` `process(collection, target);`

The `diw` command still overwrites the unnamed register, but it leaves the yank register untouched. We can safely paste from the yank register by pressing `"0P`, and Vim gives us the text that we want.

If we inspect the contents of the unnamed and yank registers, we'll see that they contain the text that we deleted and yanked, respectively:

```
⇒ :reg "0
‹ --- Registers ---
  ""   somethingInTheWay
  "0   collection
```

The Named Registers ("a–"z)

Vim has one named register for each letter of the alphabet (see :h quote_alpha ⓘ). That means that we can cut (`"ad{motion}`), copy (`"ay{motion}`), or paste (`"ap`) up to twenty-six pieces of text.

We could use a named register to solve our problem from *Oops! I Clobbered My Yank*, on page 147:

Keystrokes	Buffer Contents
`"ayiw`	`collection = getCollection();` `process(somethingInTheWay, target);`
`jww`	`collection = getCollection();` `process(somethingInTheWay, target);`
`diw`	`collection = getCollection();` `process( , target);`
`"aP`	`collection = getCollection();` `process(collection, target);`

Using a named register requires extra keystrokes, so for a simple example like this we're better off using the yank register (`"0`). Named registers can become really useful when we've got one or more pieces of text that we want to paste in several places.

When we address a named register with a lowercase letter, it *overwrites* the specified register, whereas when we use an uppercase letter, it *appends to* the specified register. Skip ahead to Tip 100, *Collect TODO Items in a Register*, on page 244, to see a demonstration of appending to a register.

The Black Hole Register ("_)

The black hole register is a place from which nothing returns. It's addressed by the underscore symbol (see :h quote_ ⓘ). If we run the command `"_d{motion}`, then Vim deletes the specified text without saving a copy of it. This can be useful if we want to delete text without overwriting the contents of the unnamed register.

We could use the black hole register to solve our problem from *Oops! I Clobbered My Yank*, on page 147:

Keystrokes	Buffer Contents
`yiw`	`collection = getCollection();` `process(somethingInTheWay, target);`
`jww`	`collection = getCollection();` `process(somethingInTheWay, target);`
`"_diw`	`collection = getCollection();` `process(, target);`
`P`	`collection = getCollection();` `process(collection, target);`

The System Clipboard ("+) and Selection ("*) Registers

All of the registers that we've discussed so far are internal to Vim. If we want to copy some text from inside of Vim and paste it into an external program (or vice versa), then we have to use one of the system clipboards.

Vim's plus register references the system clipboard and is addressed by the + symbol (see :h quote+ ⓘ).

If we use the cut or copy command to capture text in an external application, then we can paste it inside Vim using `"+p` command (or `<C-r>+` from the Insert mode). Conversely, if we prefix Vim's yank or delete commands with `"+`, the specified text will be captured in the system clipboard. That means we can easily paste it inside other applications.

The X11 windowing system has a second kind of clipboard called the *primary*. This represents the most recently selected text, and we can use the middle mouse button (if we have one) to paste from it. Vim's quotestar register maps to the primary clipboard and is addressed by the * symbol (:h quotestar ⓘ).

Keystrokes	Buffer Contents
`"+`	The X11 clipboard, used with cut, copy, and paste
`"*`	The X11 primary, used with middle mouse button

In Windows and Mac OS X, there is no primary clipboard, so we can use the "+ and "* registers interchangeably: they both represent the system clipboard.

Vim can be compiled with or without support for X11 clipboard integration. To find out whether your version of Vim has the feature enabled, run the

:version command and look for xterm_clipboard. If it's prefixed with a minus sign, then your version of Vim does not support this feature. A plus sign means that the feature is available.

The Expression Register ("=)

Vim's registers can be thought of simply as containers that hold a block of text. The expression register, referenced by the = symbol (:h quote=), is an exception. When we fetch the contents of the expression register, Vim drops into Command-Line mode, showing an = prompt. We can enter a Vim script expression and then press <CR> to execute it. If the expression returns a string (or a value that can be easily coerced into a string), then Vim uses it.

For examples of the expression register in action, check out Tip 16, *Do Back-of-the-Envelope Calculations in Place*, on page 33, Tip 96, *Swap Two or More Words*, on page 234, Tip 95, *Perform Arithmetic on the Replacement*, on page 233, and Tip 71, *Evaluate an Iterator to Number Items in a List*, on page 177.

More Registers

We can set the contents of the named, unnamed, and yank registers explicitly using the delete and yank commands. In addition, Vim provides a handful of registers whose values are set implicitly. These are known collectively as the read-only registers (:h quote.). The following table summarizes them:

Register	Contents
"%	Name of the current file
"#	Name of the alternate file
".	Last inserted text
":	Last Ex command
"/	Last search pattern

Technically, the "/ register is not read-only—it can be set explicitly using the :let command (see :h quote/)—but it's included in this table for convenience.

Tip 62

Replace a Visual Selection with a Register

When used from Visual mode, Vim's put command has some unusual qualities. We'll find out how these can be exploited in this tip.

When we use the `p` command in Visual mode, Vim *replaces the selection* with the contents of the specified register (see `:h v_p`ⓘ). We can exploit this feature to solve our problem from *Oops! I Clobbered My Yank*, on page 147:

Keystrokes	Buffer Contents
`yiw`	`collection = getCollection();` `process(somethingInTheWay, target);`
`jww`	`collection = getCollection();` `process(somethingInTheWay, target);`
`ve`	`collection = getCollection();` `process(somethingInTheWay, target);`
`p`	`collection = getCollection();` `process(collection, target);`

For this particular problem, this is my favorite solution. We can get away with using the unnamed register for both the yank and put operations because there's no delete step. Instead, we combine the delete and put operations into a single step that replaces the selection.

It's important to understand that this technique has a side effect. Try pressing `u` to undo the last change. Now press `gv` to reselect the last visual selection and then press the `p` key again. What happens? Apparently nothing!

To make it work this time, we'd have to press `"0p` to replace the visual selection with the contents of the yank register. We got away with using `p` the first time because the unnamed register happened to contain the text that we wanted to use. The second time around, the unnamed register contains the text that was overwritten.

To illustrate how strange this is, let's consider an imaginary API for the standard cut, copy, and paste model. This API has methods called setClipboard() and getClipboard(). The cut and copy operations both call setClipboard(), while the paste operation calls getClipboard(). When we use Vim's `p` command in Visual mode, it does both: it *gets* the contents of the unnamed register, and it *sets* the contents of the unnamed register.

Think of it this way: the visual selection in the document *swaps places* with the text in the register. Is it a feature? Is it a bug? You decide!

Swap Two Words

We can exploit this quirk in Vim's visual put behavior. Let's say that we want to swap the order of two words in this sentence to make it read "fish and chips":

Keystrokes	Buffer Contents
{start}	I like chips and fish.
fc	I like chips and fish.
de	I like and fish.
mm	I like and fish.
ww	I like and fish.
ve	I like and fish.
p	I like and chips.
`m	I like and chips.
P	I like fish and chips.

We use `de` to cut the word "chips," copying it into the unnamed register. Then we visually select the word "fish," which we want to replace. When we use the `p` command, the word "chips" goes into the document, and the word "fish" is copied into the unnamed register. Then we can snap back to the gap and paste the word "fish" from the unnamed register back into the document.

In this case, it would be quicker to delete "chips and fish" and then type out "fish and chips" instead, using the `c3w` command for example. But this same technique can also be used to swap the order of longer phrases.

The `m{char}` command sets a mark, and the `` `{char} `` command jumps to the mark. Refer to Tip 54, *Mark Your Place and Snap Back to It*, on page 131, for more information.

Tip 63

Paste from a Register

The Normal mode put command can behave differently, depending on the nature of the text that is being inserted. It can be helpful to adopt different strategies, depending on whether we're pasting a line-wise or a character-wise region of text.

In Tip 60, *Delete, Yank, and Put with Vim's Unnamed Register*, on page 145, we saw that we could transpose the order of two characters by pressing `xp`, while `ddp` would transpose the order of two lines. We use the `p` command in both cases, but the outcome is subtly different.

The `p` command puts the text from a register after the cursor position (`:h p ⓘ`). As a complement, Vim also provides the (uppercase) `P` command, which inserts text before the cursor position. What is meant by *before* or *after* the cursor position can differ, depending on the contents of the register that is being inserted.

In the case of `xp`, the register contains a single character. The `p` command puts the contents of the register directly after *the character that the cursor is positioned on.*

In the case of `ddp`, the register contains one complete line. The `p` command puts the contents of the register on *the line below the one that the cursor is positioned on.*

Whether the `p` command puts the text from the register after the current character or after the current line depends on how the specified register was set. A line-wise yank or delete operation (such as `dd`, `yy`, or `dap`) creates a line-wise register, whereas a character-wise yank or delete (such as `x`, `diw`, or `das`) creates a character-wise register. In general, the outcome of using the `p` command is fairly intuitive (see `:h linewise-register` ⓘ for more details).

Pasting Character-wise Regions

Suppose that our default register contains the text `collection`, and that we want to paste as the first argument to a method call. Whether we use the `p` or `P` command depends on where the cursor is positioned. Take this buffer:

```
collection = getCollection();
process(, target);
```

Compare it with this:

```
collection = getCollection();
process(, target);
```

In the first case we would use `p`, whereas in the second case we would use `P`. I don't find this to be very intuitive. In fact, I get it wrong often enough that `puP` and `Pup` are practically muscle memory for me!

I don't like having to think about whether a character-wise region of text needs to go in front of the cursor or after it. For that reason, I sometimes prefer to paste character-wise regions of text from Insert mode using the `<C-r>{register}` mapping rather than using the Normal mode `p` and `P` commands. Using this technique, the text from the register is always inserted in front of the cursor position, just as though we were typing it in Insert mode.

From Insert mode, we can insert the contents of the unnamed register by pressing `<C-r>"`, or we can insert the contents of the yank register by pressing `<C-r>0` (see Tip 15, *Paste from a Register Without Leaving Insert Mode*, on page

31, for more details). We can use this technique to solve our problem from *Oops! I Clobbered My Yank*, on page 147:

Keystrokes	Buffer Contents
`yiw`	`collection = getCollection();` `process(somethingInTheWay, target);`
`jww`	`collection = getCollection();` `process(somethingInTheWay, target);`
`ciw<C-r>0<Esc>`	`collection = getCollection();` `process(collection, target);`

Using the `ciw` command gives us an added bonus: the dot command now replaces the current word with "collection."

Pasting Line-Wise Regions

When pasting from a line-wise register, the `p` and `P` commands put the text below or above the current line. This is more intuitive than the character-wise behavior.

It's worth noting that Vim also provides `gp` and `gP` commands. These also put the text before or after the current line, but they leave the cursor positioned at the end of the pasted text instead of at the beginning. The `gP` command is especially useful when duplicating a range of lines, as demonstrated here:

Keystrokes	Buffer Contents

`yap`	`<table>`
	
	  `<tr>`
	    `<td>Symbol</td>`
	    `<td>Name</td>`
	  `</tr>`
	
	`</table>`

`gP`	`<table>`
	
	  `<tr>`
	    `<td>Symbol</td>`
	    `<td>Name</td>`
	  `</tr>`
	
	  `<tr>`
	    `<td>Symbol</td>`
	    `<td>Name</td>`
	  `</tr>`
	
	`</table>`

We can use the duplicated text as a template, changing the contents of the table cells to make it look how we want. Both the `P` and `gP` commands would have worked fine, except that the first one would leave our cursor positioned above the inserted text. The `gP` command leaves our cursor positioned on the second duplicate, which sets us up conveniently so that we can change it to suit our needs.

Discussion

The `p` and `P` commands are great for pasting multiline regions of text. But for short sections of character-wise text, the `<C-r>{register}` mapping can be more intuitive.

Tip 64

Interact with the System Clipboard

Besides Vim's built-in put commands, we can sometimes use the system paste command. However, using this can occasionally produce unexpected results when running Vim inside a terminal. We can avoid these issues by enabling the 'paste' option before using the system paste command.

Preparation

This tip is only applicable when running Vim inside the terminal, so you can safely skip it if you always use GVim. We'll start by launching Vim in the terminal:

⇒ `$ vim -u NONE -N`

Enabling the 'autoindent' setting is a sure way to induce strange effects when pasting from the system clipboard:

⇒ `:set autoindent`

Finally, we'll need to copy the following code into the system clipboard. Copying code listings from a PDF can produce strange results, so I recommend downloading the sample code and then opening it in another text editor (or a web browser) and using the system copy command:

copy_and_paste/fizz.rb
```
[1,2,3,4,5,6,7,8,9,10].each do |n|
  if n%5==0
    puts "fizz"
  else
```

```
    puts n
  end
end
```

Locating the System Paste Command

Throughout this tip, we'll refer to the *system paste command*, and you can substitute the appropriate mapping for your system. On OS X, the system paste command is triggered by the `Cmd-v` mapping. We can use this inside the Terminal or in MacVim, and it inserts the contents of the system clipboard.

Things aren't quite so tidy on Linux and Windows. The standard mapping for the system paste command is normally `Ctrl-v`. In Normal mode, this mapping enables Visual-Block mode (Tip 21, *Define a Visual Selection*, on page 41), and in Insert mode it enables us to insert characters literally or by a numeric code (Tip 17, *Insert Unusual Characters by Character Code*, on page 34).

Some terminal emulators on Linux provide a modified version of `Ctrl-v` for pasting from the system clipboard. It might be `Ctrl-Shift-v` or perhaps `Ctrl-Alt-v`, depending on the system. Don't worry if you can't figure out what the system paste command is for your setup. An alternative using the "* register is presented at the end of this tip.

Using the System Paste Command in Insert Mode

If we switch to Insert mode and then use the system paste command, we get this strange result:

```
[1,2,3,4,5,6,7,8,9,10].each do |n|
  if n%5==0
    puts "fizz"
      else
    puts n
      end
      end
```

Something is wrong with the indentation. When we use the system paste command in Insert mode, Vim acts as though each character has been typed by hand. When the 'autoindent' option is enabled, Vim preserves the same level of indentation each time we create a new line. The leading whitespace at the start of each line in the clipboard is added on top of the automatic indent, and the result is that each line wanders further and further to the right.

GVim is able to discern when text is pasted from the clipboard and adjust its behavior accordingly, but when Vim runs inside a terminal this information is not available. The 'paste' option allows us to manually warn Vim that we're about to use the system paste command. When the 'paste' option is enabled,

Vim turns off all Insert mode mappings and abbreviations and resets a host of options, including 'autoindent' (look up :h 'paste' ⓘ for the full list). That allows us to safely paste from the system clipboard with no surprises.

When we're finished using the system paste command, we should disable the 'paste' option again. That means switching back to Normal mode and then running the Ex command :set paste!. Don't you think it would be handy if there were a way of toggling this option without leaving Insert mode?

The way that Vim behaves when 'paste' is enabled means that the usual methods for creating custom mappings won't work in Insert mode. Instead, we can assign a key to the 'pastetoggle' option (:h 'pastetoggle' ⓘ):

⇒ `:set pastetoggle=<f5>`

Try executing that command line: it sets up the `<f5>` to toggle the paste option on and off. It should work both in Insert and Normal modes. If you find the mapping useful, add that line (or a variation of it) to your vimrc.

Avoid Toggling 'paste' by Putting from the Plus Register

If you're running a version of Vim with system clipboard integration, then you can avoid fiddling with the 'paste' option entirely. The Normal mode `"+p` command pastes the contents of the plus register, which mirrors the system clipboard (see *The System Clipboard ("+) and Selection ("*) Registers*, on page 152, for more details). This command preserves the indentation of the text in the clipboard so you can expect no surprises, regardless of how the 'paste' and 'autoindent' options are set.

CHAPTER 11

Macros

Vim offers more than one way to repeat changes. We've already learned about the dot command, which is useful for repeating small changes. But when we want to repeat anything more substantial, we should reach for Vim's macros. Using these, we can record any number of keystrokes into a register and then play them back.

Macros are ideal for repeating changes over a set of similar lines, paragraphs, or even files. We'll discover that there are two ways of executing a macro across a set of targets—playing it back in series or running it multiple times in parallel—and we'll learn when to use each one.

When recording a sequence of commands, there's always the chance that we'll make a mistake. But we needn't discard a bad take. We can easily append commands to the end of an existing macro. For more extensive amendments, we can even paste the macro into a document, edit the sequence of commands in place, and then yank it back into a register.

Sometimes we need to insert consecutive numbers into our text. In Tip 67, *Play Back with a Count*, on page 166, we'll learn how to do that with a method that uses rudimentary Vim script in combination with the expression register.

Like the game of Othello, Vim's macros take a minute to learn and a lifetime to master. But everyone—from beginners to experts—can get a lot of value from this feature that makes it easy to automate tasks. Let's see how.

Tip 65

Record and Execute a Macro

Macros allow us to record a sequence of changes and then play them back. This tip shows how.

Many repetitive tasks involve making multiple changes. If we want to automate these, we can record a macro and then execute it.

Capture a Sequence of Commands by Recording a Macro

The q key functions both as the "record" button and the "stop" button. To begin recording our keystrokes, we type q{register}, giving the address of the register where we want to save the macro. We can tell that we've done it right if the word "recording" appears in the status line. Every command that we execute will be captured, right up until we press q again to stop recording.

Let's see this in action:

Keystrokes	Buffer Contents
qa	foo = 1 bar = 'a' foobar = foo + bar
A;<Esc>	foo = 1; bar = 'a' foobar = foo + bar
Ivar_<Esc>	var foo = 1; bar = 'a' foobar = foo + bar
q	var foo = 1; bar = 'a' foobar = foo + bar

Pressing qa begins recording and saves our macro into register a. We then perform two changes on the first line: appending a semicolon and prepending the word var. Having completed both of those changes, we press q to stop recording our macro (:h q ⓘ).

We can inspect the contents of register a by typing the following:

⇒ `:reg a`
‹ `--- Registers ---`
`"a   A;^[Ivar ^[`

It doesn't make for easy reading, but the same sequence of commands that we recorded moments ago should be recognizable. The only surprise might be that the symbol ^[is used to stand for the Escape key. See *Keyboard Codes in Macros,* on page 181, for an explanation.

Play Back a Sequence of Commands by Executing a Macro

The `@{register}` command executes the contents of the specified register (see :h @ ⓘ). We can also use `@@`, which repeats the macro that was invoked most recently.

Here's an example:

Keystrokes	Buffer Contents

{start}	`var █foo = 1;`
	`bar = 'a'`
	`foobar = foo + bar`

j	`var foo = 1;`
	`bar█= 'a'`
	`foobar = foo + bar`

@a	`var foo = 1;`
	`var█bar = 'a';`
	`foobar = foo + bar`

j@@	`var foo = 1;`
	`var bar = 'a';`
	`var█foobar = foo + bar;`

We've executed the macro that we just recorded, repeating the same two changes for each of the subsequent lines. Note that we use `@a` on the first line and then `@@` to replay the same macro on the next line.

In this example, we played the macro back by running `j@a` (and subsequently `j@@`). Superficially, this has some resemblance to the Dot Formula. It involves one keystroke to move (`j`) and two to act (`@a`). Not bad, but there's room for improvement.

We have a couple of techniques at our disposal for executing a macro multiple times. The setup differs slightly for each technique, but more importantly, they react differently on encountering an error. I'll explain the differences by way of a comparison with Christmas tree lights.

If you buy a cheap set of party lights, the chances are that they will be wired in series. If one bulb blows, they all go out. If you buy a premium set, they're more likely to be wired in parallel. That means any bulb can go out, and the rest will be unaffected.

I've borrowed the expressions *in series* and *in parallel* from the field of electronics to differentiate between two techniques for executing a macro multiple times. The technique for executing a macro in series is brittle. Like cheap Christmas tree lights, it breaks easily. The technique for executing a macro in parallel is more fault tolerant.

Execute the Macro in Series

Picture a robotic arm and a conveyor belt containing a series of items for the robot to manipulate.

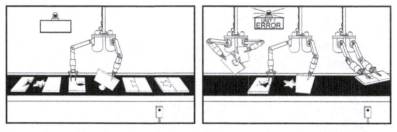

Recording a macro is like programming the robot to do a single unit of work. As a final step, we instruct the robot to move the conveyor belt and bring the next item within reach. In this manner, we can have a single robot carry out a series of repetitive tasks on similar items.

One consequence of this approach is that if the robot encounters any surprises, it sounds an alarm and aborts the operation. Even if items on the conveyor belt still need to be manipulated, the work stops.

Execute the Macro in Parallel

When we execute the macro in parallel, it's as though we've dispensed with the conveyor belt entirely. Instead, we deploy an assemblage of robots,[1] all programmed to do the same simple task. Each is given a single job to do. If it succeeds, very well. If it fails, no matter.

Under the hood, Vim always executes macros sequentially, no matter which of these two techniques we use. The term *in parallel* is intended to draw an analogy with the robustness of parallel circuits. It is not meant to suggest that Vim executes multiple changes concurrently.

In Tip 68, *Repeat a Change on Contiguous Lines*, on page 168, as well as Tip 70, *Act Upon a Collection of Files*, on page 173, we'll see examples of a macro being executed both in series and in parallel.

---

1. http://all-sorts.org/of/robots

Tip 66

Normalize, Strike, Abort

Executing a macro can sometimes produce unexpected results, but we can achieve better consistency if we follow a handful of best practices.

When we execute a macro, Vim blindly repeats the sequence of canned keystrokes. If we aren't careful, the outcome when we replay a macro might diverge from our expectations. But it's possible to compose macros that are more flexible, adapting to do the right thing in each context.

The golden rule is this: when recording a macro, ensure that every command is repeatable.

Normalize the Cursor Position

As soon as you start recording a macro, ask yourself these questions: where am I, where have I come from, and where am I going? Before you do anything, make sure your cursor is positioned so that the next command does what you expect, where you expect it.

That might mean moving the cursor to the next search match (`n`) or the start of the current line (`0`) or perhaps the first line of the current file (`gg`). Always starting on square one makes it easier to strike the right target every time.

Strike Your Target with a Repeatable Motion

Vim has many motion commands for getting around a text file. Use them well.

Don't just hammer the `l` key until your cursor reaches its target. Remember, Vim executes your keystrokes blindly. Moving your cursor ten characters to the right might get you where you need to go as you record the macro, but what about when you play it back later? In another context, moving the cursor ten places to the right might overshoot the mark or stop short of it.

Word-wise motions, such as `w`, `b`, `e`, and `ge` tend to be more flexible than character-wise `h` and `l` motions. If we recorded the motion `0` followed by `e`, we could expect consistent results each time we executed the macro. The cursor would end up on the last character of the first word of the current line. It wouldn't matter how many characters that word contained, so long as the line contained at least one word.

Navigate by search. Use text objects. Exploit the full arsenal of Vim's motions to make your macros as flexible and repeatable as you can. Don't forget: when recording a macro, using the mouse is *verboten*!

Abort When a Motion Fails

Vim's motions can fail. For example, if our cursor is positioned on the first line of a file, the `k` command does nothing. The same goes for `j` when our cursor is on the last line of a file. By default, Vim beeps at us when a motion fails, although we can mute it with the 'visualbell' setting (see :h 'visualbell' ⓘ).

If a motion fails while a macro is executing, then Vim aborts the rest of the macro. Consider this a feature, not a bug. We can use motions as a simple test of whether or not the macro should be executed in the current context.

Consider this example: We start by searching for a pattern. Let's say that the document has ten matches. We start recording a macro using the `n` command to repeat the last search. With our cursor positioned on a match, we make some small change to the text and stop recording the macro. The result of our edit is that this particular region of text no longer matches our search pattern. Now the document has only nine matches.

When we execute this macro, it jumps to the next match and makes the same change. Now the document has only eight matches. We execute the macro again and again, until eventually no matches remain. If we attempt to execute the macro now, the `n` command will fail because there are no more matches. The macro aborts.

Suppose that the macro was stored in the a register. Rather than executing `@a` ten times, we could prefix it with a count: `10@a`. The beauty of this technique is that we can be unscrupulous about how many times we execute this macro. Don't care for counting? It doesn't matter! We could execute `100@a` or even `1000@a`, and it would produce the same result.

Tip 67

Play Back with a Count

The Dot Formula can be an efficient editing strategy for a small number of repeats, but it can't be executed with a count. Overcome this limitation by recording a cheap one-off macro and playing it back with a count.

In Tip 3, *Take One Step Back, Then Three Forward,* on page 6, we used the Dot Formula to transform this:

```
the_vim_way/3_concat.js
var foo = "method("+argument1+","+argument2+")";
```

What we want is for it to look like this:

```
var foo = "method(" + argument1 + "," + argument2 + ")";
```

The Dot Formula meant that we could complete the task simply by repeating `;.` a few times. What if we faced the same problem but on a larger scale?

```
x = "("+a+","+b+","+c+","+d+","+e+")";
```

We can approach this in exactly the same way. But when we have to invoke the two commands `;.` so many times to complete the job, it starts to feel like a lot of work. Isn't there some way that we could apply a count?

It's tempting to think that running `11;.` would do the trick, but it's no use. This instructs Vim to run the `;` command eleven times, and then the `.` command once. The equivalent mistake is more obvious if we run `;11.`, which tells Vim to invoke `;` once and then `.` eleven times. We really want to run `;.` eleven times.

We can simulate this by recording one of the simplest possible macros: `qq;.q`. Here, `qq` tells Vim to record the following keystrokes and save them to the q register. Then we type our commands `;.` and finish recording the macro by pressing `q` one final time. Now we can execute the macro with a count: `11@q`. This executes `;.` eleven times.

Let's put all of that together.

Keystrokes	Buffer Contents
{start}	x = "("+a+","+b+","+c+","+d+","+e+")";
f+	x = "("+a+","+b+","+c+","+d+","+e+")";
s + \<Esc\>	x = "(" +a+","+b+","+c+","+d+","+e+")";
qq;.q	x = "(" + a +","+b+","+c+","+d+","+e+")";
22@q	x = "(" + a + "," + b + "," + c + "," + d + "," + e +")";

The `;` command repeats the `f+` search. When our cursor is positioned *after* the last + character on the line, the `;` motion fails and the macro aborts.

In our case, we want to execute the macro ten times. But if we were to play it back eleven times, the final execution would abort. In other words, we can complete the task so long as we invoke the macro with a count of ten or more.

Who wants to sit there and count the exact number of times that a macro should be executed? Not me. I'd rather give a count that I think is high enough to get the job done. I often use 22, because I'm lazy and it's easy to type. On my keyboard, the @ and 2 characters are entered with the same button.

Note that it won't always be possible to make approximations when providing a count to a macro. It works in this case because the macro has a built-in safety catch: the `;` motion will fail if no more + symbols are left on the current line. See *Abort When a Motion Fails*, on page 166, for more details.

Tip 68

Repeat a Change on Contiguous Lines

We can make light work out of repeating the same set of changes on a range of lines by recording a macro and then playing it back on each line. There are two ways to do this: executing the macro in series or in parallel.

As a demonstration, we'll transform this snippet of text:

```
macros/consecutive-lines.txt
1. one
2. two
3. three
4. four
```

We'll make it look like this:

```
1) One
2) Two
3) Three
4) Four
```

The task may look trivial, but it presents a couple of interesting challenges.

Record One Unit of Work

To begin, we record all changes made to the first line:

Keystrokes	Buffer Contents
qa	1. one 2. two
0f.	1. one 2. two
r)	1) one 2. two

Keystrokes	Buffer Contents
w~	1) O█e 2. two
j	1) One 2. t█o
q	1) One 2. t█o

Note the use of motions in this macro. We begin with the `0` command, which normalizes our cursor position by placing it at the start of the line. This means that our next motion always starts from the same place, making it more repeatable.

Some might look at the next motion, `f.`, and consider it wasteful. It moves the cursor only one step to the right, same as the `l` command. Why use two keystrokes when one would do?

Once again, it's a matter of repeatability. In our sample set, we have lines numbered only one to four, but suppose the numbers ran into double digits?

```
1. one
2. two
...
10. ten
11. eleven
```

On the first nine lines, `0l` takes us to the second character of the line, which happens to be a period. But from line ten onward, that motion stops short of the target, whereas `f.` works on all of these lines and would continue to work into triple digits and beyond.

Using the `f.` motion also adds a safety catch. If no . characters are found on the current line, the `f.` command raises an error and macro execution aborts. We'll exploit this later, so keep that thought at the back of your mind.

Execute Macro in Series

We can execute the macro we just recorded by pressing `@a`. This carries out the following steps: jump to the first . character on the line, change it to `)`, uppercase the first letter of the next word, and finish by advancing to the next line.

We could invoke the `@a` command three times to complete the task, but running `3@a` is quicker:

Keystrokes	Buffer Contents
{start}	1) One 2. t█o 3. three 4. four
3@a	1) One 2) Two 3) Three 4) F█ur

Let's introduce a new obstacle. Suppose our file contains comments.

macros/broken-lines.txt

```
1. one
2. two
// break up the monotony
3. three
4. four
```

Now watch what happens if we attempt to replay the same macro on this file.

Keystrokes	Buffer Contents
{start}	█. one 2. two // break up the monotony 3. three 4. four
5@a	1) One 2) Two █/ break up the monotony 3. three 4. four

The macro stalls on line three—the one containing the comment. When the `f.` command is executed, it finds no . characters and the macro aborts. We've tripped the safety catch, and it's a good thing too. If the macro had successfully executed on this line, then it would have made changes that were probably unwanted.

But we are left with a problem. We asked Vim to execute the macro five times, and it bailed out on the third repetition. So we have to invoke it again on the next lines to complete the job. Let's look at an alternative technique.

Execute Macro in Parallel

Tip 30, *Run Normal Mode Commands Across a Range*, on page 63, demonstrated a method for running the dot command on a series of consecutive lines. We can apply the same technique here:

Keystrokes	Buffer Contents
qa	1. one
0f.r)w~	1) One
q	1) One
jVG	1) One 2. two // break up the monotony 3. three 4. four
:'<,'>normal @a	1) One 2) Two // break up the monotony 3) Three 4) Four

We've re-recorded the macro from scratch. This one is almost identical, except that we've omitted the final j command to advance to the next line. We won't be needing it this time.

The :normal @a command tells Vim to execute the macro once for each line in the selection. Just as before, the macro succeeds on the first two lines and then aborts on line three, but it doesn't stall there this time—it completes the job. Why?

Previously, we queued up five repetitions in series by running 5@a. When the third iteration aborted, it killed the remaining items in the queue. This time, we've lined up five iterations *in parallel*. Each invocation of the macro is independent from the others. So when the third iteration fails, it does so in isolation.

Deciding: Series or Parallel

Which is better, series or parallel? The answer (as always): it depends.

Executing a macro on multiple items in parallel is more robust. In this scenario, it's the better solution. But if we raise an error when we execute a macro, maybe we want those alarms to go off. Executing a macro on multiple items in series makes it clear when and where any errors occur.

Learn both techniques, and you'll develop a knack for knowing which one is right for the occasion.

Tip 69

Append Commands to a Macro

Sometimes we miss a vital step when we record a macro. There's no need to re-record the whole thing from scratch. Instead, we can tack extra commands onto the end of an existing macro.

Suppose that we record this macro (borrowed from Tip 68, *Repeat a Change on Contiguous Lines*, on page 168):

Keystrokes	Buffer contents
qa	1. one 2. two
0f.r)w~	1) One 2. two
q	1) One 2. two

Immediately after pressing `q` to stop recording, we realize that we should have finished by pressing `j` to advance to the next line.

Before we fix it, let's inspect the contents of register a:

⇒ `:reg a`
❮ `"a        0f.r)w~`

If we type `qa`, then Vim will record our keystrokes, saving them into register a by *overwriting* the existing contents of that register. If we type `qA`, then Vim will *append* our keystrokes to the existing contents of register a.

Keystrokes	Buffer Contents
qA	1) One 2. two
j	1) One 2. two
q	1) One 2. two

Let's see what's in the a register now:

⇒ `:reg a`
❮ `"a        0f.r)w~j`

All of the commands that we recorded the first time around are still there, but now it ends with j.

Discussion

This little trick saves us from having to re-record the entire macro from scratch. But we can use it only to tack commands on at the end of a macro. If we wanted to add something at the beginning or somewhere in the middle of a macro, this technique would be of no use to us. In Tip 72, *Edit the Contents of a Macro*, on page 180, we'll learn about a more powerful method for amending a macro after it has been recorded.

Tip 70

Act Upon a Collection of Files

So far, we've stuck to tasks that were repeated in the same file, but we can play back a macro across a collection of files. Once again, we'll consider how to execute the macro in parallel and in series.

Let's start with a set of files that look something like this:

macros/ruby_module/animal.rb
```
# ...[end of copyright notice]
class Animal
  # implementation
end
```

We'll wrap the class in a module to end up with this:

```
# ...[end of copyright notice]
module Rank
  class Animal
    # implementation...
  end
end
```

Preparation

Source these lines of configuration to reproduce the examples in this tip:

macros/rc.vim
```
set nocompatible
filetype plugin indent on
set hidden
if has("autocmd")
  autocmd FileType ruby setlocal ts=2 sts=2 sw=2 expandtab
endif
```

The 'hidden' option is discussed in more depth in *Enable the 'hidden' Setting Before Running ':*do' Commands*, on page 91.

If you'd like to follow along, consult *Downloading the Examples*, on page xxiv. The folder code/macros/ruby_module contains the files we'll be working with.

Build a List of Target Files

Let's stake out the terrain by building a list of the files that we want to act upon. We'll keep track of them using the argument list (for more details, see Tip 38, *Group Buffers into a Collection with the Argument List*, on page 86):

⇒ `:cd code/macros/ruby_module`
⇒ `:args *.rb`

Running :args without arguments reveals the contents of the list:

⇒ `:args`
❮ `[animal.rb] banker.rb frog.rb person.rb`

We can navigate through this list of files using :first, :last, :prev, and :next.

Record a Unit of Work

Before we begin, let's make sure we're at the start of the arguments list:

⇒ `:first`

Now let's record a macro that performs the necessary work:

Keystrokes	Buffer Contents

qa	`# ...[end of copyright notice]`
	`class Animal`
	`  # implementation...`
	`end`

gg/class <CR>	`# ...[end of copyright notice]`
	`class Animal`
	`  # implementation...`
	`end`

O module Rank<Esc>	`# ...[end of copyright notice]`
	`module Rank`
	`class Animal`
	`  # implementation...`
	`end`

j>G	`# ...[end of copyright notice]`
	`module Rank`
	`  class Animal`
	`    # implementation...`
	`  end`

Keystrokes	Buffer Contents

`Go end<Esc>`	`# ...[end of copyright notice]`
	`module Rank`
	`  class Animal`
	`    # implementation...`
	`  end`
	`end`

`q`	`# ...[end of copyright notice]`
	`module Rank`
	`  class Animal`
	`    # implementation...`
	`  end`
	`end`

Each of these files begins with a copyright notice, so we have to take care to properly normalize the cursor position. Pressing `gg` places the cursor at the start of the file, and `/class<CR>` jumps forwards to the first occurrence of the word "class." Having made these preparatory steps, we can now proceed to make the changes.

We use the `O` command to open a new line above the cursor, inserting the new text. Then we advance our cursor to the next line, where we use the `>G` command to indent each line up to the end of the file. Finally, we jump to the end of the file by pressing `G` and then using the `o` command to create a new line below the cursor, inserting the end keyword there.

If you're following along with your editor, try to resist the urge to save your changes to the file by running :w. We'll see why in a moment.

Execute the Macro in Parallel

The :argdo command allows us to execute an Ex command once for each buffer in the argument list (see :h :argdo ⓘ). But if we were to run :argdo normal @a right now, there would be side effects.

Think about it. Running :argdo normal @a executes the macro that we just recorded in all of the buffers in the argument list, including the first one: the one that we changed as we recorded the macro. As a result, the first buffer gets wrapped in a module twice over.

To prevent this, we'll revert all of the changes we just made to the first buffer in the argument list by running :edit! (see :h :edit! ⓘ):

⇒ **`:edit!`**

If you had already written the changes to a file, then :edit! won't work. In this case, you could just use the `u` command repeatedly until the file looked as it did when you opened it.

Now we can go ahead and execute the macro in all of the buffers in the argument list:

⇒ `:argdo normal @a`

This technique takes a bit of setup, but that one command does a lot of work for us. Now let's see how we could adapt this macro to run in series.

Execute the Macro in Series

Our macro performs a single unit of work on a single buffer. If we want to make it act upon multiple buffers, we could append a final step that advances to the next buffer in the list. (See Table 12, *Executing the Macro in Series*, on page 177.)

While we could run `3@a` to execute the macro on each of the remaining files in the buffer list, there's no need to be so precise about it. When we reach the last buffer in the argument list, the :next command fails and the macro aborts. So, rather than specifying an exact count, we only have to ensure that we provide a number that's large enough: 22 will do, and it's easy to type.

Save Changes to All Files

We've changed four files, but we haven't saved any of them yet. We could run :argdo write to save all files in the argument list, but it would be quicker simply to run this:

⇒ `:wall`

Note that this saves all files in the buffer list, so it's not exactly equivalent to :argdo write (see :h :wa ⓘ).

Another useful command is :wnext (see :h :wn ⓘ), which is equivalent to running :write followed by :next. If you are executing a macro in series across several files in the argument list, you may prefer to use this.

Discussion

Suppose that something caused the macro to fail while executing on the third buffer in the argument list. If we were using the :argdo normal @a command, then the macro would fail only in that one buffer, whereas if we executed the macro in series by using a count, then it would abort, and any items that follow in the argument list would be left unchanged.

Keystrokes	Buffer Contents
| qA | ```
module Rank
    class Animal
        # implementation...
    end
end
``` |
| :next | ```
class Banker
    # implementation...
end
``` |
| q | ```
class Banker
    # implementation...
end
``` |
| 22@a | ```
module Rank
    class Person
        # implementation...
    end
end
``` |

Table 12—Executing the Macro in Series

We've already seen this effect in Tip 68, *Repeat a Change on Contiguous Lines*, on page 168. But the consequences are slightly different this time. When we performed the same task on a block of adjacent lines, we could see everything at a glance. If anything went wrong, it was there right in front of our eyes.

This time we're working on a set of files, so we can't see everything in a single glance. If we execute the macro in series and it fails, then it will halt at the place where the error occurs, whereas if we execute the macro in parallel and it fails, we'll have to browse through the argument list until we find the buffer where the error was raised.

In the case where an error is raised, running the macro in parallel may complete the job faster, but it conceals useful information.

Tip 71

Evaluate an Iterator to Number Items in a List

Being able to insert a value that changes for each execution of a macro can be useful. In this tip, we'll learn a technique for incrementing a number as we record a macro so that we can insert the numbers 1 to 5 on consecutive lines.

Suppose that we want to create a numbered list from a series of items on adjacent lines. To demonstrate, we'll start with this text:

```
macros/incremental.txt
partridge in a pear tree
turtle doves
French hens
calling birds
golden rings
```

We'll transform it to look like this:

```
1) partridge in a pear tree
2) turtle doves
3) French hens
4) calling birds
5) golden rings
```

We've already learned a couple of ways to make Vim perform simple arithmetic. We can either use the `<C-a>` and `<C-x>` commands with a count (see Tip 10, *Use Counts to Do Simple Arithmetic*, on page 20), or we can use the expression register (see Tip 16, *Do Back-of-the-Envelope Calculations in Place*, on page 33). For this solution, we'll use the expression register with a touch of Vim script.

Rudimentary Vim Script

Let's begin by stepping through a few simple command-line invocations. Using the let keyword, we can create a variable called i and assign it a value of 0. The :echo command allows us to inspect the current value assigned to a variable.

```
⇒ :let i=0
⇒ :echo i
❮ 0
```

We can increment the value of i:

```
⇒ :let i += 1
⇒ :echo i
❮ 1
```

The :echo command is fine for revealing the value that is assigned to a variable, but ideally we want to insert that value into the document. We can do that using the expression register. In Tip 16, *Do Back-of-the-Envelope Calculations in Place*, on page 33, we saw that the expression register can be used to do simple sums and to insert the result into the document. We can insert the value stored in variable i just by running `<C-r>=i<CR>` in Insert mode.

Record the Macro

Now let's put all of this together:

Keystrokes	Buffer Contents
:let i=1	partridge in a pear tree
qa	partridge in a pear tree
I<C-r>=i<CR>) <Esc>	1) partridge in a pear tree
:let i += 1	1) partridge in a pear tree
q	1) partridge in a pear tree

Before we begin recording the macro, we set the variable i to 1. Inside the macro, we use the expression register to insert the value stored in i. Then, before we finish recording the macro, we increment the value stored in the variable, which should now contain the value 2.

Execute the Macro

We can then play it back for the remaining lines.

Keystrokes	Buffer Contents
{start}	1) partridge in a pear tree turtle doves French hens calling birds golden rings
jVG	1) partridge in a pear tree turtle doves French hens calling birds golden rings
:'<,'>normal @a	1) partridge in a pear tree 2) turtle doves 3) French hens 4) calling birds 5) golden rings

The :normal @a command tells Vim to execute the macro on each of the selected lines (see *Execute Macro in Parallel*, on page 170). The value of i is 2 to begin with, but it gets incremented each time the macro executes. The end result is that each line is prefixed with consecutive digits.

We could also use the yank, put, and <C-a> commands to accomplish this same task. Try it yourself for exercise!

Tip 72

Edit the Contents of a Macro

In Tip 69, Append Commands to a Macro, on page 172, we saw that adding commands at the end of a macro is straightforward. But what if we want to remove the last command? Or change something at the beginning of the macro? In this tip, we'll learn how to edit the content of a macro as if it were plain text.

The Problem: Nonstandard Formatting

Suppose that we've just followed the steps in *Record One Unit of Work*, on page 168, saving our keystrokes into register a. Now we're faced with this file, which is formatted slightly differently:

macros/mixed-lines.txt
```
1. One
2. Two
3. three
4. four
```

Some of the lines already use a capital letter. In our macro, we used the ~ command, which toggles the case of the letter under the cursor (see :h ~ ⓘ). Instead of using ~, let's update the macro to use the command vU, which uppercases the letter under the cursor (see :h v_U ⓘ).

Paste the Macro into a Document

The registers that we use for recording macros are the very same with which the yank and put operations interact. So if we want to make changes to the macro saved in register a, we simply have to paste it into the document, where we can edit it as plain text.

Let's press G and jump to the end of the current document. We want to paste the contents of register a into a new line. The simplest way of doing that is with the :put command:

⇒ **:put a**

Why didn't we just use the `"ap` command? In this context, the p command would paste the contents of the a register after the cursor position *on* the current line. The :put command, on the other hand, always pastes *below* the current line, whether the specified register contains a line-wise or a character-wise set of text.

> ## Keyboard Codes in Macros
>
> In this example, we are working with a relatively simple register. But things can get messy quickly if we attempt to edit a larger macro. For example, let's inspect the macro that was recorded in Tip 70, *Act Upon a Collection of Files*, on page 173:
>
> ```
> :reg a
> --- Registers ---
> "a     Omoul<80>kb<80>kbdule Rank^[j>GGoend^[
> ```
>
> Notice anything strange? First of all, the ^[symbol appears a couple of times. No matter whether you press `<Esc>` or `<C-[>`, that's how Vim represents the Escape key.
>
> Stranger still is the `<80>kb` symbol, which represents the backspace key. Study the keystrokes. When I recorded this macro, I started off by typing "moul." Upon seeing my mistake, I hit the backspace key a couple of times and then typed out "dule," the rest of the word.
>
> This action is of no practical consequence. If I replay those keystrokes, Vim will reproduce my mistake followed by my correction. The net result will be correct. But it does make the register harder to read and more fiddly to edit.

Edit the Text

Now we can edit the macro as plain text. The sequence of commands shown in Table 13, *Editing the Macro as Plain Text*, on page 181 replaces the ~ character with vU.

Keystrokes	Buffer Contents
{start}	`0f.r)w~j`
f~	`0f.r)w~j`
s vU<Esc>	`0f.r)wvUj`

Table 13—Editing the Macro as Plain Text

Yank the Macro from the Document Back into a Register

We've got the sequence of commands looking just the way we want it to, so we can yank it from the document back into a register. The simplest way is to run `"add` (or `:d a`), but this could cause us problems later. The `dd` command performs a line-wise deletion. The register contains a trailing ^J character:

```
:reg a
0f.r)wvUj^J
```

This character represents a newline, which in most circumstances won't matter. But sometimes this trailing newline could change the meaning of the macro. As a precaution, using a character-wise yank to get the characters from the document back into the register is a safer bet:

Keystrokes	Buffer Contents
{start}	`// last line of the file proper` `0f.r)wvUj`
`0`	`// last line of the file proper` `0f.r)wvUj`
`"ay$`	`// last line of the file proper` `0f.r)wvUj`
`dd`	`// last line of the file proper`

When we run the command `0` followed by `"ay$`, we yank every character on that line except for the carriage return. Having captured everything that we want to keep into register a, we can then run `dd` to delete the line. This will end up in the default register, but we won't use it.

Having followed these steps, register a now contains a new and improved macro. We can use it on the example text that we met at the start of this tip.

Discussion

Being able to paste a macro into the document, edit it right there, and then yank it back into a register and execute it is very handy. But the register can be fussy to work with for the reasons noted in *Keyboard Codes in Macros*, on page 181. If you only have to append a command at the end of your macro, following the procedure outlined in Tip 69, *Append Commands to a Macro*, on page 172, is simpler.

Since Vim's registers are no more than containers for strings of text, we can also manipulate them programmatically using Vim script. For example, we could use the substitute() function (which is not the same as the :substitute command! See :h substitute() ⓘ) to perform the same edit as before:

➭ `:let @a=substitute(@a, '\~', 'vU', 'g')`

If you're curious about this approach, look up :h function-list ⓘ for more ideas.

Part V

Patterns

This part of the book is devoted to patterns, which are integral to some of Vim's most powerful commands. We'll look at some tricks that make it easier to compose regular expressions and to search for text verbatim. We'll study the mechanics of the search command itself and then explore two powerful Ex commands: :substitute, which allows us to find occurrences of one pattern and replace them with something else, and :global, which lets us run any Ex command on each line that matches a particular pattern.

CHAPTER 12

Matching Patterns and Literals

In this part of the book, we'll talk about search, substitute, and global commands. But first, we'll focus on the core that drives each of them: Vim's search engine. Have you ever wondered how Vim's regular expressions work or how to turn them off?

Vim's regular expression engine may be somewhat different from the one you're accustomed to using. We'll see that the most confusing discrepancies can be smoothed out with the very magic pattern switch. Certain characters have a special meaning *by default* in Vim's search field, which can complicate matters when we just want to match something verbatim. We'll learn how to disable all of these special meanings at a stroke, with the very nomagic literal switch.

We'll focus on a couple of special items that can be used in Vim's patterns: zero-width delimiters that can mark the boundaries of a word or a search match. We'll finish with an in-depth discussion of how to deal with the handful of characters that retain special meaning, even when we use the \V literal switch.

Tip 73

Tune the Case Sensitivity of Search Patterns

We can tune the case sensitivity of Vim's search globally or on a per-search basis.

Setting Case Sensitivity Globally

We can make Vim's search patterns *case insensitive* by enabling the 'ignorecase' setting:

⇒ `:set ignorecase`

Be aware that this setting has a side effect that influences the behavior of Vim's keyword autocompletion, as discussed in *Autocompletion and Case Sensitivity*, on page 282.

Setting Case Sensitivity per Search

We can override Vim's default case sensitivity using the \c and \C items. Lowercase \c causes the search pattern to ignore case, while the uppercase \C item forces case sensitivity. If either of these items is used in a search pattern, the value of 'ignorecase' is overridden for that search.

Note that these items can be used anywhere in a pattern. If you realize that you need a case sensitive search *after* you typed out the full pattern, just tack \C on at the end and it will apply to the entire pattern.

Enabling Smarter Default Case Sensitivity

Vim provides an extra setting that makes an effort to predict our case sensitivity intentions. This is the 'smartcase' option. When enabled, 'smartcase' has the effect of canceling out the 'ignorecase' setting any time that we include an uppercase character in our search pattern. In other words, if our pattern is all lowercase, then the search will be case insensitive. But as soon as we include an uppercase letter, the search becomes case sensitive.

Does that sound complicated? Try it out and you'll find that it feels quite intuitive. And remember that we can always force case sensitivity or insensitivity for an individual search by including the \C or \c items. The following table illustrates a matrix of case sensitivity options. A similar table can be found in Vim's built-in documentation by looking up :h /ignorecase ⓘ.

Pattern	'ignorecase'	'smartcase'	Matches
foo	off	-	foo
foo	on	-	foo Foo FOO
foo	on	on	foo Foo FOO
Foo	on	on	Foo
Foo	on	off	foo Foo FOO
\cfoo	-	-	foo Foo FOO
foo\C	-	-	foo

Tip 74

Use the \v Pattern Switch for Regex Searches

Vim's regular expression syntax is closer in style to POSIX than to Perl. For programmers who already know Perl's regexes, this can be a source of frustration. Using the very magic pattern switch, we can make Vim adopt a more familiar syntax for regular expressions.

Let's say that we want to compose a regular expression that matches each of the color codes in this snippet of CSS:

patterns/color.css
```
body    { color: #3c3c3c; }
a       { color: #0000EE; }
strong { color: #000; }
```

We need to match a # character followed by either three or six hexadecimal characters. That includes all numeric digits, plus the letters A through F in upper- or lowercase.

Find Hex Colors with Magic Search

The following regular expression meets these requirements:

⇒ `/#\([0-9a-fA-F]\{6}\|[0-9a-fA-F]\{3}\)`

Try it out if you like. It works ok, but look at all of those backslashes—five in total!

We're using three types of brackets here. Square brackets have a special meaning by default, so we don't need to escape them. Parentheses match the (and) characters literally, so we have to escape them to make them take on a special meaning. The same goes for curly braces, but get this: we have to

> ## Two Regular Expression Engines
>
> Version 7.4 of Vim introduced a new regular expression engine (see :h new-regexp-engine ⓘ). Whereas the old engine uses a backtracking algorithm, the new engine uses a state machine, which performs better for complex patterns and long text. In turn, this enhancement has improved the performance of all features that use regular expressions, such as syntax highlighting, the search command, and vimgrep.
>
> The new regex engine is enabled by default in Vim 7.4, but the old engine is still available. Some features of Vim's regular expressions are not supported by the new engine. Vim will automatically use the old engine for a pattern that uses those features. See :h two-engines ⓘ for more information.

escape only the opening member of the pair. We can leave the closing brace unescaped, and Vim will figure out our intentions. This is *not* the case for parentheses, where both the opening and closing member of the pair must be escaped.

Each of the three bracket types is governed by a different set of rules. Read the previous paragraph again, and commit them to memory. I'll wait. Tell you what: don't bother!

Find Hex Colors with Very Magic Search

We can normalize the rules for all special symbols with the \v pattern switch. This enables very magic search, where all characters assume a special meaning, with the exception of "_", uppercase and lowercase letters, and the digits 0 through 9 (see :h \v ⓘ).

The \v pattern switch makes Vim's regular expression engine behave much more like that of Perl, Python, or Ruby. There are still differences, which we'll draw attention to throughout this chapter, but they're easier to remember than arbitrary rules about what must and must not be escaped.

Let's rewrite that regular expression for matching hex colors, this time using the \v pattern switch:

⇒ `/\v#([0-9a-fA-F]{6}|[0-9a-fA-F]{3})`

The \v switch at the start causes all subsequent characters to take on a special meaning. It looks much more readable without all of those backslash characters, don't you think?

Use the Hex Character Class to Further Refine the Pattern

We can make one further refinement to this pattern: instead of spelling out the character collection [0-9a-fA-F] in full, we can replace it with the character class \x (see :h /character-classes ⓘ). This pattern has exactly the same meaning as the previous one:

⇒ `/\v#(\x{6}|\x{3})`

Discussion

This table presents each of the regular expressions for easy comparison:

Pattern	Remarks
`#\([0-9a-fA-F]\{6}|[0-9a-fA-F]\{3}\)`	Using magic search, we have to escape (,), |, and { characters to confer special meaning upon them.
`\v#([0-9a-fA-F]{6}|[0-9a-fA-F]{3})`	Using the \v pattern switch, the (,), |, and { characters assume special meaning.
`\v#(\x{6}|\x{3})`	We can compact the expression further by using the \x character class, which stands for [0-9A-Fa-f].

One final note: # has no special meaning and is matched literally. Remember how very magic search treats all characters as special, except for "_", letters, and numbers? It looks like we've found an exception to this rule!

Vim's answer is that any characters that do not yet have a special meaning are "reserved for future expansions" (see :h /\\ ⓘ). In other words, just because # has no special meaning today does not mean that will be true for future versions. If # were to take on a special meaning, then we would have to escape it to match the "#" character literally. But don't let that thought keep you awake at night.

Tip 75

Use the \V Literal Switch for Verbatim Searches

*The special characters used for defining regular expressions are handy when searching for patterns, but they can get in the way if we want to search for text verbatim. Using the verynomagic literal switch, we can cancel out most of the special meanings attached to characters such as ., *, and ?.*

History Lesson: On the Heritage of Vim's Pattern Syntax

Vim has two older syntaxes for patterns besides the ones enabled by \v and \V switches. Vim's default is *magic* search, while *nomagic* search emulates the behavior of vi. They can be enabled with the \m and \M switches, respectively.

The \M nomagic switch has a similar effect to the \V literal switch, except that a couple of characters automatically take on a special meaning: namely, the ^ and $ symbols.

Magic search automatically assigns a special meaning to a handful of extra symbols, such as the ., *, and square brackets. Magic search was created to make it easier to build simple regexes, but it stopped short of adding special meaning to symbols such as +, ?, parentheses, and braces, each of which must be escaped to assign them with their special meaning.

Magic search goes halfway toward making regular expressions easier to compose. As a result, the rules over what to escape seem haphazard, making them difficult to memorize. The \v pattern search switch fixes this by assigning a special meaning to every symbol except _, numbers, and letters. That's easily remembered and happens to be consistent with the rules for Perl's regular expressions.

Take this excerpt of text:

patterns/excerpt-also-known-as.txt

```
The N key searches backward...
...the \v pattern switch (a.k.a. very magic search)...
```

Now suppose that we want to jump to the occurrence of "a.k.a." (which stands for *also known as*) by searching for it. The most natural thing to do would be to run this search:

⇒ **/a.k.a.**

But when we press Enter, we'll find that this pattern matches more than we bargained for. The "." symbol has a special meaning: it matches any character. As chance would have it, the word "backward" contains a fragment that matches our pattern. This table illustrates the outcome.

Keystrokes	Buffer Contents
{start}	The N key searches backward... ...the \v pattern switch (a.k.a. very magic search)...
/a.k.a.<CR>	The N key searches backward... ...the \v pattern switch (a.k.a. very magic search)...
/a\.k\.a\.<CR>	The N key searches backward... ...the \v pattern switch (a.k.a. very magic search)...
/\Va.k.a.<CR>	The N key searches backward... ...the \v pattern switch (a.k.a. very magic search)...

In this example, the result is merely an irritation. We can jump to the next match—the one we're aiming for, let's hope—just by pressing the `n` key. But in some circumstances, a false positive match could be more insidious. Imagine if we were to go ahead and run a substitute command, such as :%s//also known as/g, without realizing that our search pattern was too broad (leaving the search field of the :substitute command blank tells Vim to use the last search pattern, as discussed in Tip 91, *Reuse the Last Search Pattern*, on page 225). That could lead to some surprising typos!

We can cancel out the special meaning of the . character by escaping it. The following pattern would not match the fragment inside the word *backward*, but it would still match "a.k.a.":

⇒ `/a\.k\.a\.`

Alternatively, we could use the \V literal switch to enable very nomagic search:

⇒ `/\Va.k.a.`

As Vim's documentation says, "use of \V means that in the pattern after it, only the backslash has a special meaning" (see :h /\V ⓘ). As we'll see in Tip 79, *Escape Problem Characters*, on page 195, this is a slight oversimplification, but it will do for the purposes of this discussion.

Creating regular expressions in a very nomagic search is still possible, but it's awkward because we have to escape every symbol. As a general rule, if you want to search for a regular expression, use the \v pattern switch, and if you want to search for verbatim text, use the \V literal switch.

Tip 76

Use Parentheses to Capture Submatches

When specifying a pattern, we can capture submatches and then reference them elsewhere. This feature is especially useful in combination with the sub-stitute command, but it can also be used to define patterns where a word is repeated.

Take this excerpt of text:

patterns/springtime.txt
```
I love Paris in the
the springtime.
```

Can you spot the grammatical error? It's surprisingly hard to see because of a trick that our mind plays on us, but it should pop out with emphasis: "Paris in *the the* springtime." When a line break separates two occurrences of the same word, our brain tends to ignore the duplicate. The effect is called a *lexical illusion.*[1]

Here's a regular expression that matches duplicate words:

⇒ `/\v<(\w+)\_s+\1>`

Now try searching for this pattern on the springtime excerpt, and you should see "the the" light up as a search match. Now try joining the two lines together (`vipJ` will do it), and you should find that it still matches. Best of all, this pattern doesn't just match "the the," it works for *any* pair of duplicate words. Let's pick the regular expression apart and see how it works.

The trick to matching the same word twice lies in the combination of () and \1. Anything that matches inside of parentheses is automatically assigned to a temporary silo. We can reference the captured text as \1. If our pattern contained more than one set of parentheses, then we could reference the submatch for each pair of () by using \1, \2, and so on, up to \9. The \0 item always refers to the entire match, whether or not parentheses were used in the pattern.

The regular expression for matching lexical illusions contains several other tricks. We've already seen in Tip 74, *Use the \v Pattern Switch for Regex Searches*, on page 187, that the \v pattern switch enables very magic search. The < and > symbols match word boundaries, as discussed in Tip 77, *Stake the Boundaries of a Word*, on page 193. Finally, the \s item matches whitespace or a line break (see :h _ ⓘ and :h 27.8 ⓘ, respectively).

There aren't many scenarios where submatches are useful in a search pattern. One more example springs to mind: matching opening and closing pairs of XML or HTML tags. But as we'll see in Tip 94, *Rearrange CSV Fields Using Submatches*, on page 232, we can also use submatches in the replacement {string} of the :substitute command.

---

1.   http://matt.might.net/articles/shell-scripts-for-passive-voice-weasel-words-duplicates/

Use Parentheses Without Capturing Their Contents

Sometimes we may want to use parentheses for grouping, while we may have no interest in capturing the submatch. For example, take this pattern, which matches both forms of my name:

⇒ `/\v(And|D)rew Neil`

Here we're using parentheses to match either "Andrew" or "Drew," but we're probably not interested in capturing the "And or D" fragment that is wrapped in parentheses. We can tell Vim not to bother assigning it to the \1 register by prepending a % in front of the parentheses, like this:

⇒ `/\v%(And|D)rew Neil`

What difference does this make? Well, it's a smidge faster, not that you're likely to notice. But it can be useful if you find yourself using several sets of parentheses. Suppose we wanted to replace all occurrences of FIRSTNAME LASTNAME with LASTNAME, FIRSTNAME for both forms of my name. We could do so like this:

⇒ `/\v(%(And|D)rew) (Neil)`
⇒ `:%s//\2, \1/g`

The search pattern assigns either "Andrew" or "Drew" to capture register \1 and assigns "Neil" to register \2. If we hadn't used %() for the second set of parentheses, then it would have captured a fragment of text unnecessarily, cluttering up our replacement field.

Tip 77

Stake the Boundaries of a Word

When defining a pattern, specifying where a word begins and ends can be useful. Vim's word-delimiter items let us do that.

Some words, especially short ones, have a habit of showing up inside other words. For example, "the" appears inside "these," "they," "their," and many other words besides. So if we search the following excerpt by running /the`<CR>`, we'll find more matches than we may have bargained for:

```
the problem with these new recruits is that
they don't keep their boots clean.
```

If we specifically want to match "the" as a word rather than a fragment, we can use word boundary delimiters. In very magic searches, these are represented by the < and > symbols. So if we amended our search to /\v<the>`<CR>`, it would find only one match in the excerpt.

These are *zero-width* items, meaning that they don't match any characters themselves. They represent the boundary between a word and the whitespace or punctuation that surrounds it.

We can approximate the meaning of < and > by combining the \w and \W character classes with the \zs and \ze match delimiters (which we'll meet in Tip 78, *Stake the Boundaries of a Match*, on page 194). \w matches word characters, including letters, numbers, and the "_" symbol, while \W matches everything except for word characters. Combining these, we could approximate the < item as \W\zs\w, and the > item as \w\ze\W.

In a very magic search, the naked < and > characters are interpreted as word delimiters, but in magic, nomagic, and very nomagic searches we have to escape them. Hence, to look up these items in Vim's documentation, we must prepend a backslash: :h /\< ⓘ. Note that if we wanted to match the angle bracket characters literally in a very magic search, we would have to escape them.

Even if we don't make a habit of using the word boundary items when composing our own search patterns, we use them indirectly each time we trigger the * or # commands (see :h * ⓘ). These search forward and backward, respectively, for the word under the cursor. If we examine the search history after using either of these commands (by pressing /<Up>), we'll see that the last search pattern is wrapped with word delimiters. Incidentally, the g* and g# variants perform the same searches *without* word delimiters.

Tip 78

Stake the Boundaries of a Match

Sometimes we might want to specify a broad pattern and then focus on a subset of the match. Vim's \zs and \ze items allow us to do just that.

Up until now, we've assumed a complete overlap between search patterns and the matches they generate. It's time to pry these apart into two separate concepts. Let's start by defining them. When we talk of a *pattern*, we refer to the regular expression (or literal text) that we type into the search field. When we talk of a *match*, we refer to any text in the document that appears highlighted (assuming the 'hlsearch' option is enabled).

The boundaries of a match normally correspond to the start and end of a pattern. But we can use the \zs and \ze items to crop the match, making it a subset of the entire pattern (see :h /\zs ⓘ). The \zs item marks the start of a match, while the \ze item matches the end of a match. Together, they allow us to specify a pattern that entirely matches a range of characters and then zoom in on a subset of the match. Just like the word delimiters (from the previous tip), \zs and \ze are zero-width items.

An example would help at this point. If we searched for /Practical Vim`<CR>` then any occurrences of "Practical Vim" in our document would light up. If we were to modify the search pattern to /Practical \zsVim`<CR>`, then only the word "Vim" would be highlighted. The word "Practical" would be excluded from the match, even though it is still part of the pattern. As a result, occurrences of the word "Vim" that directly follow the word "Practical" will be highlighted, but any occurrences of the word "Vim" that do not follow the word "Practical" will not match. The outcome is quite different from simply searching for /Vim`<CR>`.

Here's another example, this time using both \zs and \ze to tweak the start and end of the match:

Keystrokes	Buffer Contents
{start}	Match "quoted words"---not quote marks.
/\v"[^"]+"`<CR>`	Match "quoted words"---not quote marks.
/\v"\zs[^"]+\ze"`<CR>`	Match "quoted words"---not quote marks.

The basic pattern uses a common regex idiom: "[^"]+". The pattern begins and ends with a quote mark and then matches one or more characters in between that are anything but a quote. In the final rendition of the pattern, we add the \zs item after the opening quote mark and the \ze item before the closing quote mark. This excludes the quote marks from the match, leaving only the contents of the quotes highlighted. Note that the quote marks are still a critical element in the pattern, even though they are excluded from the match.

Tip 79

Escape Problem Characters

*The \V literal switch makes it easier to search for text verbatim because it disables the special meanings for the ., +, and * symbols, but there are a few characters whose special meaning can't be turned off. In this advanced tip, we'll look at how to handle these.*

Escape / Characters When Searching Forward

Take this excerpt from a Markdown document:

Lookaround Expressions

Vim's \zs and \ze are conceptually similar to Perl's *lookaround* assertions.[a] Although the syntax differs between the regex engines in Perl and Vim, the \zs item is roughly equivalent to *positive lookbehind*, while \ze is equivalent to *positive lookahead*.

As you might expect, Perl also supports negative variants of the lookaround assertions. These are zero-width items that match only if the specified pattern is *not* present. Vim also supports the full matrix of negative/positive lookahead/lookbehind assertions, but again, the syntax differs from Perl. For a side-by-side comparison, look up :h perl-patterns ⓘ.

Instead of using \zs and \ze, we could rewrite the /\v"\zs[^"]+\ze"<CR> pattern from Tip 78, *Stake the Boundaries of a Match*, on page 194, using Vim's positive lookaround items, like so:

⇒   `/\v"@<=[^"]+"@=`

I don't know about you, but I find the version using \zs and \ze easier to parse. Negative lookaround expressions are used heavily in some of Vim's syntax highlighting definitions, but I've found little need for them in everyday usage. However, I've found many uses for positive lookaround expressions, so it seems fitting that they should have their own shorthand tokens, namely \zs and \ze.

———————

a.   http://www.regular-expressions.info/lookaround.html

patterns/search-url.markdown
```
Search items: [http://vimdoc.net/search?q=/\\][s]
...
[s]: http://vimdoc.net/search?q=/\\
```

Suppose that we want to search for all instances of the URL http://vim-doc.net/search?q=/\\. Rather than typing it out in full, we'll just yank it into a register so that we can paste it into our search field. We want to match this text exactly as is, so we'll use the \V literal switch.

With our cursor placed anywhere inside the brackets, we can yank the URL into register u with the command `"uyi[` (mnemonic: *u* stands for *URL*). We then type /\V<C-r>u<CR> to populate the search field with the contents of that same register. Our search prompt looks like this:

⇒   **/\Vhttp://vimdoc.net/search?q=/**

When we execute the search, we get this result:

```
Search items: [http://vimdoc.net/search?q=/\\][s]
...
[s]: http://vimdoc.net/search?q=/\\
```

What's going on here? When we pasted the full URL into the search field, Vim interpreted the first / character as a search field terminator (see *Search Field Terminators*, on page 199). Everything after that first forward slash was ignored, so our search string became merely http:.

When searching forward, we have to escape / characters. This is required whether we are doing a very magic search (with the \v pattern switch) or a very nomagic search (with the \V literal switch). Let's amend the previous search, prefixing each / character with a backslash:

⇒ `/\Vhttp:\/\/vimdoc.net\/search?q=\/\\`

This time, the result is closer to what we would expect:

```
Search items: [http://vimdoc.net/search?q=/\\][s]
...
[s]: http://vimdoc.net/search?q=/\\
```

It's still not perfect. The match stops short of the final backslash. We'll find out why soon, but first, let's consider searching backward.

Escape ? Characters When Searching Backward

When searching backward, the ? symbol acts as the search field terminator. That means we don't have to escape / characters, but instead we have to escape the ? symbol. Watch what happens if we search backward for the URL that we yanked into register u:

⇒ `?http://vimdoc.net/search?q=/\\`

Without escaping anything, Vim matches the string "http://vimdoc.net/search":

```
Search items: [http://vimdoc.net/search?q=/\\][s]
...
[s]: http://vimdoc.net/search?q=/\\
```

That's a better result than when we searched forward without escaping anything, but it still doesn't match the full URL. We can do better if we prepend the ? character with a backslash:

⇒ `?http://vimdoc.net/search\?q=/\\`

That matches the following:

```
Search items: [http://vimdoc.net/search?q=/\\][s]
...
[s]: http://vimdoc.net/search?q=/\\
```

Escape \ Characters Every Time

There's one more character that we have to escape in the search field: the backslash. Normally, a \ indicates that the next character is to be given some special treatment. If we double it up as \\, the first backslash cancels out the special meaning of the second one. In effect, we're telling Vim to search for a single backslash character.

In our example text, we're searching for a URL that includes two consecutive backslashes. We have to include two backslashes in the search field for each of them. Searching forward, we end up with this:

⇒ `/\Vhttp:\/\/vimdoc.net\/search?q=\/\\\\`

At last! Our search query matches the entire URL:

```
Search items: [http://vimdoc.net/search?q=/\\][s]
...
[s]: http://vimdoc.net/search?q=/\\
```

The backslash character always needs to be escaped, whether we're searching forward or backward.

Escape Characters Programmatically

Escaping characters by hand is laborious, error-prone work. Fortunately, Vim script includes a library function that can do the hard work for us: escape({string}, {chars}) (see :h escape() ⓘ).

The {chars} argument specifies which characters must be escaped with a backslash. If we're searching forward, we could call escape(@u, '/\'), which would prefix each / and \ character with a backslash. If we were searching backward, we could instead call escape(@u, '?\').

First, make sure that the URL we want to search for is still stored in the u register. Then we'll bring up the search prompt by pressing / or ?; either one will work just fine. Enter the \V literal switch and then type `<C-r>=`. That switches from the search prompt to the expression register prompt. Now we type this:

⇒ `=escape(@u, getcmdtype().'\')`

When we press `<CR>`, the escape() function is evaluated, and the returned value gets inserted into the search field. The getcmdtype() function simply returns a / symbol if we're searching forward or a ? symbol if we're searching backward (see :h getcmdtype() ⓘ). In Vim script, the . operator performs string concatenation, so getcmdtype().'\' produces '/\' if we're searching forward and '?\' if we're searching backward. The end result is that no matter which way we're searching, this expression escapes the contents of the u register so that we can find it.

Switching to the expression register and calling the escape() function by hand still involves a lot of typing. With just a little bit more Vim script, we could automate this, making it more convenient to use. Skip ahead to Tip 87, *Search for the Current Visual Selection*, on page 216, for an example.

Search Field Terminators

You might be wondering why the search field has to treat any character as a terminator. Why not just accept that everything following the search prompt is to be included in the search match? The behavior of Vim's search command can be tuned by appending certain flags after the search field terminator. For example, if we run the command /vim/e<CR>, then our cursor will be placed at the *end* of any matches rather than at the start. In Tip 83, *Offset the Cursor to the End of a Search Match*, on page 206, we'll learn how to exploit this feature rather than let it exploit us.

There is one way of entering a pattern without having to worry about search field terminators, but it works only in GVim: use the :promptfind command (see :h :promptfind ⓘ). This brings up a graphical dialog window with a field labeled "Find." You can enter the / and ? characters here without having to escape them. However, the \ and newline characters still cause problems.

CHAPTER 13

Search

Having studied Vim's regular expression engines in the previous chapter, let's see how we can put them to use with the search command. We'll start with the basics: how to execute a search, highlight matches, and jump between them. Then we'll learn a couple of tricks that exploit Vim's incremental search feature, which not only gives us instant feedback but can also save us typing by autocompleting our match. We'll also learn how to count the number of matches that occur in a document.

The search offsets feature allows us to position our cursor relative to a match. We'll look at one scenario where search offsets can streamline our workflow. Then we'll see how search offsets can be exploited to operate on a complete search match.

Composing a regular expression—and getting it right—often takes a few attempts, so developing a workflow that allows us to iterate on a pattern is important. We'll learn about two methods for doing this: calling up our search history and working in the command-line window.

Have you ever wished for a simple way of searching for text that's already present in your document? We'll finish by devising a simple customization that overrides the * command to search for the current visual selection.

Tip 80

Meet the Search Command

In this tip, we'll cover the basics of using the search command, including how to specify the direction of a search, repeat (or reverse) the last search, and work with the search history.

Execute a Search

From Normal mode, the `/` key brings up Vim's search prompt. Here we can enter the pattern, or literal text, that we want to search for. Vim does nothing until we press the `<CR>` key to execute the search. If we press the `<Esc>` key instead, the search prompt will be dismissed and we'll return to Normal mode.

When we execute a search, Vim scans forward from the current cursor position, stopping on the first match that it finds. If nothing is found before the end of the document, Vim informs us "search hit BOTTOM, continuing at TOP." This means that in some circumstances, a forward search can take us backward. That's not as disorienting as it might sound. Just remember that the search command wraps around the document, and it'll make sense.

If you ever need to search from the current cursor position to the end of the document *without* wrapping around, you can disable the 'wrapscan' option (see :h 'wrapscan' ⓘ).

Specify the Search Direction

When a search is initiated with the `/` key, Vim scans the document forward. If we use the `?` key to bring up the search prompt, Vim searches backward instead. The search prompt always begins with either the / or ? character, which indicates in what direction the search will scan.

Repeat the Last Search

The `n` command jumps to the next match, and the `N` command jumps to the previous match. We can easily navigate between matches in the current document with the `n` and `N` commands. But the definition of "next match" depends on context.

The `n` command preserves the direction as well as any offsets that were applied to the previous search. (We'll meet offsets in Tip 83, *Offset the Cursor to the End of a Search Match*, on page 206.) So if we execute a forward search using `/`, then `n` will continue searching forward. Whereas if we used `?` for the original search, then `n` will continue backward. Meanwhile, the `N` command always goes in the opposite direction to `n`.

Sometimes we might want to repeat a search using the same pattern but changing the direction or offset. In this case, it's useful to know that if we execute a search without providing a pattern, Vim will just reuse the pattern from the previous search. The following table summarizes the matrix of options for repeating a search:

Command	Effect
n	Jump to next match, preserving direction and offset
N	Jump to previous match, preserving direction and offset
/<CR>	Jump forward to next match of same pattern
?<CR>	Jump backward to previous match of same pattern
gn	Enable character-wise Visual mode and select next search match
gN	Enable character-wise Visual mode and select previous search match

Suppose we use ? to initiate a search. Having jumped backward to the previous match, we then decide that we want to skip forward through the remainder of the matches. We could do it with the N key, but somehow that makes everything feel upside down. Instead, we could execute /<CR>. This executes a forward search, reusing the same pattern. Now, we can use the n key to skip forward through the rest of the matches in the document.

The n and N commands move the cursor, placing it on a match for the current pattern. But what if we want to select the matching text using Visual mode so that we can make some modifications to it? That's where the gn command comes in. When used from Normal mode, gn moves the cursor to the next match, then enables Visual mode and selects the matching text. If your cursor is already on a match, then gn will select the current match without you having to move the cursor. We'll look at this command in in more detail in Tip 84, *Operate on a Complete Search Match*, on page 208.

Recall Historical Searches

Vim records our search patterns so we can easily recall them. When the search prompt is visible, we can scroll through the previous searches by pressing the <Up> key. In fact, the interface for browsing the search history is just the same as for browsing the command-line history. We covered this in more depth in Tip 34, *Recall Commands from History*, on page 70. We'll put these techniques into action in Tip 85, *Create Complex Patterns by Iterating upon Search History*, on page 211.

Tip 81

Highlight Search Matches

Vim can highlight search matches, but this feature is not enabled by default. Learn how to enable it, and (just as importantly) how to mute it for those times when the highlighting takes over.

The search command allows us to jump quickly between matches, but by default, Vim does nothing to make them stand out visually. We can fix this by enabling the 'hlsearch' option, (see :h 'hlsearch' ⓘ), which causes all matches to be highlighted throughout the active document as well as in any other open split windows.

Mute Search Highlighting

Search highlighting is a useful feature, but sometimes it can make itself unwelcome. If we search for a common string, for example, or a pattern with hundreds of matches, we'll soon find that our workspace is riddled with yellow (or whatever hue the active color scheme uses).

In this scenario, we could run :set nohlsearch to disable the feature entirely (:se nohls and :se hls! also work). But when we come to execute another search, we might wish to reenable the feature again.

Vim has a more elegant solution. The :nohlsearch command can be used to mute the search highlighting temporarily (see :h :noh ⓘ). It will stay muted until the next time you execute a new or repeat search command. See *Create a Shortcut to Mute Highlighting*, on page 204, for a suggested mapping.

Create a Shortcut to Mute Highlighting

Typing :noh<CR> to mute search highlighting is laborious. We can speed things up by creating a mapping such as this:

```
nnoremap <silent> <C-l> :<C-u>nohlsearch<CR><C-l>
```

Normally, <C-l> clears and redraws the screen (see :h CTRL-L ⓘ). This mapping builds on top of the usual behavior by muting search highlighting.

Tip 82

Preview the First Match Before Execution

Vim's search command is much more useful when the incremental search feature is enabled. Here are a couple of ways that this option can improve your workflow.

By default, Vim sits idle as we prepare our search pattern, only springing into action when we press `<CR>`. My favorite enhancement is enabled with the 'incsearch' setting (see :h 'incsearch' ⓘ). This tells Vim to show a preview of the first match based on what has been entered so far into the search field. Each time we enter another character, Vim instantly updates the preview. This table illustrates how it works:

Keystrokes	Buffer Contents
{start}	`The car was the color of a carrot.`
/car	`The car was the color of a carrot.`
/carr	`The car was the color of a carrot.`
/carr`<CR>`	`The car was the color of a carrot.`

After typing "car" into the search field, Vim highlights the first match, which in this case is the word "car" itself. As soon as we enter the next "r" character, our preview ceases to match, and Vim skips forward to the next matching word. This time, it's "carrot." If we were to press the `<Esc>` key at this point, the search prompt would be dismissed and our cursor restored to its original position at the start of the line. But instead, we press `<CR>` to execute the command, causing our cursor to jump to the start of the word "carrot."

This instant feedback lets us know when we've hit our target. If our intention was simply to move the cursor to the start of the word "carrot," then there's no need to type the full word into the search field. In this case, /carr`<CR>` is enough. Without the 'incsearch' feature enabled, we wouldn't know whether or not our pattern would hit the target until we executed the search.

Check for the Existence of a Match

In our example, we have two partial matches for "car" on the same line. But imagine if the words "car" and "carrot" were separated by several hundred words. When we updated our search field from "car" to "carr," Vim would have to scroll the document to bring the word "carrot" into view. And that is exactly what happens.

Suppose that we just want to check if the word "carrot" is present in the current document without moving our cursor. With the 'incsearch' option enabled, we would simply have to dial up the search prompt and then type as many characters of the word "carrot" as it takes to bring the first occurrence of the word into view. If the word is found, we can just press `<Esc>`, and we'll end up right back where we started. No need to interrupt our train of thought.

Autocomplete the Search Field Based on Preview Match

In that last example, we executed the search command before completing the word "carrot." That's good enough if our intention was simply to move our cursor to the first match. But suppose that we needed our pattern to match the entire word "carrot": for example, if we were planning to follow the search command with a substitute command.

Of course, we could simply type out the "carrot" in full. But here's a handy shortcut: `<C-r><C-w>`. This autocompletes the search field using the remainder of the current preview match. If we used this command after entering "carr" into the search field, it would append "ot," causing the match to encompass the entire word "carrot."

Note that the `<C-r><C-w>` autocompletion is slightly brittle in this context. If you prefix your search with the \v item, then `<C-r><C-w>` will complete the entire word under the cursor (creating /\vcarrcarrot`<CR>`, for example) instead of the remainder of the word. As long as you are searching for words and not patterns, the autocomplete feature of incremental search can be a nice little time-saver.

Tip 83

Offset the Cursor to the End of a Search Match

A search offset can be used to position the cursor a fixed number of characters away from the start or end of a match. In this tip, we'll study an example where, by placing the cursor at the end of a match, we're able to complete a series of changes using the Dot Formula.

Each time we execute a search command, our cursor is positioned on the first character of the match. This default seems reasonable, but sometimes we might rather have the cursor positioned at the end of a search match. Vim makes this possible using its search offset feature (see :h search-offset ⓘ).

Let's study an example. In this excerpt, the author has consistently abbreviated the word "language":

search/langs.txt

```
Aim to learn a new programming lang each year.
Which lang did you pick up last year?
Which langs would you like to learn?
```

How would you go about expanding all three occurrences of "lang" to the full word? One solution would be to use the substitute command: :%s/lang/language/g. But let's see if we can find an alternative that uses the Dot Formula. We might learn something along the way.

First let's tackle this without using a search offset. We'll start by searching for the string that we want to modify: /lang`<CR>`. That places our cursor at the start of the first match. From there, we can append at the end of the word by typing `ea`uage<Esc>. Appending at the end of a word is such a common task that `ea` should flow from your fingers as though it were a single command.

Now we just need to maneuver our cursor into the right position, and the dot command should take care of the rest. We can amend the next occurrence of "lang" by typing `ne.` - `n` jumps to the start of the next match; then `e` moves us to the end of the word, and `.` appends the letters required to complete the word. That's three keystrokes. We haven't achieved the ideal Dot Formula, but at least it gets the job done.

Or does it? If we bash out the same command sequence a second time, `ne.`, we'll end up mangling the final word. Can you see why? The final occurrence of "lang" is actually an abbreviation of "languages" (note the plural). So if we blindly repeat our suboptimal Dot Formula, we'll create the frankenword "langsuage." Clearly, this is one scenario where placing the cursor at the end of the match, rather than at the end of the word, would be preferable.

Table 14, *Improved Workflow Using Search Offset*, on page 208 shows an improved workflow.

Here, we search for /lang/e`<CR>`, which places the cursor at the end of the search match, exactly where we need it. Each time we use the `n` command, our cursor is positioned at the end of the next search match, setting us up perfectly to use the dot command. The search offset has enabled us to achieve an ideal Dot Formula.

Keystrokes	Buffer Contents
{start}	Aim to learn a new programming lang each year. Which lang did you pick up last year? Which langs would you like to learn?
/lang/e<CR>	Aim to learn a new programming lang each year. Which lang did you pick up last year? Which langs would you like to learn?
auage<Esc>	Aim to learn a new programming language each year. Which lang did you pick up last year? Which langs would you like to learn?
n	Aim to learn a new programming language each year. Which lang did you pick up last year? Which langs would you like to learn?
.	Aim to learn a new programming language each year. Which language did you pick up last year? Which langs would you like to learn?
n.	Aim to learn a new programming language each year. Which language did you pick up last year? Which languages would you like to learn?

Table 14—Improved Workflow Using Search Offset

In the real world, it won't always be obvious when a search offset will come in handy. Suppose that we started off by executing the search command without the offset. Then, after pressing n a couple of times, we realize that we'd prefer to place the cursor at the end of the match. That's no problem: we could simply run //e<CR>. When we leave the search field blank like this, Vim reuses the pattern from the previous search. So this repeats the last search but with an offset.

Tip 84

Operate on a Complete Search Match

Vim's search command allows us to highlight matches and jump between them quickly. We can also operate on regions of text that match our current pattern using the gn command.

Vim's search command is convenient for jumping between occurrences of a pattern, but what if we want to make a change to each match? This used to be awkward, but the gn command (available since Vim 7.4.110) offers a very efficient workflow for operating on search matches.

Let's look at an example. In this excerpt, we're dealing with classes called XmlDocument, XhtmlDocument, XmlTag, and XhtmlTag:

```
search/tag-heirarchy.rb
class XhtmlDocument < XmlDocument; end
class XhtmlTag < XmlTag; end
```

Suppose we want to rename each class to look like this instead:

```
class XHTMLDocument < XMLDocument; end
class XHTMLTag < XMLTag; end
```

To do this we can use the `gU{motion}` operator to convert a range of text to uppercase (see :h gU ⓘ). For the motion, we'll use the `gn` command, which operates on the next match (see :h gn ⓘ). If the cursor is positioned on a match, then `gn` will act upon the current match. But if the cursor is not currently on a match, then `gn` will jump forward to the next match and apply the operation there. Table 15, *Operating on a Complete Search Match*, on page 210, demonstrates how we can use this.

To begin with, we write a regular expression to match either Xml or Xhtml. That's easy enough: `/\vX(ht)?ml\C<CR>` does the job. The `\C` item enforces case sensitivity, so the pattern won't match XML or XHTML. After searching for this pattern, the four ranges of text that we want to operate on light up with search highlighting, and our cursor is positioned at the start of the first match.

The `gUgn` command transforms the matching text to uppercase. The beauty of this command is that it's easily repeated. We can jump to the next match by pressing `n` and repeat the change with `.`. That's two keystrokes per change: our classic Dot Formula. But this is a rare case where we can be even more economical with our keystrokes.

Improving Upon the Dot Formula

We could describe the `gUgn` operation as: convert the *next match* to uppercase. If the cursor is already positioned on a match, then pressing `.` will affect the match under the cursor. But if the cursor is not positioned on a match, then `.` will jump forward to the next match and apply the operation there. We don't even have to press the `n` key. We only have to press `.`, which means we can repeat the change for each match with only one keystroke per change.

The classic Dot Formula has two parts: one keystroke to move, another to make the change. The `gn` command lets us condense these two steps into one, because `gn` operates on *the next match*, rather than at the current cursor location. If we can arrange things such that pressing the `.` command jumps

Keystrokes	Buffer Contents
{start}	class XhtmlDocument < XmlDocument; end class XhtmlTag < XmlTag; end
/\vX(ht)?ml\C<CR>	class XhtmlDocument < XmlDocument; end class XhtmlTag < XmlTag; end
gUgn	class XHTMLDocument < XmlDocument; end class XhtmlTag < XmlTag; end
n	class XHTMLDocument < XmlDocument; end class XhtmlTag < XmlTag; end
.	class XHTMLDocument < XMLDocument; end class XhtmlTag < XmlTag; end
n.	class XHTMLDocument < XMLDocument; end class XHTMLTag < XmlTag; end
.	class XHTMLDocument < XMLDocument; end class XHTMLTag < XMLTag; end

Table 15—Operating on a Complete Search Match

to the next match *and* applies the last operation, then we can use one keystroke to repeat each change. I call this the *Improved Dot Formula*.

Try working through the same example with a case-insensitive pattern, by changing the \C item to \c. You'll find that you can still repeat each change by pressing n. (the classic Dot Formula), but pressing . by itself won't advance through the matches in the document. That's because the case-insensitive pattern matches the text before and after running the gUgn command: for example, it matches both Xml and XML. In this context, the . command will repeat the change for the match under the cursor, rather than jumping to the next match. You won't see anything happen, because converting XML to uppercase makes no change.

For the Improved Dot Formula to work, our search pattern should match the target text before making a change, but not after making the change. In this particular example, our gU operation changes the case of the target text, so it's vital that our search pattern is case-sensitive. But we don't always have to use a case-sensitive pattern to make the Improved Dot Formula work.

Try working through the same example, but this time use the dgn operation to delete the matching text. Or use cgnJson<Esc> to replace each match with Json. In both cases, you should be able to repeat the change for each match just by pressing .. As long as the target text is modified so as to no longer match the search pattern, we can make use of the Improved Dot Formula.

Be careful when using the Improved Dot Formula on a large file, where the matches may be spaced far apart. If you use n., then you can pause between the two keystrokes and decide whether or not you want to repeat the change by pressing the `.` key. Whereas if you use `.` without first jumping to the next match, you won't get to look at all the matches before changing them.

Since the release of Vim version 7.4.110, the `gn` command has become a staple of my workflow. If you're using an older version of Vim, this command is a good reason to upgrade!

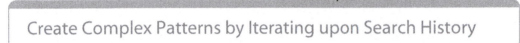

Tip 85

Create Complex Patterns by Iterating upon Search History

Writing regular expressions is hard. We won't get it right the first time, so the next best thing is to develop a frictionless workflow that allows us to develop a pattern by iteration. Being able to recall and edit previous items from our search history is the trick.

In this example text, the prime symbol has been used as a quote mark:

search/quoted-strings.txt
```
This string contains a 'quoted' word.
This string contains 'two' quoted 'words.'
This 'string doesn't make things easy.'
```

We want to compose a regular expression to match each quoted string. This will take a few tries, but when we get it right, we'll run a substitute command to transform the text to use real double-quote symbols, like this:

```
This string contains a "quoted" word.
This string contains "two" quoted "words."
This "string doesn't make things easy."
```

Draft 1: A Broad Match

Let's begin with a crude search:

➡ `/\v'.+'`

This matches a single `'` character, followed by any character one or more times, and terminates with a final `'` character. After executing this search command, our document looks like this:

```
This string contains a 'quoted' word.
This string contains 'two' quoted 'words.'
This 'string doesn't make things easy.'
```

The first line looks fine, but there's a problem with line two. The .+ item in the pattern performs a *greedy* match, meaning that it matches as many characters as possible. But we want to generate two separate matches on this line: one for each quoted word. Let's go back to the drawing board.

Draft 2: Refinement

Instead of using the . symbol to match *any* character, let's be a bit more specific. We actually want to match any character *except* ', which can be done using [^']+. We'll refine our pattern to look like this instead:

⇒ `/\v'[^']+'`

We don't have to type this out from scratch. Instead, we can press `/<Up>`, which prepopulates the search field with the most recent pattern. We only have to make a small change, so we'll use the `<Left>` and backspace keys to delete the . character from the pattern and then type in the replacement. When we execute the search, we'll get the following matches:

```
This string contains a 'quoted' word.
This string contains 'two' quoted 'words.'
This 'string doesn't make things easy.'
```

That's an improvement. The first two lines match up just as we want them to, but line three raises a new issue. The ' character is used here as an apostrophe, which shouldn't terminate the match. We'll have to refine our pattern some more.

Draft 3: Another Iteration

Now we need to consider what differentiates an apostrophe from a closing quote mark. Here are a few examples: "won't," "don't," and "we're." In each case, the ' character is followed immediately by a letter—not by a space or punctuation mark. We could update our pattern to allow ' characters as long as they are followed by a word character. Here's our next refinement:

⇒ `/\v'([^']|'\w)+'`

This involves some fairly substantial changes. Not only do we have to type in the extra '\w item, we also have to wrap the two alternatives in parentheses and separate them with a pipe. It's time to bring out the big guns.

Instead of pressing `/<Up>` to prefill the search field with our last pattern, let's press `q/` to summon the command-line window. This acts more or less like a regular Vim buffer, but it's prepopulated with our search history, one item per line (see *Meet the Command-Line Window*, on page 70). We can use the full power of Vim's modal editing to amend the last pattern.

The following sequence of edits demonstrates how we might make this particular change. If you're struggling to understand `c%(<C-r>")<Esc>`, refer to Tip 55, *Jump Between Matching Parentheses*, on page 132, and Tip 15, *Paste from a Register Without Leaving Insert Mode*, on page 31.

Keystrokes	Buffer Contents
{start}	`\v'[^']+'`
`f[`	`\v'[^']+'`
`c%(<C-r>")<Esc>`	`\v'([^'])+'`
`i|\w<Esc>`	`\v'([^']|'\w)+'`

When we've got the pattern looking how we want it, we just press the `<CR>` key to execute the search. The document should light up as follows:

```
This string contains a 'quoted' word.
This string contains 'two' quoted 'words.'
This 'string doesn't make things easy.'
```

Score!

Draft 4: One Final Tweak

Our pattern matches in all the right places, but we need to make one final change before we can execute our substitute command. We want to capture everything inside the quotes by wrapping it in parentheses. This is our final pattern:

⇒ `/\v'(([^']\|'\w)+)'`

We could either run `/<Up>` and edit the search field, or we could run `q/` and make the change in the command-line window. Use whichever you feel is more appropriate. The search highlighting won't look any different from the last time, but for each match, the text inside quotes will be assigned to the \1 capture register. That means we can run the following substitute command:

⇒ `:%s//"\1"/g`

We can leave the search field blank, and Vim will reuse the last search command (for more details, skip ahead to Tip 91, *Reuse the Last Search Pattern*, on page 225). Here's the outcome from running this command:

```
This string contains a "quoted" word.
This string contains "two" quoted "words."
This "string doesn't make things easy."
```

Discussion

What we've done here is effectively identical to this:

⇒ `:%s/\v'((['']|\w)+)'/"\1"/g`

Would you trust yourself to type that out correctly in one go?

Don't worry about getting a search pattern right the first time. Vim keeps our most recent search pattern two keystrokes away, so it's easy to refine a pattern. Start with a broad match; then take as many steps as you need to focus on your target.

Being able to edit the command line directly is great for simple edits. If we have the 'incsearch' setting enabled, then we get the added bonus of live feedback as we edit the command line. We lose this perk as soon as we call up the command-line window. But with the full power of Vim's modal editing at our fingertips, this is a fair trade-off.

Tip 86

Count the Matches for the Current Pattern

This tip shows a couple of ways that you can count the number of matches for a pattern.

Suppose we want to find out how many times the word "buttons" appears in this excerpt:

search/buttons.js
```
var buttons = viewport.buttons;
viewport.buttons.previous.show();
viewport.buttons.next.show();
viewport.buttons.index.hide();
```

We'll start by searching for that word:

⇒ `/\<buttons\>`

Now we can move from one match to another by pressing the `n` and `N` keys, but Vim's search command doesn't give us any indication of how many matches are in the current document. We can get a match count by using either the :substitute or :vimgrep command.

Count Matches with the ':substitute' Command

We can get a match count by running this command:

⇒ `/\<buttons\>`
⇒ `:%s///gn`
❮ `5 matches on 4 lines`

We're calling the :substitute command, but the n flag suppresses the usual behavior. Instead of replacing each match with the target, it simply counts the number of matches and then echoes the result below the command line. By leaving the search field blank, we instruct Vim to use the current search pattern. The replacement field is ignored anyway (because of the n flag), so we can leave it blank too.

Note that the command contains three consecutive / characters. The first and second delimit the pattern field, and the second and third delimit the replacement field. Be careful not to omit any of the / characters. Running :%s//gn would replace every match with gn!

Count Matches with the ':vimgrep' Command

The n flag of the :substitute command lets us know the total number of matches for a pattern. But sometimes it would be useful to know that a particular match is, say, number 3 out of a total of 5. We can get that information with the :vimgrep command:

⇒ `/\<buttons\>`
⇒ `:vimgrep //g %`
❮ `(1 of 5) var buttons = viewport.buttons;`

This command populates the quickfix list with each match found in the current buffer. The :vimgrep command is capable of finding matches across multiple files, but here we're asking it to look inside a single file. The % symbol expands to the filepath of the current buffer (see :h cmdline-special ⓘ). Leaving the pattern field blank tells :vimgrep to reuse the current search pattern.

As well as being able to move between matches with the n and N keys, we can now go back and forward using the :cnext and :cprev commands:

⇒ `:cnext`
❮ `(2 of 5) var buttons = viewport.buttons;`
⇒ `:cnext`
❮ `(3 of 5) viewport.buttons.previous.show();`
⇒ `:cprev`
❮ `(2 of 5) var buttons = viewport.buttons;`

I prefer using this technique over the substitute command when I want to look at each match, perhaps making some changes. It's helpful seeing (1 of 5), then (2 of 5), and so on, which gives me an idea of how much work I've still got to do.

The quickfix list is an important feature that's central to many Vim workflows. You can read more about the quickfix list in Chapter 17, *Compile Code and Navigate Errors with the Quickfix List*, on page 263.

*In Normal mode, the * command lets us search for the word under the cursor. Using a small amount of Vim script, we can redefine the * command in Visual mode so that, instead of searching for the current word, it searches for the current selection.*

Search for the Current Word in Visual Mode

In Visual mode, the * command searches for the word under the cursor:

Keystrokes	Buffer Contents
{start}	She sells sea shells by the sea shore.
*	She sells sea shells by the sea shore.

We start off in Visual mode with the first three words selected and our cursor placed on the word "sea." When we invoke the * command, it searches forward for the next occurrence of the word "sea," extending the range of the visual selection. Although this behavior is consistent with the Normal mode * command, I rarely find it useful.

Before I became hooked on Vim, I used another text editor, which included a "Use selection for find" command. I had the keyboard shortcut for this burned into my fingers and used it all the time. When I switched to Vim, I was surprised to find that it didn't have such a feature. It always felt to me that triggering the * command from Visual mode should search for the current selection, not the current word. With a small amount of Vim script, we can add this feature to Vim.

Search for the Current Selection (Prior Art)

If you look up :h visual-search ⓘ, you'll find this suggestion:

> Here is an idea for a mapping that makes it possible to do a search for the selected text:
>
> ```
> :vmap X y/<C-R>"<CR>
> ```
>
> Note that special characters (like "." and "*") will cause problems.

The y command yanks the current visual selection, and /<C-r>"<CR> brings up the search prompt, pastes the contents of the default register, and then executes the search. That solution is simple, but as the cautionary note in Vim's documentation says, it has limitations.

In Tip 79, *Escape Problem Characters*, on page 195, we learned how to overcome these limitations. Now let's put that theory into practice and create a mapping that searches for the current selection without being derailed by special characters.

Search for the Current Selection (Redux)

This snippet of Vim script does the trick:

```
patterns/visual-star.vim
xnoremap * :<C-u>call <SID>VSetSearch('/')<CR>/<C-R>=@/<CR><CR>
xnoremap # :<C-u>call <SID>VSetSearch('?')<CR>?<C-R>=@/<CR><CR>

function! s:VSetSearch(cmdtype)
  let temp = @s
  norm! gv"sy
  let @/ = '\V' . substitute(escape(@s, a:cmdtype.'\'), '\n', '\\n', 'g')
  let @s = temp
endfunction
```

You can either paste this into your vimrc file directly or install the visual star search plugin.[1]

As well as overriding the * command, we've customized the # command, which searches backward for selected text. The xnoremap keyword specifies that the mappings should apply to Visual mode but not to Select mode (see :h mapmode-x ⓘ).

---

1. https://github.com/nelstrom/vim-visual-star-search

CHAPTER 14

Substitution

You might think that the substitute command is just for simple find and replace operations, but in fact, it's one of the most powerful Ex commands available. By the time we've reached the end of this chapter, we'll have learned all the many roles that the substitute command can play, from simple to very complex.

We'll look at a few tips and tricks that allow us to compose substitution commands more quickly by reusing the last search pattern. We'll also look at a special case, where Vim allows us to eyeball every occurrence before confirming the substitution. We'll learn how we can fill out the replacement field without typing, and we'll examine some of the special behaviors that are available through the replacement field. We'll also learn how to repeat the last substitute command over a different range without having to retype the whole command.

We can execute Vim script expressions in the replacement field. We'll study an advanced example that exploits this to perform arithmetic on a series of numerical matches. Then we'll learn how to swap two (or more) words with a single substitute command.

We'll finish by looking at a couple of strategies for performing search and replace across multiple files.

Tip 88

Meet the Substitute Command

The :substitute command is complex: in addition to providing a search pattern and replacement string, we have to specify the range over which it will execute. Optionally, we can also provide flags to tweak its behavior.

The substitute command allows us to find and replace one chunk of text with another. The command's syntax looks like this:

```
:[range]s[ubstitute]/{pattern}/{string}/[flags]
```

The substitute command has many parts to it. The rules for the [range] are just the same as for every other Ex command, which we covered in-depth in Tip 28, *Execute a Command on One or More Consecutive Lines*, on page 56. As for the {pattern}, that was covered in Chapter 12, *Matching Patterns and Literals*, on page 185.

Tweak the Substitute Command Using Flags

We can tweak the behavior of the substitute command using flags. The best way to understand what a flag does is to see it in action, so let's briefly define a handful of flags that are used in other tips. (For a complete reference, look up :h :s_flags ⓘ.)

The g flag makes the substitute command act *globally*, causing it to change all matches within a line rather than just changing the first one. We'll meet it in Tip 89, *Find and Replace Every Match in a File*, on page 222.

The c flag gives us the opportunity to *confirm* or reject each change. We'll see it in action in Tip 90, *Eyeball Each Substitution*, on page 223.

The n flag suppresses the usual substitute behavior, causing the command to report the *number* of occurrences that would be affected if we ran the substitute command. Tip 86, *Count the Matches for the Current Pattern*, on page 214, gives an example of usage.

If we run the substitute command using a pattern that has no matches in the current file, Vim will report an error saying "E486: Pattern not found." We can silence these errors by including the e flag.

The & flag simply tells Vim to reuse the same flags from the previous substitute command. Tip 93, *Repeat the Previous Substitute Command*, on page 229, shows a scenario where it comes in handy.

Special Characters for the Replacement String

In Chapter 12, *Matching Patterns and Literals*, on page 185, we saw that some characters take on special meaning when used in search patterns. The replacement field also has a handful of special characters. You can find the complete list by looking up :h sub-replace-special ⓘ, but some of the highlights are summarized in this table:

Symbol	Represents
\r	Insert a carriage return
\t	Insert a tab character
\\	Insert a single backslash
\1	Insert the first submatch
\2	Insert the second submatch (and so on, up to \9)
\0	Insert the entire matched pattern
&	Insert the entire matched pattern
~	Use {string} from the previous invocation of :substitute
\={Vim script}	Evaluate {Vim script} expression; use result as replacement {string}

The \r, \t and \\ tokens should be fairly self-explanatory. In Tip 93, *Repeat the Previous Substitute Command*, on page 229, we'll see how the ~ token works, but we'll also learn about a couple of shortcuts that make it even faster to repeat a substitute command. We'll see \1 and \2 in use in Tip 94, *Rearrange CSV Fields Using Submatches*, on page 232.

The \={Vim script} token is very powerful. It allows us to execute code and use the result as our replacement {string}. In Tip 95, *Perform Arithmetic on the Replacement*, on page 233, and Tip 96, *Swap Two or More Words*, on page 234, we'll see a couple of examples of usage.

Tip 89

Find and Replace Every Match in a File

By default, the substitute command acts on the current line, changing the first occurrence only. To change every match throughout a file, we have to specify a range and use the g flag.

For demonstration purposes, we'll use this text:

`substitution/get-rolling.txt`
```
When the going gets tough, the tough get going.
If you are going through hell, keep going.
```

Let's try and replace every occurrence of the word *going* with *rolling*. First, we'll enable the 'hlsearch' option so that we can see what we're doing (see Tip 81, *Highlight Search Matches*, on page 204, for more details):

⇒ `:set hlsearch`

The simplest thing that we could do with the substitute command is to provide a target {pattern} and replacement {string}:

Keystrokes	Buffer Contents
:s/going/rolling	When the rolling gets tough, the tough get going.
	If you are going through hell, keep going.

See what's happened? Vim has replaced the first occurrence of "going" with "rolling," but it's left every other match untouched.

To understand why, it helps to think of a file as a two-dimensional board made up of characters along the *x*-axis and lines down the *y*-axis. By default, the substitute command only acts upon the first match on the current line. Let's see what's required to expand its scope to cover the *x*- and *y*-axes in their entirety.

To keep going on the horizontal axis we need to include the g flag. This stands for *global*, which is a rather misleading name. One might expect that this flag would cause the substitution to be carried out across the entire file, but in fact, it just means "globally within the current line." This makes more sense if you remember that Vim is a direct descendent of the line editor ed, as discussed in *On the Etymology of Vim (and Family)*, on page 55.

We'll press u to undo the last change and then try running a variation of the substitute command. This time, we'll tack the /g flag on at the end:

Keystrokes	Buffer Contents
:s/going/rolling/g	When the rolling gets tough, the tough get rolling. If you are going through hell, keep going.

This time, all occurrences of *going* on the current line have been changed to *rolling*, but that still leaves a couple of instances unchanged elsewhere in the file. So how do we tell the substitute command to act on the entire vertical axis of our file?

The answer is to provide a range. If we prefix a % at the start of the substitute command, it will be executed on every line of the file:

Keystrokes	Buffer Contents
:%s/going/rolling/g	When the rolling gets tough, the tough get rolling. If you are rolling through hell, keep rolling.

The substitute command is just one of many Ex commands, all of which can accept a range in the same manner. Tip 28, *Execute a Command on One or More Consecutive Lines*, on page 56, goes into greater depth.

To recap, if we want to find and replace all occurrences in the current file, we have to explicitly tell the substitute command to operate on the entire *x*- and *y*-axes. The g flag deals with the horizontal axis, while the % address deals with the vertical axis.

It's easy enough to forget one or the other of these details. In Tip 93, *Repeat the Previous Substitute Command*, on page 229, we'll look at a couple of techniques for repeating a substitute command.

Tip 90

Eyeball Each Substitution

Finding all occurrences of a pattern and blindly replacing them with something else won't always work. Sometimes we need to look at each match and decide if it should be substituted. The c flag modifies the :substitute command to make this possible.

Remember this example from Tip 5, *Find and Replace by Hand*, on page 9?

the_vim_way/1_copy_content.txt
```
...We're waiting for content before the site can go live...
...If you are content with this, let's go ahead with it...
...We'll launch as soon as we have the content...
```

We couldn't use find and replace to change "content" to "copy." Instead, we used the Dot Formula to solve our problem. However, we could also have used the c flag on the substitute command:

⇒ `:%s/content/copy/gc`

The c flag causes Vim to show us each match and ask "Replace with copy?" We can then say `y` to perform the change or `n` to skip it. Vim does what we ask and then moves to the next match and asks us again.

In our example, we would respond `yny`, changing the first and last occurrences while leaving the middle one untouched.

We aren't limited to just two answers. In fact, Vim helpfully reminds us of our options with the prompt "y/n/a/q/l/^E/^Y." This table shows what each answer means:

Trigger	Effect
`y`	Substitute this match
`n`	Skip this match
`q`	Quit substituting
`l`	"last"—Substitute this match, then quit
`a`	"all"—Substitute this and any remaining matches
`<C-e>`	Scroll the screen up
`<C-y>`	Scroll the screen down

You can also find this information in Vim's help by looking up `:h :s_c` ⓘ.

Discussion

Unusually, most buttons on the keyboard do nothing in Vim's Substitute-Confirmation mode. As always, the `<Esc>` key allows us to return to Normal mode, but apart from that, the landscape feels unfamiliar.

On the up side, this allows us to complete the task with a minimum of keystrokes. On the down side, all of the functionality that we're used to is unavailable to us. By contrast, if we use the Dot Formula (as in Tip 5, *Find and Replace by Hand*, on page 9), then we're in plain old Normal mode throughout. Everything works just as we expect it to.

Try both methods, and use whichever one you feel more comfortable with.

Reuse the Last Search Pattern

Leaving the search field of the substitute command blank instructs Vim to reuse the most recent search pattern. We can exploit this fact to streamline our workflow.

Let's face it: to execute a substitute command, we have to do a lot of typing. First we specify the range, then we fill out the pattern and replacement fields, and finally we append any necessary flags. That's a lot to think about, and making a mistake in any of these fields could change the outcome.

Here's the good news: leaving the search field blank tells Vim to use the current pattern.

Take this monolithic substitute command (from Tip 85, *Create Complex Patterns by Iterating upon Search History*, on page 211):

⇒ `:%s/\v'((['^']|'\w)+)'/"\1"/g`

It's equivalent to these two separate commands:

⇒ `/\v'((['^']|'\w)+)'`
⇒ `:%s//"\1"/g`

So what? One way or another, we'll still have to type out the full pattern, right? That's not the point. The substitute command involves two steps: composing a pattern and devising a suitable replacement string. This technique allows us to decouple those two tasks.

When composing a nontrivial regular expression, it usually takes a few attempts to get it right. If we were to test our pattern by executing a substitute command, we would change the document each time we tried it out. That's messy. When we execute a search command, the document is not changed, so we can make as many mistakes as we like. In Tip 85, *Create Complex Patterns by Iterating upon Search History*, on page 211, we see an effective workflow for building regular expressions. Separating the two tasks allows for a cleaner workflow. We can measure twice and cut once.

Besides, who says we have to type out the pattern? In Tip 87, *Search for the Current Visual Selection*, on page 216, we used a smidgen of Vim script to add a Visual mode equivalent of the * command. This mapping allows us to select any text in our document and then hit the * key to search for the selection.

We could then run the substitute command with an empty search field to replace our selection (and any similar matches) with something else. Talk about being lazy!

It's Not Always Appropriate

I'm not saying that you should never fill out the search field of the substitute command. Here, for example, we have a substitute command that joins every line of a file by replacing newlines with commas:

⇒ `:%s/\n/,`

It's such a simple command that you won't gain anything by splitting it in two. In fact, doing so would probably add work.

Implications for Command History

Another point to consider is that leaving the search field blank creates an incomplete record in our command history. Patterns are saved in Vim's search history, while substitute commands are saved in the history of Ex commands (:h cmdline-history ⓘ). Decoupling the search and replacement tasks causes the two pieces of information to be placed in separate silos, which could cause difficulty if you want to reuse an old substitute command later.

If you think that you'll want to recall a substitute command in its complete form from history, you can always fill out the search field explicitly. Pressing `<C-r>/` at the command line pastes the contents of the last search register in place. Typing out the following would create a complete entry in our command history:

⇒ `:%s/<C-r>//"\1"/g`

Sometimes leaving the search field of the substitute command blank is convenient. Other times it's not. Try both ways, and you'll develop an intuition for whether or not to use it. As always, use your judgment.

Tip 92

Replace with the Contents of a Register

We don't have to type out the replacement string by hand. If the text already exists in the document, we can yank it into a register and use it in the replacement field. Then we can pass the contents of a register either by value or by reference.

In Tip 91, *Reuse the Last Search Pattern*, on page 225, we saw that Vim makes an intelligent assumption when we leave the search field of the substitute command blank. It's tempting to think that leaving the replacement field blank would also reuse the string from the previous substitute command, but this isn't the case. Instead, a blank replacement field instructs the substitute command to replace each match with an empty string. In other words, it deletes each match.

Pass by Value

We can insert the contents of a register by typing `<C-r>{register}`. Suppose that we have yanked some text and want to paste it into the replacement field of the substitute command. We could do so by typing this:

⇒ `:%s//<C-r>0/g`

When we type `<C-r>0`, Vim pastes the contents of register 0 in place, which means we can examine it before we execute the substitute command. In many cases, this works just fine, but complications could ensue.

If the text in register 0 contains any characters that have special meaning within the replacement field (such as & or ~, for example), we would have to edit the string by hand to escape those characters. Also, if register 0 contained a multiline excerpt of text, it might not fit on the command line.

To avoid these problems, we could simply pass a reference to the register containing the text we want to use in the substitution field.

Pass by Reference

Suppose that we've yanked a multiline selection of text, and it's stored in register 0. Now we want to use that text as the replacement field of the substitute command. We could do so by running this:

⇒ `:%s//\=@0/g`

In the replacement field, the `\=` item tells Vim to evaluate a Vim script expression. In Vim script, we can reference the contents of a register as `@{register}`. `@0` returns the contents of the yank register, while `@"` returns the contents of the default register. So the expression `:%s//\=@0/g` tells Vim to substitute the last pattern with the contents of the yank register.

Comparison

Look at this command:

⇒ `:%s/Pragmatic Vim/Practical Vim/g`

Compare it with this sequence of commands:

```
⇒ :let @/='Pragmatic Vim'
⇒ :let @a='Practical Vim'
⇒ :%s//\=@a/g
```

:let @/='Pragmatic Vim' is a programmatic way of setting the search pattern. It has the same effect as executing the search /Pragmatic Vim`<CR>` (except that running :let @/='Pragmatic Vim' does not create a record in the search history).

Likewise, :let @a='Practical Vim' sets the contents of the a register. The end result is the same as if we had visually selected the text "Practical Vim" and then typed `"ay` to yank the selection into register a.

Both substitute commands do the same thing—they replace all occurrences of "Pragmatic Vim" with "Practical Vim." But think about the consequences of each approach.

In the first case, we create a record in our command history that reads :%s/Pragmatic Vim/Practical Vim/g. That's unambiguous. Later in our editing session, if we realize that we need to repeat this substitute command, we can dial it up from the command history and play it back as is. No surprises.

In the second case, we create a record in our command history that reads :%s/\=@a/g. That looks pretty cryptic, don't you think?

When we ran this substitute command for the first time, the search pattern was "Pragmatic Vim," while the a register contained the text "Practical Vim." But half an hour later, our current search pattern could have changed dozens of times, and we might have overwritten the a register to contain something else. So if we repeated the :%s/\=@a/g command, it could have a completely different effect!

We could exploit this. We could search for the text we want to act upon and yank its replacement into register a. Then we could replay the :%s/\=@a/g command, and it would use the values of @/ and @a that we had just prepared. Next we could search for something else and yank another replacement string into register a, and when we replayed the :%s/\=@a/g command, it would do something else entirely.

Try it out. You might love it or you might hate it. But either way, it's a pretty neat trick!

Tip 93

Repeat the Previous Substitute Command

At times, we might have to amend the range of a substitute command. We might have made a mistake on our first try, or maybe we just want to rerun the command exactly but on a different buffer. A couple of shortcuts make it easy to repeat the substitute command.

Repeat a Line-Wise Substitution Across the Entire File

Suppose that we've just executed this command, which acts upon the current line:

⇒ `:s/target/replacement/g`

We realize our mistake at once: we should have prepended %. No harm done. We can repeat the command across the entire file just by pressing g& (see :h g& ⓘ), which is equivalent to running the following:

⇒ `:%s//~/&`

This longhand command spells out the following instruction: repeat the last substitute command using the same flags, the same replacement string, and the current search pattern, but use the % range. In other words, repeat the last substitution across the entire file.

The next time you catch yourself tweaking the search history to prepend a % to a substitute command that is otherwise all right, try hitting g& instead.

Amend the Range of a Substitute Command

Start with this code:

substitution/mixin.js
```
mixin = {
    applyName: function(config) {
        return Factory(config, this.getName());
    },
}
```

Suppose that we want to extend it to look like this:

```
mixin = {
    applyName: function(config) {
        return Factory(config, this.getName());
    },
```

```
    applyNumber: function(config) {
        return Factory(config, this.getNumber());
    },
}
```

The new applyNumber function is almost identical to the existing one. So let's start off by duplicating the applyName function. Then we can use the substitute command to change some occurrences of "Name" to "Number." But there's a mistake in the following workflow:

Keystrokes	Buffer Contents
| {start} | ```
mixin = {
    applyName: function(config) {
        return Factory(config, this.getName());
    },
}
``` |
| Vjj | ```
mixin = {
    applyName: function(config) {
        return Factory(config, this.getName());
    },
}
``` |
| yP | ```
mixin = {
    applyName: function(config) {
        return Factory(config, this.getName());
    },
    applyName: function(config) {
        return Factory(config, this.getName());
    },
}
``` |
| :%s/Name/Number/g | ```
mixin = {
    applyNumber: function(config) {
        return Factory(config, this.getNumber());
    },
    applyNumber: function(config) {
        return Factory(config, this.getNumber());
    },
}
``` |

Can you see what went wrong? We used the % symbol as a range, so it changed every occurrence of "Name" to "Number." Instead, we should have specified a range to focus the substitute command on the lines of the second function (the duplicate).

Not to worry. We can easily undo the mistake and fix it. Have a look at the following:

Keystrokes	Buffer Contents
| u | ```
mixin = {
    applyName: function(config) {
        return Factory(config, this.getName());
    },
    applyName: function(config) {
        return Factory(config, this.getName());
    },
}
``` |
| gv | ```
mixin = {
    applyName: function(config) {
        return Factory(config, this.getName());
    },
    applyName: function(config) {
        return Factory(config, this.getName());
    },
}
``` |
| :'<,'>&& | ```
mixin = {
    applyName: function(config) {
        return Factory(config, this.getName());
    },
    applyNumber: function(config) {
        return Factory(config, this.getNumber());
    },
}
``` |

The gv command enables Visual mode and rehighlights the last selection (we discussed it in Tip 21, *Define a Visual Selection*, on page 41). When we press : in Visual mode, the command line is prepopulated with the range :'<,'>, which focuses the next Ex command on the selected lines.

The :&& command requires some explanation, since the first and second & symbols have different meanings. The first one forms the :& Ex command, which repeats the last :substitute command (see :h :& ⓘ), while the second one indicates that the flags from the previous :s command should be reused.

Discussion

We can always specify a new range and replay the substitution using the :&& command. It doesn't matter what range was used the last time. :&& by itself acts on the current line, :'<,'>&& acts on the visual selection, and :%&& acts on the entire file. As we saw already, the g& command is a handy shortcut for :%&&.
```

Fixing the & Command

The & command is a synonym for :s, which repeats the last substitution. Unfortunately, if any flags were used, the & command disregards them, meaning that the outcome could be quite different from the previous substitution.

Making & trigger the :&& command is more useful. It preserves flags and therefore produces more consistent results. These mappings fix the & command in Normal mode and create a Visual mode equivalent:

```
nnoremap & :&&<CR>
xnoremap & :&&<CR>
```

Tip 94

Rearrange CSV Fields Using Submatches

In this tip, we'll see how submatches captured from the search pattern can be referenced in the replacement field.

Let's say that we have a CSV file containing a list of email addresses along with first and last names:

substitution/subscribers.csv
```
last name,first name,email
neil,drew,drew@vimcasts.org
doe,john,john@example.com
```

Now suppose that we want to swap the order of the fields so that the email comes first, then the first name, and finally the last name. We could use this substitute command to do it:

⇒ `/\v^([^,]*),([^,]*),([^,]*)$`
⇒ `:%s//\3,\2,\1`

In the pattern, [^,] matches anything that isn't a comma. So ([^,]*) matches zero or more consecutive non-commas and captures the result as a submatch (refer to Tip 76, *Use Parentheses to Capture Submatches*, on page 191). We repeat this three times to capture each of the three fields in the CSV file.

We can reference these submatches using the \n notation. So, in the replacement field, \1 will refer to the last name field, \2 refers to the first name field, and \3 refers to the email field. Having sliced each line into the individual fields, we can rearrange them into the order we want, namely \3,\2\,1—email, first name, last name.

The result of running this command looks like this:

```
email,first name,last name
drew@vimcasts.org,drew,neil
john@example.com,john,doe
```

Tip 95

Perform Arithmetic on the Replacement

The replacement field needn't be a simple string. We can evaluate a Vim script expression and then use the result as the replacement string. Thus with a single command, we can promote every HTML header tag in a document.

Suppose that we have an HTML document like this:

substitution/headings.html
```
<h2>Heading number 1</h2>
<h3>Number 2 heading</h3>
<h4>Another heading</h4>
```

We want to promote each heading, turning `<h2>` into `<h1>`, `<h3>` into `<h2>`, and so on. To put it another way, we want to subtract one from the numeral part of all HTML header tags.

We'll harness the substitute command to do it. Here's the general idea: we write a pattern that matches the numeral portion of HTML header tags. Then we write a substitute command that uses a Vim script expression to subtract one from the number that was captured. When we run the substitute command globally across the entire file, all HTML header tags will be changed with that single command.

The Search Pattern

The only thing that we want to change is the numeral part of the header tags, so ideally we want to create a pattern that matches that and nothing else. We don't want to match all digits. We only want to match the ones that immediately follow `<h` or `</h`. This pattern should do the trick:

⇒ `/\v\<\/?h\zs\d`

The \zs item allows us to zoom in on part of the match. To simplify our example, we could say that a pattern of h\zs\d would match the letter h followed by any digit (h1, h2, and so on). The placement of \zs indicates that the h itself would be excluded from the match, even though it is an integral part of the broader pattern (we met the \zs item in Tip 78, *Stake the Boundaries of a Match*, on page 194, where we compared it to Perl's positive lookbehind assertion). Our pattern looks slightly more complex, because we don't just match h1 and h2, but <h1, </h1, <h2, </h2, and so on.

Try executing this search for yourself. You should see that the numeral part of each header tag is highlighted, while the freestanding digits are not.

The Substitute Command

We want to perform arithmetic inside the replacement field of our substitute command. To do this, we'll have to evaluate a Vim script expression. We can fetch the current match by calling the submatch(0) function. Since our search pattern matched a digit and nothing else, we can expect that submatch(0) will return a number. From this, we subtract one and return the result to be substituted in place of the match.

This substitute command should work:

⇒ `:%s//\=submatch(0)-1/g`

When we execute the search followed by this substitute command on our fragment of HTML, it produces this result:

```
<h1>Heading number 1</h1>
<h2>Number 2 heading</h2>
<h3>Another heading</h3>
```

All HTML header tags have been changed, but the freestanding numerals have been left untouched.

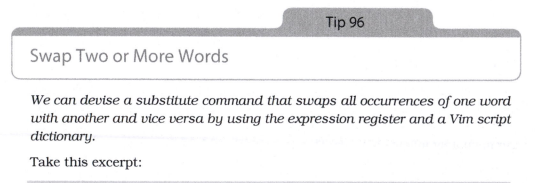

Tip 96

Swap Two or More Words

We can devise a substitute command that swaps all occurrences of one word with another and vice versa by using the expression register and a Vim script dictionary.

Take this excerpt:

substitution/who-bites.txt
```
The dog bit the man.
```

Suppose that we want to swap the order of the words "dog" and "man." We could, of course, use a succession of yank and put operations, as demonstrated in *Swap Two Words*, on page 154. But let's consider how we would go about doing this with the substitute command.

Here's a naïve attempt at a solution:

⇒ `:%s/dog/man/g`
⇒ `:%s/man/dog/g`

The first command replaces the word "dog" with "man," leaving us with the phrase "the man bit the man." Then the second command replaces both occurrences of "man" with "dog," giving us "the dog bit the dog." Clearly, we have to try harder.

A two-pass solution is no good, so we need a substitute command that works in a single pass. The easy part is writing a pattern that matches both "dog" and "man" (think about it). The tricky part is writing an expression that accepts either of these words and returns the other one. Let's solve this part of the puzzle first.

Return the Other Word

We don't even have to create a function to get the job done. We can do it with a simple dictionary data structure by creating two key-value pairs. In Vim, try typing the following:

⇒ `:let swapper={"dog":"man","man":"dog"}`
⇒ `:echo swapper["dog"]`
❮ `man`
⇒ `:echo swapper["man"]`
❮ `dog`

When we pass `"dog"` as a key to our `swapper` dictionary, it returns `"man"`, and vice versa.

Match Both Words

Did you figure out the pattern? Here it is:

⇒ `/\v(<man>|<dog>)`

This pattern simply matches the whole word "man" or the whole word "dog." The parentheses serve to capture the matched text so that we can reference it in the replacement field.

All Together Now

Let's put everything together. We'll start by running the search command. This should cause all occurrences of "dog" and "man" to be highlighted. Then when we run the substitute command, we can leave the search field blank and it will simply reuse the last search pattern (as discussed in Tip 91, *Reuse the Last Search Pattern*, on page 225).

For the replacement, we'll have to evaluate a little bit of Vim script. That means using the \= item in the replacement field. This time, we won't bother assigning the dictionary to a variable, we'll just create it inline for a single use.

Normally we could refer to captured text using Vim's \1, \2 (and so on) notation. But in Vim script, we have to fetch the captured text by calling the submatch() function (see :h submatch() ⓘ).

When we put everything together, this is what we get:

```
⇒ /\v(<man>|<dog>)
⇒ :%s//\={"dog":"man","man":"dog"}[submatch(1)]/g
```

Discussion

This is a daft example! We have to type out the words "man" and "dog" three times each. Obviously, it would be quicker to change the two words in the document, one time each. But if we were working with a large body of text with multiple occurrences of each word, then this extra effort could quickly pay for itself. Note that this technique could easily be adapted to swap three or more words in a single pass.

There still remains the issue of all that typing. With a little bit more Vim script, we could write a custom command that exposed a more user-friendly interface that would do all of the repetitive work for us under the hood. That's beyond the scope of this book, but check out *Abolish.vim: A Supercharged Substitute Command*, on page 237, for inspiration.

Tip 97

Find and Replace Across Multiple Files

The substitute command operates on the current file. So what do we do if we want to make the same substitution throughout an entire project? Although this scenario is common, Vim doesn't include a dedicated command for project-wide

> ## Abolish.vim: A Supercharged Substitute Command
>
> One of my favorite plugins from Tim Pope is called Abolish.[a] It adds a custom command called :Subvert (or :S for short), which acts like a supercharged version of Vim's :substitute command. Using this plugin, we could swap the words "man" and "dog" by issuing the following command:
>
> ⇨ `:%S/{man,dog}/{dog,man}/g`
>
> Not only is this easier to type, but it's much more flexible too. As well as replacing "man" with "dog" (and vice versa), it would also replace "MAN" with "DOG" and "Man" with "Dog." This example merely scratches the surface of this terrific plugin. I encourage you to explore its other capabilities.
>
> _____
>
> a. https://github.com/tpope/vim-abolish

find and replace. We can get this functionality by combining a few of Vim's primitive commands that operate with the quickfix list.

As a demonstration, we'll use the refactor-project directory, which you can find in the source files that come distributed with this book. It contains the following files, reproduced here with their contents:

```
refactor-project/
  about.txt
  Pragmatic Vim is a hands-on guide to working with Vim.

  credits.txt
  Pragmatic Vim is written by Drew Neil.

  license.txt
  The Pragmatic Bookshelf holds the copyright for this book.

  extra/
    praise.txt
    What people are saying about Pragmatic Vim...

    titles.txt
    Other titles from the Pragmatic Bookshelf...
```

Each of these files contains the word "Pragmatic," either as part of the phrase "Pragmatic Bookshelf" or "Pragmatic Vim." We'll do a find and replace to change each occurrence of "Pragmatic Vim" to "Practical Vim" while leaving each occurrence of "Pragmatic Bookshelf" unchanged.

If you'd like to follow along, download the source code from *Practical Vim*'s book page on the Pragmatic Bookshelf site. Before opening Vim, change to the refactor-project directory.

The workflow described here depends on the :cfdo command, which first became available in Vim version 7.4.858. If you are using an older version of Vim you should upgrade to get access to this command.

The Substitute Command

Let's start by devising the substitute command. We want to compose a pattern that matches the word "Pragmatic" when it appears in the phrase "Pragmatic Vim," but not when it appears in the phrase "Pragmatic Bookshelf." This pattern will do the trick:

⇒ `/Pragmatic\ze Vim`

This uses the \ze item to exclude the word "Vim" from the match (see Tip 78, *Stake the Boundaries of a Match*, on page 194). Then we can run this substitute command:

⇒ `:%s//Practical/g`

Next we just need to figure out how to execute that command across the entire project. We'll do this in two steps. First we'll perform a project-wide search for our target pattern. Then we'll run the substitute command on the files that returned a positive match.

Execute a Project-Wide Search Using ':vimgrep'

To perform a project-wide search, we'll reach for the :vimgrep command (see Tip 111, *Grep with Vim's Internal Search Engine*, on page 277). Since this uses Vim's built-in search engine, we can reuse the exact same pattern. Try running this:

⇒ `/Pragmatic\ze Vim`
⇒ `:vimgrep // **/*.txt`

The search field for this command is delimited by the two adjacent / characters. We've left the search field blank, which tells Vim to run :vimgrep using the last search pattern. We use the **/*.txt wildcard to tell vimgrep to look inside all files contained in the current directory that use the .txt extension.

Execute a Project-Wide Substitute Command Using ':cfdo'

Each match returned by vimgrep is recorded in the quickfix list (see Chapter 17, *Compile Code and Navigate Errors with the Quickfix List*, on page 263). We can browse the results by running :copen, which opens the quickfix window. But instead of stepping through the results one at a time, we want to run the substitute command on every file that appears in the quickfix list. We can do so using the :cfdo command (see :h :cfdo ⓘ).

Before using the :cfdo command, make sure the hidden setting is enabled:

⇒ `:set hidden`

This setting enables us to navigate away from a modified file without first saving it. Refer to Tip 38, *Group Buffers into a Collection with the Argument List*, on page 86, for a more detailed discussion.

Now we can execute our substitution command across all the files in the quickfix list by running this:

⇒ `:cfdo %s//Practical/gc`

The c flag is optional here. It lets us view each match and decide whether we want to perform the substitution (see Tip 90, *Eyeball Each Substitution*, on page 223). We'll finish by writing the changes to disk:

⇒ `:cfdo update`

The :update command saves the file, but only if it has been changed (see :h update ⓘ).

Note that the last two commands could be combined into one, like this:

⇒ `:cfdo %s//Practical/g | update`

The | character has a different meaning on Vim's command line than shell users might expect. In Unix, the pipe character passes standard output from one command into the standard input of the next command (creating a "pipeline"). In Vim, | is simply a command separator, making it equivalent to the semicolon in the Unix shell. Look up :h :bar ⓘ for more details.

Summary

Here's the complete sequence of commands:

⇒ `/Pragmatic\ze Vim`
⇒ `:vimgrep // **/*.txt`
⇒ `:cfdo %s//Practical/gc`
⇒ `:cfdo update`

We start by composing a search pattern and checking that it works in the current buffer. Then we use :vimgrep to search the whole project for the same pattern, populating the quickfix list with the results. We can then iterate through the files in the quickfix list using :cfdo to run the :substitute and :update commands.

Global Commands

The :global command combines the power of Ex commands with Vim's pattern matching abilities—it runs an Ex command on each line that matches a specified pattern. Alongside the Dot Formula and macros, the :global command is one of Vim's power tools for performing repetitive work efficiently.

Tip 98

Meet the Global Command

The :global command allows us to run an Ex command on each line that matches a particular pattern. Let's start by studying its syntax.

The :global command takes the following form (see :h :g ⓘ):

```
:[range] global[!] /{pattern}/ [cmd]
```

The default range for the :global command is the entire file (%). That sets it apart from most other Ex commands, including :delete, :substitute, and :normal, whose range is the current line (.) by default.

The {pattern} field integrates with search history. That means we can leave it blank and Vim will automatically use the current search pattern.

The [cmd] could be any Ex command except for another :global command. In practice, Ex commands that interact with the text in the document prove most useful, such as those in Table 7, *Ex Commands That Operate on the Text in a Buffer*, on page 54. If we don't specify a [cmd], then Vim will use :print by default.

We can invert the behavior of the :global command either by running :global! or :vglobal (mnemonic: in*vert*). Each of these tells Vim to execute [cmd] on each line that *doesn't* match the specified pattern. In the next tip, we'll see examples of both :global and :vglobal in action.

The :global command works by making two passes through the lines specified by [range]. In the first pass, Vim marks each line that matches the specified {pattern}. Then on the second pass, the [cmd] is executed for each marked line. The [cmd] can accept a range of its own, which allows us to operate on multiline regions. This powerful technique is demonstrated by Tip 101, *Alphabetize the Properties of Each Rule in a CSS File*, on page 246.

On the Etymology of Grep

Consider this abbreviated form of the :global command:

➡ `:g/re/p`

re stands for regular expression, and p is short for :print, which is the default [cmd]. If we ignore the / symbols, we find the word "grep."

Tip 99

Delete Lines Containing a Pattern

Combining the :global and :delete commands allows us to cut down the size of a file rapidly. We can either keep or discard all lines that match a {pattern}.

This file contains links to the first few episodes from the Vimcasts.org archive:

```
global/episodes.html
<ol>
  <li>
    <a href="/episodes/show-invisibles/">
      Show invisibles
    </a>
  </li>
  <li>
    <a href="/episodes/tabs-and-spaces/">
      Tabs and Spaces
    </a>
  </li>
  <li>
    <a href="/episodes/whitespace-preferences-and-filetypes/">
      Whitespace preferences and filetypes
    </a>
  </li>
</ol>
```

Each list item contains two pieces of data: the title of an episode and its URL. We'll use a :global command to expose each of these.

Delete Matching Lines with ':g/re/d'

What if we wanted to throw away everything except for the contents of each <a> tag? In this file, the contents of each link appear on a line of their own, while every other line of the file contains either an opening or a closing tag. So if we can devise a pattern that matches HTML tags, we could use it with the :global command to reject any lines that match the pattern.

These commands would do the trick:

⇒ `/\v\<\/?\w+>`
⇒ `:g//d`

If we run these two commands on the Vimcasts.org archive file, we're left with this:

```
Show invisibles
Tabs and Spaces
Whitespace preferences and filetypes
```

Just like with the :substitute command, we can leave the search field of the :global command blank, and Vim will reuse the last search pattern (see Tip 91, *Reuse the Last Search Pattern*, on page 225). That means that we can build our regular expression by starting with a broad match and then narrowing it, as demonstrated in Tip 85, *Create Complex Patterns by Iterating upon Search History*, on page 211.

The regular expression uses very magic mode (covered in Tip 74, *Use the \v Pattern Switch for Regex Searches*, on page 187). It matches an opening angle bracket (\<), followed by an optional forward slash (\/?), and then one or more word characters (\w+) followed by an end-of-word delimiter (>). This is not an all-purpose tag-matching regex, but it's good enough for this particular case.

Keep Only Matching Lines with ':v/re/d'

This time we'll switch things around. The :vglobal command, or :v for short, does the opposite of the :g command. That is, it executes a command on each line that does not match the specified pattern.

The lines containing the URLs are easy to identify: they all contain the href attribute. We can select only those lines by running this command:

⇒ `:v/href/d`

This can be read as "Delete each line that *doesn't* contain href." The result looks like this:

```
<a href="/episodes/show-invisibles/">
<a href="/episodes/tabs-and-spaces/">
<a href="/episodes/whitespace-preferences-and-filetypes/">
```

With a single command, we've condensed the file to the lines that interest us.

Tip 100

Collect TODO Items in a Register

Combining the :global and :yank commands allows us to collect all lines that match a {pattern} in a register.

This excerpt of code contains a couple of comments that lead with "TODO":

global/markdown.js
```
Markdown.dialects.Gruber = {
    lists: function() {
        // TODO: Cache this regexp for certain depths.
        function regex_for_depth(depth) { /* implementation */ }
    },
    "`": function inlineCode( text ) {
        var m = text.match( /(`+)(([\s\S]*?)\1)/ );
        if ( m && m[2] )
            return [ m[1].length + m[2].length ];
        else {
            // TODO: No matching end code found - warn!
            return [ 1, "`" ];
        }
    }
}
```

Suppose that we wanted to collect all of the TODO items in one place. We could view them all at a glance by running this command:

⇒ **:g/TODO**

‹
```
    // TODO: Cache this regexp for certain depths.
        // TODO: No matching end code found - warn!
```

Remember, :print is the default [cmd] for the :global command. This simply echoes each line containing the word "TODO." It's not a great deal of use though, because the messages disappear as soon as we execute another command.

Here's an alternative strategy: let's yank each line containing the word "TODO" into a register. Then we can paste the contents of that register into another file and keep them around for later.

We'll use the a register. First we'll need to clear it by running `qaq`. Let's break that down: `qa` tells Vim to start recording a macro into the a register, and then `q` stops the recording. We didn't type anything while the macro was recording, so the register ends up empty. We can check that by running the following:

```
⇒   :reg a
‹   --- Registers ---
    "a
```

Now we can go ahead and yank the TODO comments into the register:

```
⇒   :g/TODO/yank A
⇒   :reg a
‹   "a   // TODO: Cache this regexp for certain depths.
         // TODO: No matching end code found - warn!
```

The trick here is that we've addressed our register with an uppercase A. That tells Vim to *append* to the specified register, whereas a lowercase a would overwrite the register's contents. We can read the global command as "For each line that matches the pattern /TODO/, append the entire line into register a."

This time, when we run `:reg a`, we can see that the register contains the two TODO items from the document. (For the sake of legibility, I've formatted these items on two separate lines, but in Vim it actually shows a ^J symbol for newlines.) We could then open up a new buffer in a split window and run `"ap` to paste the a register into the new document.

Discussion

In this example, we've just collected two TODO items, which we could have done by hand quite rapidly. But this technique scales well. If the document contained a dozen TODO items, it would require the same effort on our part.

We could even combine the `:global` command with either `:bufdo` or `:argdo` to collect all TODO items from a set of files. I'll leave that as an exercise for you, but look to Tip 36, *Run Multiple Ex Commands as a Batch*, on page 76, for a hint at the workflow.

Here's an alternative solution:

```
⇒   :g/TODO/t$
```

It uses the :t command, which we met in Tip 29, *Duplicate or Move Lines Using ':t' and ':m' Commands*, on page 61. Rather than appending each TODO item to a register, we simply copy it to the end of the file. After running this command, we could jump to the end of the file to review the TODO items. This technique is more straightforward because it avoids messing around with registers. But it won't work as neatly with the :argdo and :bufdo commands.

Tip 101

Alphabetize the Properties of Each Rule in a CSS File

When combining an Ex command with :global, we can also specify a range for our chosen [cmd]. Vim allows us to set the range dynamically using the :g/{pattern} as a reference point. Here we'll see how we can exploit this fact to alphabetize the properties within each block of a CSS file.

We'll use this CSS file for demonstration purposes:

global/unsorted.css
```
Line 1  html {
            margin: 0;
            padding: 0;
            border: 0;
     5      font-size: 100%;
            font: inherit;
            vertical-align: baseline;
        }
        body {
    10      line-height: 1.5;
            color: black;
            background: white;
        }
```

Suppose that we want to sort the properties of each rule into alphabetical order. We could do so using Vim's built-in :sort command (:h :sort ⓘ).

Sort Properties for a Single Block of Rules

Let's start by trying out the :sort command on a subset of the file. (See Table 16, *Sort a Subset of a File*, on page 247.)

We can easily select the lines inside a {} block using the `vi{` text object. Running :'<,'>sort then rearranges the lines into alphabetical order. This technique works great if we just have to sort one block of rules at a time, but

Keystrokes	Buffer Contents
| {start} | ```
html {
    margin: 0;
    padding: 0;
    border: 0;
    font-size: 100%;
    font: inherit;
    vertical-align: baseline;
}
``` |
| vi{ | ```
html {
    margin: 0;
    padding: 0;
    border: 0;
    font-size: 100%;
    font: inherit;
    vertical-align: baseline;
}
``` |
| :'<,'>sort | ```
html {
    border: 0;
    font-size: 100%;
    font: inherit;
    margin: 0;
    padding: 0;
    vertical-align: baseline;
}
``` |

Table 16—Sort a Subset of a File

suppose that we had a style sheet containing hundreds of rules. Wouldn't it be better if we could automate the process somehow?

Sort Properties for Every Block of Rules

We can sort the properties for every block of rules in the file with a single :global command. Say we run this command on our style sheet:

```
:g/{/ .+1,/}/-1 sort
```

We should end up with this result:

```
html {
  border: 0;
  font-size: 100%;
  font: inherit;
  margin: 0;
  padding: 0;
  vertical-align: baseline;
}
```
```

```
body {
  background: white;
  color: black;
  line-height: 1.5;
}
```

The sort command has been executed inside the {} block for each rule. Our sample style sheet only contains a dozen lines, but this technique would work just as well for a longer CSS file.

This command is complex, but understanding how it works will help us to appreciate just how powerful the :global command can be. The standard form looks like this:

`:g/{pattern}/[cmd]`

Remember: Ex commands can usually accept a range themselves (as discussed in Tip 28, *Execute a Command on One or More Consecutive Lines*, on page 56). This is still true for the [cmd] in the context of a :global command. So we could expand the template as follows:

`:g/{pattern}/[range][cmd]`

The [range] for our [cmd] can be set dynamically using the match from :g/{pattern} as a reference point. Normally the . address stands for the line that the cursor is positioned on. But in the context of a :global command, it stands for each line in turn that matches the specified {pattern}.

We can break our command into two separate Ex commands. Let's work our way backward from the end. This is a valid Ex command:

⇒ `:.+1,/}/-1 sort`

If we strip out the offsets from our range, it becomes simply .,/}/. We can interpret this as "from the current line up until the next line that matches the /}/ pattern." The +1 and -1 offsets simply narrow the range to focus on the contents of the {} block. If we place our cursor on either line 1 or line 9 of our original unsorted CSS file, then this Ex command would alphabetize the rules inside the corresponding {} block.

We just need to position our cursor at the start of each {} block and then run the :.,/}/sort command to alphabetize the rules inside that block. Got that? Now try executing a search using the {pattern} from our :global command:

⇒ `/{/`

That places our cursor at the top of a {} block, right where we need it. Now let's put our :global and [cmd] Ex commands back together:

⇒ `:g/{/ .+1,/}/-1 sort`

The { pattern matches the first line of each {} block. For every line that matches, the :sort command is executed on a [range] that terminates at the end of the {} block. The end result is that all CSS properties are alphabetized within each block of rules.

Discussion

A generalized form of this :global command goes like this:

`:g/{start}/ .,{finish} [cmd]`

We can read this as "For each range of lines beginning with {start} and ending with {finish}, run the specified [cmd]."

We could use the same formula for a :global command in combination with any Ex command. For example, suppose that we wanted to indent the specified ranges. We could do so with the :> Ex command (see :h :> ⓘ):

⇒ `:g/{/ .+1,/}/-1 >`
❮ 6 lines >ed 1 time
  3 lines >ed 1 time

Note that the :> command echoes a message each time it is invoked, whereas :sort doesn't. We can mute these messages by prefixing our [cmd] with :silent (see :h :sil ⓘ):

⇒ `:g/{/sil .+1,/}/-1 >`

This technique is especially useful in cases where the :g/{pattern} matches a large number of lines.

Part VI

Tools

"Do one thing, and do it well" is a principle of Unix philosophy. Vim provides wrapper commands that make it easy to call external programs such as make or grep. Some tasks require deeper integration with the text editor, so Vim provides native tools for spell checking and autocompletion and also provides a built-in :vimgrep command. In this part of the book we'll study Vim's toolbox and its interface for working with external tools.

CHAPTER 16

Index and Navigate Source Code with ctags

ctags is an external program that scans through a codebase and generates an index of keywords. It was originally built into Vim, but with the release of Vim version 6, ctags became a separate project. That heritage is evident today in Vim's tight integration with ctags.

Vim's ctags support allows us to navigate around a codebase by quickly jumping to definitions of functions and classes. We'll see how in Tip 104, *Navigate Keyword Definitions with Vim's Tag Navigation Commands*, on page 258. As a secondary benefit, we can also use the output from ctags to generate a word list for autocompletion, as we'll see in *Tag Files*, on page 287.

Tag navigation and tag autocompletion won't work unless Vim knows where to look for an up-to-date index file. Tip 103, *Configure Vim to Work with ctags*, on page 256, shows how to configure Vim to work with ctags. But first, let's find out how to install and execute ctags.

Tip 102

Meet ctags

To use Vim's tag navigation features, we must first install ctags. Then we'll learn how to execute the program and understand the index that it generates.

Installing Exuberant Ctags

Linux users should be able to get ctags with their package manager. For example, on Ubuntu you can install it by running the following:

```
$ sudo apt-get install exuberant-ctags
```

OS X ships with a BSD program called ctags. Beware: this is not the same thing as Exuberant Ctags. You'll have to install Exuberant Ctags yourself. Using homebrew, it's as easy as this:

```
$ brew install ctags
```

Check that ctags is installed and that it's in your path by running the following:

```
$ ctags --version
Exuberant Ctags 5.8, Copyright (C) 1996-2009 Darren Hiebert
Compiled: Dec 18 2010, 22:44:26
...
```

If you don't get this message, you might have to modify your $PATH. Make sure that /usr/local/bin takes precedence over /usr/bin.

Indexing a Codebase with ctags

We can invoke ctags from the command line, giving it the path for one or more files that we would like it to index. The source code distributed with this book includes a small demo program consisting of three Ruby files. Let's run ctags on this codebase:

```
$ cd code/ctags
$ ls
anglophone.rb francophone.rb speaker.rb
$ ctags *.rb
$ ls
anglophone.rb francophone.rb speaker.rb tags
```

Note that ctags has created a plain-text file called tags. It contains an index of the keywords from the three source files that ctags analyzed.

The Anatomy of a tags File

Let's look inside the tags file we just generated. Note that some lines have been truncated to fit the page:

```
ctags/tags-abridged
!_TAG_FILE_FORMAT       2       /extended format/
!_TAG_FILE_SORTED       1       /0=unsorted, 1=sorted, 2=foldcase/
!_TAG_PROGRAM_AUTHOR    Darren Hiebert //
!_TAG_PROGRAM_NAME      Exuberant Ctags //
```

```
!_TAG_PROGRAM_URL        http://ctags.sourceforge.net    /official site/
!_TAG_PROGRAM_VERSION    5.8    //
Anglophone      anglophone.rb   /^class Anglophone < Speaker$/;"        c
Francophone     francophone.rb  /^class Francophone < Speaker$/;"       c
Speaker speaker.rb      /^class Speaker$/;"     c
initialize      speaker.rb      /^  def initialize(name)$/;"    f
speak   anglophone.rb   /^  def speak$/;"        f       class:Anglophone
speak   francophone.rb  /^  def speak$/;"        f       class:Francophone
speak   speaker.rb      /^  def speak$/;"        f       class:Speaker
```

The tags file begins with a few lines of metadata. After that it lists one keyword per line, along with the filename and address where that keyword is defined in the source code. The keywords are arranged in alphabetical order, so Vim (or any text editor, for that matter) can rapidly locate them with a binary search.

Keywords Are Addressed by Pattern, Not by Line Number

The specification for the tags file format states that the address could be any Ex command. One option would be to use absolute line numbers. For example, we could make the cursor jump to an address on line 42 with the Ex command :42. But think of how brittle that could be. Adding just one new line at the top of a file would throw every address out of step.

Instead, ctags uses the search command to address each keyword (if you're not convinced that search is an Ex command, try entering :/pattern). This method is more robust than using line numbers, but it's still not perfect. What if the search command used to address a particular keyword had more than one match for a given file?

That situation shouldn't arise, because the pattern can match as many lines of code as is necessary to produce a unique address. So long as the line length doesn't exceed 512 characters, a tags file will remain backward compatible with vi. Of course, as a search pattern becomes longer, it, too, becomes brittle in its own way.

Keywords Are Tagged with Metadata

The classic tags file format only required three tab-separated fields: the keyword, the filename, and the address. But the extended format used today allows for additional fields at the end to provide metadata about the keyword. In this example, we can see that the Anglophone, Francophone, and Speaker keywords are labeled c for class, while initialize and speak are labeled f for function.

> ## Extending ctags or Using a Compatible Tag Generator
>
> ctags can be extended to work with languages that are not supported out of the box. By using the --regex, --langdef, and --langmap options, we can define regular expressions to create simple rules for indexing the key constructs of any language. We also have the option of droping down into C to write a parser. Parsers written in C tend to perform better than parsers specified as regular expressions, so if you're working with a large codebase, this could make a big difference.
>
> Instead of extending ctags, another option is to create a dedicated tool for indexing your chosen language. For example, gotags is a ctags-compatible tag generator for Go, itself implemented in Go.[a] It produces output in the same format as ctags, so it works seamlessly with Vim.
>
> There's nothing proprietary about the tags file format; it's plain text. Anybody can write a script to generate tags files that Vim understands.
>
> _____
>
> a.   https://github.com/jstemmer/gotags

Tip 103

Configure Vim to Work with ctags

If we want to use Vim's ctag navigation commands, we must ensure that the tags file is up-to-date and that Vim knows where to look for it.

Tell Vim Where to Find the Tags File

The 'tags' option specifies where Vim should look to find a tags file (:h 'tags' ⓘ). When ./ is used in the 'tags' option, Vim replaces it with the path of the currently active file. We can inspect the defaults:

```
⇒ :set tags?
❮ tags=./tags,tags
```

With these settings, Vim looks for a tags file in the directory of the current file and in the working directory. Under certain conditions, if a match is found in the first tags file, Vim won't even look in the second file (see :h tags-option ⓘ for more details). Using Vim's default settings, we could keep a tags file in every subdirectory of our project. Or we could keep it simple by creating a global tags file in the project root directory.

If you run ctags often enough to keep the index up-to-date, then your tags file (or files) could show up in every source code check-in. To keep your commit history clean, tell your source control to ignore tags files.

Generate the tags File

As we saw in *Indexing a Codebase with ctags*, on page 254, ctags can be executed from the command line. But we needn't leave Vim to regenerate the tags file.

Simple Case: Execute ctags Manually

We can invoke ctags directly from Vim by running the following:

⇒ `:!ctags -R`

Starting from Vim's current working directory, this command would recurse through all subdirectories, indexing every file. The resulting tags file would be written in the current working directory.

If we were to tweak the command by adding such options as --exclude=.git or --languages=-sql, typing it out would become more of a chore. We could save ourselves some time by creating a mapping for it:

⇒ `:nnoremap <f5> :!ctags -R<CR>`

That lets us rebuild the index just by pressing the <F5> key, but we still have to remember periodically to generate the tags file. Now let's consider a couple of options for automating this process.

Automatically Execute ctags Each Time a File is Saved

Vim's autocommand feature allows us to invoke a command on each occurrence of an event, such as a buffer being created, opened, or written to file. We could set up an autocommand that invokes ctags every time we save a file:

⇒ `:autocmd BufWritePost * call system("ctags -R")`

This would re-index our entire codebase each time we saved changes to a single file.

Automatically Execute ctags with Version Control Hooks

Most source control systems provide hooks that allow us to execute a script in response to events on the repository. We can use these to instruct our source control to re-index the repository every time we commit our code.

In "Effortless Ctags with Git," Tim Pope demonstrates how to set up hooks for the post-commit, post-merge, and post-checkout events.[1] The beauty of this solution is that it uses global hooks, so configuring each individual repository on your system is unnecessary.

Discussion

Each strategy for indexing our source code has its pros and cons. The manual solution is simplest, but having to remember to regenerate the index means that it's more likely to go stale.

Using an autocommand to invoke ctags every time a buffer is saved ensures that our tags file is always up-to-date, but at what cost? For a small codebase, the time taken to run ctags may be imperceptible, but for larger projects, the lag may be long enough to interrupt our workflow. Also, this technique is blind to any changes that happen to a file outside of the editor.

Re-indexing our codebase on each commit strikes a good balance. Sure, the tags file might fall out of step with our working copy, but the errors are tolerable. The code that we're actively working on is the code we're least likely to want to navigate using tags. And remember that keywords in the tags file are addressed with a search command (see *The Anatomy of a tags File*, on page 254), which makes them reasonably robust in the face of changes.

Tip 104

Navigate Keyword Definitions with Vim's Tag Navigation Commands

Vim's ctags integration turns the keywords in our code into a kind of hyperlink, allowing us to jump rapidly to a definition. We'll see how to use the Normal mode `<C-]>` and `g<C-]>` commands as well as their complementary Ex commands.

Jump to a Keyword Definition

Pressing `<C-]>` makes our cursor jump from the keyword under the cursor to the definition. Here it is in action:

---

1. http://tbaggery.com/2011/08/08/effortless-ctags-with-git.html

Keystrokes	Buffer Contents

{start}	```require './speaker.rb'```
	```class Anglophone < Speaker```
	``` def speak```
	``` puts "Hello, my name is #{@name}"```
	``` end```
	```end```
	```Anglophone.new('Jack').speak```

`<C-]>`	```require './speaker.rb'```
	```class Anglophone < Speaker```
	``` def speak```
	``` puts "Hello, my name is #{@name}"```
	``` end```
	```end```
	```Anglophone.new('Jack').speak```

In this case, the definition of the Anglophone class happens to be in the same buffer, but if we move our cursor onto the Speaker keyword and invoke the same command, we'll switch to the buffer where that class is defined:

Keystrokes	Buffer Contents

`fS`	```require './speaker.rb'```
	```class Anglophone < Speaker```
	``` def speak```
	``` puts "Hello, my name is #{@name}"```
	``` end```
	```end```
	```Anglophone.new('Jack').speak```

`<C-]>`	```class Speaker```
	``` def initialize(name)```
	``` @name = name```
	``` end```
	``` def speak```
	``` puts "#{name}"```
	``` end```
	```end```

As we navigate our codebase in this fashion, Vim maintains a history of the tags we've visited. The `<C-t>` command acts as the back button for our tag history. If we pressed it now, we would jump from the Speaker definition back to the Francophone definition, and if we pressed it a second time, it would take us back to where we started. For more information on interacting with the tag jump list, look up :h tag-stack ⓘ.

Specify Where to Jump to When a Keyword Has Multiple Matches

Our previous example was straightforward because the demo codebase contains only one definition for the Speaker and Anglophone keywords. But suppose that our cursor was positioned on an invocation of the speak method, like this:

```
Anglophone.new('Jack').speak
```

The Speaker, Francophone, and Anglophone classes all define a function called speak, so which one will Vim jump to if we invoke the `<C-]>` command now? Try it yourself.

If a tag in the current buffer matches the keyword, it gets the highest priority. So in this case, we would jump to the definition of the speak function in the Anglophone class. Look up :h tag-priority ⓘ if you want to know more about how Vim ranks matching tags.

Instead of `<C-]>`, we could use the `g<C-]>` command. Both of these commands behave identically in the case when the current keyword has only a single match. But if it has multiple matches, then the `g<C-]>` command presents us with a list of choices from the tag match list:

```
# pri kind tag             file
1 F C f    speak           anglophone.rb
             class:Anglophone
             def speak
2 F   f    speak           francophone.rb
             class:Francophone
             def speak
3 F   f    speak           speaker.rb
             class:Speaker
             def speak
Type number and <Enter> (empty cancels):
```

As the prompt indicates, we can choose which destination we want to jump to by typing its number and pressing `<CR>`.

Suppose that we invoked `<C-]>` and found ourselves on the wrong definition. We could use the :tselect command to retrospectively pull up the menu of the tag match list. Or we could use the :tnext command to jump to the next matching tag without showing a prompt. As you might expect, this command is complemented with :tprev, :tfirst, and :tlast. Refer to the discussion of the unimpaired plugin on page 85, for a suggested set of mappings for these commands.

Use Ex Commands

We don't have to move the cursor on top of a keyword to jump to its tag. We could just as well call an Ex command. For example, :tag {keyword} and :tjump {keyword} behave like the <C-]> and g<C-]> commands, respectively (see :h :tag ⓘ and :h :tjump ⓘ).

At times, typing these commands can be quicker than maneuvering the cursor onto a keyword in the document—especially since Vim provides tab-completion for all keywords in the tags file. For example, we could type :tag Fran<Tab>, and Vim would expand our fragment to Francophone.

Also, these Ex commands can accept a regular expression when used in the form :tag /{pattern} or :tjump /{pattern} (note the leading / before {pattern}). For example, to navigate between any definitions whose keywords end with phone, we could invoke the following:

```
⇒ :tjump /phone$
‹ # pri kind tag
  1 F C c    Anglophone        anglophone.rb
                class Anglophone < Speaker
  2 F   c    Francophone       francophone.rb
                class Francophone < Speaker
  Type number and <Enter> (empty cancels):
```

Here are the commands that we can use to navigate our codebase using tags:

Command	Effect
<C-]>	Jump to the first tag that matches the word under the cursor
g<C-]>	Prompt user to select from multiple matches for the word under the cursor. If only one match exists, jump to it without prompting.
:tag {keyword}	Jump to the first tag that matches {keyword}
:tjump {keyword}	Prompt user to select from multiple matches for {keyword}. If only one match exists, jump to it without prompting.
:pop or <C-t>	Reverse through tag history
:tag	Advance through tag history
:tnext	Jump to next matching tag
:tprev	Jump to previous matching tag
:tfirst	Jump to first matching tag
:tlast	Jump to last matching tag
:tselect	Prompt user to choose an item from the tag match list

CHAPTER 17

Compile Code and Navigate Errors with the Quickfix List

Vim's quickfix list is a core feature that allows us to integrate external tools into our workflow. At its simplest, it maintains a sequence of annotated addresses comprising the filename, line number, column number (optional), and a message. Traditionally, these addresses would be a list of error messages generated by a compiler, but they could just as well be warnings from a syntax checker, linter, or any other tool that emits such output.

We'll start off by looking at an example workflow: running make in an external shell and navigating to error messages by hand. Then we'll introduce the :make command, seeing how it can streamline our workflow by parsing error messages from the compiler and making them navigable in the form of the quickfix list.

Tip 106, *Browse the Quickfix List*, on page 266, provides a tour of the most useful commands for navigating the results of running :make. Then in Tip 107, *Recall Results from a Previous Quickfix List*, on page 269, we'll learn that the quickfix feature has its own form of the undo command.

In Tip 108, *Customize the External Compiler*, on page 269, we'll walk through the steps required to configure Vim so that calling :make puts the contents of a JavaScript file through JSLint, generating a navigable quickfix list from the output.

Tip 105

Compile Code Without Leaving Vim

Calling an external compiler from Vim saves us from having to leave our editor—and if the compiler reports any errors, Vim provides the means for us to jump between them quickly.

Preparation

We'll use a small C program to demonstrate. The source files are distributed with this book (for more details, refer to *Downloading the Examples*, on page xxiv). In the shell, change to the code/quickfix/wakeup directory:

⇒ **$ cd code/quickfix/wakeup**

You'll need gcc to build this program, but don't feel that you need to install a compiler just to follow this tip. The workflow here demonstrates the task for which the quickfix list was originally conceived (and from which it takes its name). As we'll soon see, this feature has many other uses.

Compile the Project in the Shell

The wakeup program provided consists of three files: Makefile, wakeup.c, and wakeup.h. From the shell, we could compile it by running make:

⇒ **$ make**
❮ gcc   -c -o wakeup.o wakeup.c
wakeup.c:68: error: conflicting types for 'generatePacket'
wakeup.h:3: error: previous declaration of 'generatePacket' was here
make: *** [wakeup.o] Error 1

The compiler helpfully reports a couple of errors. It's all very well having this information printed in the terminal, but now we need to navigate to each of the errors so that we can fix them in Vim.

Compile the Project from Inside Vim

Instead of running make in the shell, let's try building the project from inside Vim. Make sure that you're in the code/quickfix/wakeup directory and that it includes a Makefile file, and then launch Vim like this:

❮ $ pwd; ls
~/code/quickfix/wakeup
Makefile wakeup.c wakeup.h
⇒ **$ vim -u NONE -N wakeup.c**

From inside Vim, we can now run the :make command:

⇒ `:make`

❮
```
gcc      -c -o wakeup.o wakeup.c
wakeup.c:68: error: conflicting types for 'generatePacket'
wakeup.h:3: error: previous declaration of 'generatePacket' was here
make: *** [wakeup.o] Error 1

Press ENTER or type command to continue
```

We get the same result as when we ran make in the shell—except that Vim does something smart with the output. Instead of just echoing the output from make, Vim parses each line, extracting the filename, line number, and error message. For each warning, Vim creates a record in the quickfix list. We can navigate backward and forward through these records, and Vim jumps to the exact line corresponding to the error message. As Vim's documentation on quickfix says (:h quickfix ⓘ), it allows us to "speed up the edit-compile-edit cycle."

Vim jumps to the first record in the quickfix list when we run :make. In our case, we should find ourselves in the file wakeup.c at the top of this function:

```
void generatePacket(uint8_t *mac, uint8_t *packet)
{
  int i, j, k;
  k = 6;
  for (i = 0; i <= 15; i++)
  {
    for (j = 0; j <= 5; j++, k++)
    {
      packet[k] = mac[j];
    }
  }
}
```

The error message reports "conflicting types for 'generatePacket'." We can skip to the next location in the quickfix list by running the command :cnext. In this case, we jump to the file wakeup.h and find ourselves on this line:

```
void generatePacket(char *, char *);
```

That explains why the compiler was complaining: the signature for this function in the header file doesn't match the one used in the implementation. Let's change the line in the header file to use the uint8_t type. Make it so:

```
void generatePacket(uint8_t *, uint8_t *);
```

Save the changes to the file, and then we'll call :make again:

⇒ `:write`

⇒ `:make`

‹
```
gcc    -c -o wakeup.o wakeup.c
gcc -o wakeup wakeup.o
```

This time the program compiles successfully. Our quickfix list is updated to use the output from the latest invocation of make. No errors are reported, so our cursor stays put.

Don't Lose the Place

When we run the :make command, Vim automatically jumps to the first error (unless there are none). If we prefer that our cursor remain where it is, we can instead run this:

⇒ `:make!`

The trailing ! character tells Vim to update the quickfix list without jumping to the first item. Now suppose that we run :make and immediately realize that we should have used the bang version. How can we get back to where we were before we ran :make? Simple: use the `<C-o>` command to jump back to the previous position in the jump list. See Tip 56, *Traverse the Jump List*, on page 135, for more details.

Tip 106

Browse the Quickfix List

The quickfix list holds a collection of locations from one or more files. Each record could be an error raised by the compiler when running :make, or it could be a search match from running :grep. No matter how the list was forged, we must be able to navigate these records. In this tip, we'll review the ways of browsing the quickfix list.

An exhaustive list of commands for navigating the quickfix list can be found by looking up :h quickfix ⓘ. Table 17, *Commands for Working with the Quickfix List*, on page 267 shows some of the most useful.

They all begin with :c. The location list (see *Meet the Location List*, on page 267) has equivalents for all of these commands, each beginning with :l, such as :lnext, :lprev, and so on. The :ll N command, which jumps to the *n*th item in the location list, makes a natural diversion from this pattern.

Command	Action
:cnext	Jump to next item
:cprev	Jump to previous item
:cfirst	Jump to first item
:clast	Jump to last item
:cnfile	Jump to first item in next file
:cpfile	Jump to last item in previous file
:cc N	Jump to nth item
:copen	Open the quickfix window
:cclose	Close the quickfix window
:cdo {cmd}	Execute {cmd} on each line listed in the quickfix list
:cfdo {cmd}	Execute {cmd} once for each file listed in the quickfix list

Table 17—Commands for Working with the Quickfix List

Meet the Location List

For every command that populates the quickfix list, there's a variant that places the results in a location list instead. While :make, :grep, and :vimgrep use the quickfix list, :lmake, :lgrep, and :lvimgrep use the location list. So what's the difference? At any given moment, there can be only one quickfix list, but we can create as many location lists as we want.

Suppose that we've followed the steps in Tip 108, *Customize the External Compiler*, on page 269, so that running :make in a JavaScript file passes the contents of the file through JSLint. Now let's say that we've got two different JavaScript files open in split windows. We run :lmake to compile the contents of the active window, which saves any error messages to the location list. Then we switch to the other window and run :lmake again. Rather than overwriting the existing location list, Vim creates a new one. Now we have two location lists, each containing errors for a different JavaScript file.

Any commands that interact with a location list (:lnext, :lprev, and so on) will act on the list that is bound to the currently active window. Compare this with the quickfix list, which is available globally throughout Vim: no matter which tab page or window is active, when you run :copen, the quickfix window will show the same list.

Basic Quickfix Motions

We can iterate forward and backward through the items in the quickfix list with the :cnext and :cprevious commands. If we want to skip to the start or end of the list, we can do so with the :cfirst and :clast commands. We'll use these four commands a lot, so it's a good idea to map them to something easier to reach. See the discussion of the unimpaired plugin on page 85 for a suggestion.

Quickfix Fast Forward/Rewind

Both :cnext and :cprev can be prepended with a count. So instead of stepping through every item in the quickfix list one by one, we could skip through them five at a time by running this:

⇒   `:5cnext`

Suppose that we're browsing through the quickfix list and we come upon a file with dozens of matches, none of which are of much interest to us. In this scenario, rather than stepping through the results one at a time (or even ten at a time), it would be handy if we could just skip all of the results in that file by jumping to the first record in the *next* file. That's what the :cnfile command does. As you'd expect, the :cpfile does the same in reverse, jumping to the last quickfix record in the previous file.

Use the Quickfix Window

We can open a window containing the contents of the quickfix list by running :copen. In some ways, this window behaves like a regular Vim buffer. We can scroll up and down with the `k` and `j` keys, and we can even use Vim's search feature on the contents of the quickfix list.

The quickfix window has special behavior of its own. If we position our cursor on it and press the `<CR>` key, then that file will be opened with our cursor positioned on the line containing the match. The file usually opens in the window directly above the quickfix window, but if the file is already open in a window in the current tab page, then that buffer will be reused.

Note that each line in the quickfix window corresponds to a record in the quickfix list. If we run :cnext, then the cursor position will move down one line in the quickfix window, even when that window is not active. Conversely, if we use the quickfix window to jump to an item in the quickfix list, then the next time we run :cnext we'll go to the item after the one we selected in the quickfix window. Selecting an item from the quickfix window is much like running the :cc [nr] command but with an intuitive visual interface.

We can close the quickfix window as usual by running :q when the window is active. But we can also close it by running :cclose when any other window is active.

Tip 107

Recall Results from a Previous Quickfix List

When we update the quickfix list, Vim doesn't overwrite the previous contents. It saves the results of older quickfix lists, allowing us to refer back to them.

We can recall an older version of the quickfix list (Vim holds onto the last ten lists) by running the :colder command (sadly, there is no :warmer command). To revert from an old quickfix list back to a newer one, we run :cnewer. Note that both :colder and :cnewer commands can accept a count, which causes the respective command to be run the specified number of times.

If we open the quickfix window after running :colder or :cnewer, its status line will indicate the command that was run to generate that particular list.

You can think of the :colder and :cnewer commands as being like undo and redo for the quickfix list. That means it's cheap for us to try out commands that repopulate the quickfix list because we can always run :colder to revert to the previous list. Also, instead of repeating a :make or :grep command, we could pull up the results from the last time it was executed (unless we've changed any files). This can be a real time saver, especially if the command takes a long time to run.

Tip 108

Customize the External Compiler

Vim's :make command isn't limited to calling the external make program; it can execute any compilers available on your machine. (Note that Vim's definition of "compiler" is looser than what you may be used to; see ':compiler' and ':make' Are Not Just for Compiled Languages, on page 272.) In this tip, we'll set up the :make command so that it passes a JavaScript file through JSLint and then uses the output to populate the quickfix list.

First, we'll configure Vim so that running :make calls nodelint,[1] a command-line interface to JSLint.[2] It depends on Node.js and can be installed using NPM simply by running this:[3]

⇒ ```
$ npm install nodelint -g
```

As a test case, we'll use this JavaScript implementation of FizzBuzz:

```
quickfix/fizzbuzz.js
var i;
for (i=1; i <= 100; i++) {
    if(i % 15 == 0) {
        console.log('Fizzbuzz');
    } else if(i % 5 == 0) {
        console.log('Buzz');
    } else if(i % 3 == 0) {
        console.log('Fizz');
    } else {
        console.log(i);
    }
};
```

Configure ':make' to Invoke Nodelint

The 'makeprg' setting allows us to specify the program that will be called when we run :make (see :h 'makeprg' ⓘ). We can instruct Vim to run nodelint as follows:

⇒ ```
:setlocal makeprg=NODE_DISABLE_COLORS=1\ nodelint\ %
```

The % symbol is expanded to the path for the current file. So if we were editing a file called ~/quickfix/fizzbuzz.js, then running :make inside Vim would be equivalent to running this in the shell:

⇒ ```
$ export NODE_DISABLE_COLORS=1
```
⇒ ```
$ nodelint ~/quickfix/fizzbuzz.js
```
❮ ```
~/quickfix/fizzbuzz.js, line 2, character 22: Unexpected '++'.
for (i=1; i <= 100; i++) {
~/quickfix/fizzbuzz.js, line 3, character 15: Expected '===' ...
if(i % 15 == 0) {
~/quickfix/fizzbuzz.js, line 5, character 21: Expected '===' ...
} else if(i % 5 == 0) {
~/quickfix/fizzbuzz.js, line 7, character 21: Expected '===' ...
} else if(i % 3 == 0) {
~/quickfix/fizzbuzz.js, line 12, character 2: Unexpected ';'.
};
5 errors
```

---

1.  https://github.com/tav/nodelint
2.  http://jslint.com/
3.  http://nodejs.org/ and http://npmjs.org/, respectively.
```

By default, nodelint highlights errors in red using ANSI color codes. Setting NODE_DISABLE_COLORS=1 mutes the colors, which makes it easier to parse the error messages.

Next, we have to make Vim parse the output from nodelint so that it can build a quickfix list from the results. We can approach this problem in two ways: we could configure nodelint so that its output resembled the error messages generated by make, which Vim already understands, or we could teach Vim how to parse the default output from nodelint. We'll use the latter technique.

Populate the Quickfix List Using Nodelint's Output

The 'errorformat' setting allows us to teach Vim how to parse the output generated by running :make (see :h 'errorformat' ⓘ). We can inspect the default value by running the following:

```
⇒ :setglobal errorformat?
❮ errorformat=%*[^"]"%f"%*\D%l: %m,"%f"%*\D%l: %m, ...[abridged]...
```

If you're familiar with scanf (in C), then you'll recognize the concept. Each of the characters preceded by a percent sign has a special meaning: %f stands for the filename, %l for the line number, and %m for the error message. For the complete list, look up :h errorformat ⓘ.

To parse the output from nodelint, we could set the error format as follows:

```
⇒ :setlocal efm=%A%f\,\ line\ %l\,\ character\ %c:%m,%Z%.%#,%-G%.%#
```

Now when we run :make, Vim will use this error format to parse the output from nodelint. For each warning it will extract the filename, line number, and column number to generate an address, which becomes a record in the quickfix list. That means we can jump between warnings using all of the commands discussed in Tip 106, *Browse the Quickfix List*, on page 266.

Set Up 'makeprg' and 'errorformat' with a Single Command

This 'errorformat' string is not something we would want to commit to memory. Instead, we can save it to a file and then activate it with the :compiler command, which is a convenient shortcut for setting both 'makeprg' and 'errorformat' options (see :h :compiler ⓘ):

```
⇒ :compiler nodelint
```

The :compiler command activates a *compiler plugin*, which sets the 'makeprg' and 'errorformat' options to run and parse nodelint. It's roughly equivalent to sourcing these lines of configuration:

```
quickfix/ftplugin.javascript.vim
setlocal makeprg=NODE_DISABLE_COLORS=1\ nodelint\ %

let &l:efm='%A'
let &l:efm.='%f\, '
let &l:efm.='line %l\, '
let &l:efm.='character %c:'
let &l:efm.='%m' . ','
let &l:efm.='%Z%.%#' . ','
let &l:efm.='%-G%.%#'
```

The internals of a compiler plugin are more elaborate, but this is a fair approximation of what goes on. You can familiarize yourself with the compiler plugins that are distributed with Vim by running this command:

⇒ `:args $VIMRUNTIME/compiler/*.vim`

Note that Vim doesn't ship with a nodelint compiler plugin, but we can easily install one.[4] If we wanted to always use nodelint as the compiler for JavaScript files, we could either use an autocommand or a file-type plugin to make it so. To find out how, see *Apply Customizations to Certain Types of Files*, on page 306.

':compiler' and ':make' Are Not Just for Compiled Languages

The words *make* and *compile* have particular meanings in the context of a compiled programming language. But in Vim, the corresponding :make and :compile commands have more flexible definitions, making them just as applicable for interpreted languages and markup formats.

For example, when working on a LaTeX document, we can configure Vim so that the :make command compiles our .tex file into a PDF. Or if we're working with an interpreted language such as JavaScript, we can have :make run our source code through JSLint or some other (less opinionated) syntax checker. Alternatively, we could set up :make so that it runs the test suite.

In Vim's terminology, a compiler is any external program that *does something* with our document and produces a list of errors or warnings. The :make command simply invokes the external compiler and then parses the output to construct a navigable quickfix list from them.

---

4. https://github.com/bigfish/vim-nodelint

Search Project-Wide with grep, vimgrep, and Others

Vim's search command is great for finding all occurrences of a pattern within a file. But what if we want to find matches across an entire project? Then we have to scan many files. Traditionally, this has been the domain of grep, a dedicated Unix tool.

In this chapter, we'll discover Vim's :grep command, which allows us to call an external program without leaving our editor. While this command calls grep by default (when available), we'll see that it can easily be customized to outsource the task to other dedicated programs, such as ack.

One down side to using external programs is that their regex syntax may be incompatible with the one we use for most Vim searches. We'll see that the :vimgrep command allows us to use Vim's native search engine to find patterns in multiple files. This convenience comes at a cost: vimgrep isn't nearly as fast as dedicated programs.

Tip 109

Call grep Without Leaving Vim

Vim's :grep command acts as a wrapper to an external grep (or grep-like) program. Using this wrapper, we can have grep search for a pattern across multiple files without leaving Vim, and then we can navigate the results using the quickfix list.

First we'll step through a workflow where grep and Vim run independently without talking to each other. We'll examine the weaknesses with this approach before considering an integrated solution that solves these problems.

Using grep from the Command Line

Suppose that we're working on something in Vim and we need to find every occurrence of the word "Waldo" in all files in the current directory. Leaving Vim, we run the following in the shell:

```
$ grep -n Waldo *
department-store.txt:1:Waldo is beside the boot counter.
goldrush.txt:6:Waldo is studying his clipboard.
goldrush.txt:9:The penny farthing is 10 paces ahead of Waldo.
```

By default, grep prints one line of output for each match, displaying the contents of the matching line and the name of the file. The -n flag tells grep to include the line number in the printed output.

So what can we do with this output? Well, we could just treat it as a table of contents. For each line in the result list, we could open the file and specify the line number. For example, to open goldrush.txt at line 9, we could run this from the shell:

```
$ vim goldrush.txt +9
```

Surely our tools can integrate better than this.

Calling grep from Inside Vim

Vim's :grep command is a wrapper for the external grep program (see :h :grep ⓘ). Instead of running grep in the shell, we could execute this directly from Vim:

```
:grep Waldo *
```

Behind the scenes, Vim executes grep -n Waldo * in the shell for us. Rather than printing grep's output, Vim does something much more useful. It parses the results and builds a quickfix list from them. We can navigate through the results using the :cnext/:cprev commands and all of the other techniques that we explored in Chapter 17, *Compile Code and Navigate Errors with the Quickfix List*, on page 263.

Even though we simply called :grep Waldo *, Vim automatically included the -n flag, telling grep to include line numbers in the output. That's why when we navigate through the quickfix list, it takes us directly to each matching line.

Suppose we want to run a case-insensitive grep. We supply grep with the -i flag:

⇒ `:grep -i Waldo *`

Behind the scenes, Vim executes grep -n -i Waldo *. Note that the default -n flag is still present. We can pass along any other flags to grep in the same manner if we want to tweak its behavior.

Tip 110

Customize the grep Program

Vim's :grep command is a wrapper for the external grep program. We can customize the way that Vim delegates this task by manipulating two settings: 'grepprg' and 'grepformat'. First we'll examine the defaults, and then we'll see how tweaking them allows us to outsource the search task to any other suitable program.

Vim's Default grep Settings

The 'grepprg' setting specifies what to run in the shell when Vim's :grep command is executed (:h 'grepprg' ⓘ). The 'grepformat' setting tells Vim how to parse the output returned by the :grep command (see :h 'grepformat' ⓘ). On Unix systems, the defaults are these:

```
grepprg="grep -n $* /dev/null"
grepformat="%f:%l:%m,%f:%l%m,%f  %l%m"
```

The $* symbol used in the 'grepprg' setting is a placeholder, which is replaced with any arguments supplied to the :grep command.

The 'grepformat' setting is a string containing tokens that describe the output returned by :grep. The special tokens used in the 'grepformat' string are the same as those used by 'errorformat', which we met in *Populate the Quickfix List Using Nodelint's Output*, on page 271. For the complete list, look up :h errorformat ⓘ.

Let's see how the default %f:%l %m format stacks up against this output from grep:

```
department-store.txt:1:Waldo is beside the boot counter.
goldrush.txt:6:Waldo is studying his clipboard.
goldrush.txt:9:The penny farthing is 10 paces ahead of Waldo.
```

For each record, %f matches the filename (department-store.txt or goldrush.txt), %l matches the line number, and %m matches the text on that line.

The 'grepformat' string can contain multiple formats separated by commas. The default matches either %f:%l %m or %f %l%m. Vim will use the first format that matches the output from :grep.

Make ':grep' Call ack

ack is a grep alternative that is targeted specifically at programmers. If you're wondering how it compares to grep, visit the home page (and be sure to read the URL, http://betterthangrep.com).

First, we need to install ack. On Ubuntu, we can do so as follows:

```
$ sudo apt-get install ack-grep
$ sudo ln -s /usr/bin/ack-grep /usr/local/bin/ack
```

The first of these commands installs the program, allowing us to call it as ack-grep. The second command creates a symlink so that we can call it simply as ack.

On OS X, we can install ack using Homebrew:

```
$ brew install ack
```

Let's see how we could customize the 'grepprg' and 'grepformat' settings so that :grep calls ack instead. By default, ack lists the filename on a line of its own, followed by the line number and contents of each matched line, like this:

```
$ ack Waldo *
department-store.txt
1:Waldo is beside the boot counter.

goldrush.txt
6:Waldo is studying his clipboard.
9:The penny farthing is 10 paces ahead of Waldo.
```

We can easily massage this output so that it resembles that of grep -n by running ack with the --nogroup switch:

```
$ ack --nogroup Waldo *
department-store.txt:1:Waldo is beside the boot counter.
goldrush.txt:6:Waldo is studying his clipboard.
goldrush.txt:9:The penny farthing is 10 paces ahead of Waldo.
```

This output matches the format of grep -n, and since Vim's default 'grepformat' string knows how to parse this, we don't need to change it. So the simplest thing we could do to use ack instead of grep would be to set 'grepprg' as follows:

```
:set grepprg=ack\ --nogroup\ $*
```

Alternative grep Plugins

Outsourcing a multiple-file search to an external program is easy with Vim. We have only to change the 'grepprg' and 'grepformat' settings and then execute :grep. And just like that, our results are in the quickfix list. No matter which program is actually called, the interface is nearly identical.

But there are some important differences. grep uses POSIX regular expressions, whereas ack uses Perl regular expressions. If the :grep command calls ack in the background, a layer of misdirection is added. Wouldn't you rather create a custom command called :Ack that does what it says on the label?

The Ack.vim plugin follows this strategy and so does fugitive.vim,[a] which adds a custom :Ggrep command that executes git-grep. We can install several plugins like this, and since each one creates a custom command rather than overriding the :grep command, they can all coexist without conflict. We needn't stick to one grep-like program. We can use whichever is best for the task at hand.

_____

a.   https://github.com/mileszs/ack.vim and https://github.com/tpope/vim-fugitive, respectively.

Make ack Jump to Line and Column

But ack has another trick up its sleeve. When run with the --column option, ack will output the line *and column number* of each match. Observe:

```
$ ack --nogroup --column Waldo *
department-store.txt:1:1:Waldo is beside the boot counter.
goldrush.txt:6:1:Waldo is studying his clipboard.
goldrush.txt:9:41:The penny farthing is 10 paces ahead of Waldo.
```

If we could tweak the 'grepformat' to extract this extra information, then we could navigate search results by jumping to the precise position of each match rather than just to the right line. It's easily done using these settings:

```
:set grepprg=ack\ --nogroup\ --column\ $*
:set grepformat=%f:%l:%c:%m
```

The %c item matches the column number.

Tip 111

Grep with Vim's Internal Search Engine

The :vimgrep command allows us to search through multiple files using Vim's native regular expression engine.

As a demonstration, we'll use the files in the grep/quotes directory, which you can find in the source files that come distributed with this book. The directory contains the following files, reproduced here with their contents:

```
quotes/
  about.txt
  Don't watch the clock; do what it does. Keep going.

  tough.txt
  When the going gets tough, the tough get going.

  where.txt
  If you don't know where you are going,
  you might wind up someplace else.
```

Each of these files contains at least one occurrence of the word "going." We can ask Vim to search for that word in each of those files using the :vimgrep command, like this:

```
➾ :vimgrep /going/ clock.txt tough.txt where.txt
❮ (1 of 3): Don't watch the clock; do what it does. Keep going.
➾ :cnext
❮ (2 of 3): When the going gets tough, the tough get going.
➾ :cnext
❮ (3 of 3): If you don't know where you are going,
```

The :vimgrep command populates the quickfix list with one entry for each line that contains a match. Navigate through the results using commands such as :cnext and :cprev (see Tip 106, *Browse the Quickfix List*, on page 266).

The file tough.txt contains two occurrences of the word "going," but our :vimgrep command only counted the first match. If we supply the g flag after the pattern, then :vimgrep will match all occurrences of the specified pattern, not just the first match on each line:

```
➾ :vim /going/g clock.txt tough.txt where.txt
❮ (1 of 4): Don't watch the clock; do what it does. Keep going.
```

This time the quickfix list contains an entry for all four occurrences of the word "going." This might remind you of the way that the :substitute command works: by default it only affects the first match on the line, but when supplied with the g flag it will affect all matches on a given line. When I'm using the :substitute or :vimgrep command, I almost always want the behavior that the g flag specifies.

Specifying Which Files to Look Inside

This is the format of the :vimgrep command (:h :vimgrep ⓘ):

```
:vim[grep][!] /{pattern}/[g][j] {file} ...
```

The {file} argument must not be blank. It can include filenames, wildcards, backtick expressions, and combinations of all of the above. Each of the techniques that we can use to populate the argument list can also be used here. (See *Populate the Argument List*, on page 87 for a detailed discussion.)

In the previous examples, we spelled out the names of each file individually. We could get the same result by using a wildcard:

⇒ `:vim /going/g *.txt`
❮ `(1 of 4): Don't watch the clock; do what it does. Keep going.`

As well as being able to use * and ** wildcards, we can use the ## symbol, which is expanded to represent the names of each file in the argument list (:h cmdline-special ⓘ). This allows for an alternative workflow. First, we populate the argument list with the files we want to inspect. Then we run :vimgrep across each of the files in the argument list:

⇒ `:args *.txt`
⇒ `:vim /going/g ##`
❮ `(1 of 4): Don't watch the clock; do what it does. Keep going.`

This may look like more work because we have to run two seperate Ex commands. But I often prefer to use :vimgrep this way because it lets me address two questions separately: what files do I want to search inside, and what pattern am I looking for? Once the argument list has been populated, we can reuse that set of files with the :vimgrep command as often as we like.

Search in File, Then Search in Project

We can leave the pattern field empty, which tells :vimgrep to use the current search pattern. The same trick works for the :substitute command (as discussed in Tip 91, *Reuse the Last Search Pattern*, on page 225), and also for the :global command. This is handy if we want to search for a regular expression across multiple files. We can begin by composing a regular expression and testing it in the current file. When we're satisfied that the pattern matches where it should, we execute :vimgrep using the exact same pattern. For example, here we use the search command to look inside the current file for a regex that will match both "don't" and "Don't."

⇒ `/[Dd]on't`
⇒ `:vim //g *.txt`
❮ `(1 of 2): Don't watch the clock; do what it does. Keep going.`

The main advantage to using :vimgrep is that it understands the same patterns as Vim's search command. If we wanted to use :grep to do a project-wide search for the same pattern, we would first have to translate it into a POSIX regular expression. That won't take long for a simple pattern such as this, but you wouldn't want to do that for a complex regular expression, such as the one we constructed in Tip 85, *Create Complex Patterns by Iterating upon Search History*, on page 211.

Search History and :vimgrep

I often use this command, which looks inside each of the files in the argument list for the current search pattern:

⇒ `:vim //g ##`
❮ `(1 of 2): Don't watch the clock; do what it does. Keep going.`

One thing to watch out for with this command is that it will always use the current values from the argument list and search history. If we repeat this command later, it may behave differently depending on what's in our argument list and search history.

Alternatively, we could fill the search field with the value of the current pattern by pressing `<C-r>/` . The search results would be the same either way, but our command history would be different.

⇒ `:vim /<C-r>//g ##`

If you think that you might want to rerun the same :vimgrep command later, then it would be useful to have that pattern preserved in your command history.

Dial X for Autocompletion

Autocompletion saves us from typing out entire words. Given the first letters of a word, Vim builds a list of suggested endings and lets us choose our favorite. Whether or not this is of any use to us depends on how adept we are at interacting with that list of suggestions. We'll learn a few tricks for working with the autocomplete menu in Tip 113, *Work with the Autocomplete Pop-Up Menu*, on page 283.

Tip 112, *Meet Vim's Keyword Autocompletion*, on page 281, introduces the basics of keyword autocompletion. The list of suggested completions is created by scanning all files that have been opened in the current editing session, as well as any included files and tag files. We'll find out what this means in Tip 114, *Understand the Source of Keywords*, on page 285, and see how we can narrow down the list of suggestions.

Besides keywords, Vim has other ways of building a list of suggestions. Table 17, , on page 283, lists some of the highlights, each of which is covered by a tip in this chapter.

To make the most of Vim's autocomplete functionality, we need to understand two things: how to dial up the most relevant suggestions and how to choose the right word from the list. We'll address each of these topics in the following tips.

Tip 112

Meet Vim's Keyword Autocompletion

With keyword autocompletion, Vim attempts to guess the word that we're typing, which can save us from completing it by hand.

Autocompletion and Case Sensitivity

Vim's search command treats uppercase and lowercase letters as equivalent when the 'ignorecase' option is enabled (as discussed in Tip 73, *Tune the Case Sensitivity of Search Patterns*, on page 186), but there's a side effect: autocompletion also becomes case insensitive.

In the "She sells sea shells" example above, the word "She" is not included in the word list because it starts with an uppercase "S." However, if the 'ignorecase' option were enabled, then "She" would appear in the word list with an uppercase "S." Seeing as we've already typed a lowercase "s," this might be considered unhelpful.

We can fix this behavior by enabling the 'infercase' option (see :h 'infercase' ⓘ). This would add "she" to the word list but with a lowercase "s."

Vim's autocomplete functionality is triggered from Insert mode. When invoked, Vim builds a word list from the contents of each buffer in the current editing session and then examines the characters to the left of the cursor, looking for a partial word. If one is found, the word list is filtered to exclude anything that doesn't begin with that partial word. The resulting word list is presented in a menu from which we can select our match.

This figure shows two screenshots, one taken before and one after triggering Vim's keyword autocompletion:

```
She sells sea shells by the s|


She sells sea shells by the sea|
                              sells
                              sea
                              shells
-- match 2 of 3
```

In this case, the letter "s" is used to filter the word list, giving us three choices: "sells," "sea," and "shells." If you're wondering why "She" isn't in the list, see *Autocompletion and Case Sensitivity*, on page 282.

Trigger Autocompletion

Vim's autocompletion can be triggered from Insert mode with the `<C-p>` and `<C-n>` chords, which select the *previous* and *next* items in the word list, respectively.

The `<C-p>` and `<C-n>` commands both invoke generic keyword autocompletion. There are several variant forms of autocompletion, all of which are prefixed with the `<C-x>` chord. In this chapter, we'll discuss the methods listed in the following table (you can view the complete list at :h ins-completion ⓘ).

Command	Type of Completion
`<C-n>`	Generic keywords
`<C-x><C-n>`	Current buffer keywords
`<C-x><C-i>`	Included file keywords
`<C-x><C-]>`	tags file keywords
`<C-x><C-k>`	Dictionary lookup
`<C-x><C-l>`	Whole line completion
`<C-x><C-f>`	Filename completion
`<C-x><C-o>`	Omni-completion

If you use `<C-x><C-n>` on the "She sells sea shells" example, then you should get the same word list as is shown in the illustration. But `<C-n>` may produce more suggestions, because the word list is populated from sources beyond the current buffer. We'll take an in-depth look at how the word list for generic keywords is populated in Tip 114, *Understand the Source of Keywords*, on page 285.

No matter which form of autocompletion is triggered, the commands for interacting with the suggestions menu are the same. We'll explore these in the next tip.

Tip 113

Work with the Autocomplete Pop-Up Menu

To get the most from the autocomplete command, learn how to interact with the pop-up menu. Either refine the choices and then pick an item, or dismiss the list if it doesn't contain what you want.

When autocomplete is triggered, Vim draws a pop-up menu containing the items in the word list. We can interact with this menu using the commands shown in Table 18, *Commands for the Pop-Up Menu*, on page 284.

More details can be found in Vim's documentation: :h popupmenu-completion ⓘ.

No matter which variant of autocompletion is used, when the autocomplete pop-up menu is visible, `<C-n>` and `<C-p>` always move to the previous or next

Keystrokes	Effect
`<C-n>`	Use the next match from the word list (*next* match)
`<C-p>`	Use the previous match from the word list (*previous* match)
`<Down>`	Select the next match from the word list
`<Up>`	Select the previous match from the word list
`<C-y>`	Accept the currently selected match (*yes*)
`<C-e>`	Revert to the originally typed text (*exit* from autocompletion)
`<C-h>` (and `<BS>`)	Delete one character from current match
`<C-l>`	Add one character from current match
`{char}`	Stop completion and insert `{char}`

Table 18—Commands for the Pop-Up Menu

item in the menu. In contrast, when used from Insert mode, `<C-n>` and `<C-p>` trigger generic keyword autocompletion.

The `<C-n>` and `<Down>` keys both select the next item from the pop-up menu, while the `<C-p>` and `<Up>` keys select the previous item. The mechanics are slightly different, whether we use `<C-p>`/`<C-n>` or `<Up>`/`<Down>`.

Browse the Word List Without Changing the Document

When we press `<Down>`, the pop-up menu is updated to select the next item in the list but the text in the document is left unchanged. We can scroll through the list of words in the pop-up menu using the `<Up>` and `<Down>` keys until we find the word we want to use. Then we can insert it into the document either by hitting the `<CR>` key or by pressing `<C-y>`.

Update the Document As You Scroll Through the Word List

By contrast, the `<C-n>` key not only *selects* the next item from the list, it also updates the document to *use* the selected word. This means that we don't have to press `<CR>` to confirm our selection, because the text in the document is always synchronized with the selected item in the pop-up menu. Once we've chosen our word from the list, we simply continue typing and the pop-up menu disappears.

I prefer the `<C-p>` and `<C-n>` chords over `<Up>` and `<Down>` for a couple of reasons. I don't have to move my hand from the home row when using `<C-p>` and `<C-n>`. Also, I don't have to confirm my choice by pressing `<CR>` or `<C-y>` because the text is inserted into the document automatically. Once again, we meet our mantra from Tip 47, *Keep Your Fingers on the Home Row*, on page 114: keep your fingers on the home row.

Dismiss All Selections

Once we've summoned the autocomplete menu, we might want to dismiss it again. For instance, if the list has too many suggestions, typing out the word by hand may prove quicker. We can end autocompletion by pressing `<C-e>`, which dismisses the pop-up menu and restores the text in front of the cursor to the partial word that was typed before autocomplete was invoked.

Refine the Word List as You Type

Here's one of my favorite tricks when working with the autocomplete pop-up menu. Try pressing `<C-n><C-p>`. That's two separate commands: `<C-n>` followed immediately by `<C-p>` (although `<C-p><C-n>` would work just as well). The first command invokes autocomplete, summons the pop-up menu, and selects the first item in the word list. The second command selects the previous item in the word list, taking us back to where we started but without dismissing the pop-up menu. Now we can continue to type, and Vim will filter the word list in real time.

This can be especially handy if the word list contains too many suggestions to read in one visual gulp. Suppose that the word list contains twenty suggestions and we typed only a partial word consisting of two characters. If we type a third character, the word list will be immediately refined. We can continue typing characters in this manner until the word list is short enough to be useful and we can make our selection.

This trick works just as well with the other variants of autocompletion. For example, we could type `<C-x><C-o><C-p>` to perform live filtering on omni auto-completion, or `<C-x><C-f><C-p>` to do the same with filename completion.

Tip 114

Understand the Source of Keywords

Generic keyword autocompletion compiles its word list from a handful of sources. We can be more specific about which sources we want to use.

Several forms of autocompletion use a specific file or set of files to generate their word list. Generic keyword autocompletion uses an amalgamation of these word lists. To understand where generic keywords come from, we should first look at each of the more targeted forms of autocompletion.

The Buffer List

The simplest mechanism for populating the autocomplete word list would be to use words only from the current buffer. Current file keyword completion does just that and is triggered with `<C-x><C-n>` (see :h compl-current ⓘ). This can be useful when generic keyword completion generates too many suggestions and you know that the word you want is somewhere in the current buffer.

But current buffer keyword completion has little to offer when the current buffer has a low word count. To augment the word list, we can have Vim source keywords from each item in the buffer list. We can inspect these by running this command:

⇒ `:ls!`

Generic keywords are sourced from the contents of each file in this list, which represents all of the files that have been opened in the current Vim session. As we'll see next, we needn't even open a file for its contents to be pulled into the autocomplete word list.

Included Files

Most programming languages provide some way of loading code from an external file or library. In C, this can be done using the #include directive, whereas Python uses import and Ruby uses require. If we are working on a file that includes code from another library, then it would be useful if Vim could read the contents of those referenced files when building a word list for autocompletion. And that is exactly what happens when we trigger keyword completion with the `<C-x><C-i>` command (see :h compl-keyword ⓘ).

Vim understands the C way of including files, but it can be taught to follow the corresponding directives in other languages by tweaking the 'include' setting (see :h 'include' ⓘ). This is usually handled by a file-type plugin. And the good news is that Vim is distributed with support for many languages, so you shouldn't have to tinker with this setting unless you are working with an unsupported language. Try opening a Ruby or Python file and running :set include?, and you should find that Vim already knows how to look up included files for those languages.

Tag Files

In Chapter 16, *Index and Navigate Source Code with ctags*, on page 253, we met Exuberant Ctags, which is an external program that scans source code for keywords such as function names, class names, and any other constructs that are significant in the given language. When ctags is run on a codebase, it generates an index of keywords, which are addressed and sorted alphabetically. By convention, the index is saved in a file called tags.

The main reason for indexing a codebase with ctags is to make it easier to navigate, but a tags file creates a useful by-product: a list of keywords that can be used for autocompletion. We can dial up this list using the `<C-x><C-]>` command (see :h compl-tag ⓘ).

If the word you are trying to complete is a language object (such as a function name or class name), then tag autocompletion will give a good signal-to-noise ratio.

Put It All Together

Generic keyword autocompletion generates suggestions by combining the word list generated from the buffer list, included files, and tag files into one. If you want to tweak this behavior, see *Customizing the Generic Autocompletion*, on page 287. Remember, generic keyword autocompletion is triggered simply with the `<C-n>` chord, whereas the more focused variants are all invoked with `<C-x>` followed by another chord.

Customizing the Generic Autocompletion

We can customize the list of places that are scanned by generic keyword completion using the 'complete' option. This option holds a comma-separated list of one-letter flags, whose presence enables scanning of a particular place. The default setting is complete=.,w,b,u,t,i. We could disable scanning of included files by running the following:

⇒ `:set complete-=i`

Or we could enable completion of words in the spelling dictionary by running this:

⇒ `:set complete+=k`

Look up :h 'complete' ⓘ to find out what each of the flags does.

Tip 115

Autocomplete Words from the Dictionary

Vim's dictionary autocompletion builds a list of suggestions from a word list. We can configure Vim so that dictionary autocompletion uses the same word list as the built-in spell checker.

Sometimes we might want to use autocompletion on a word that isn't present in any of our open buffers, included files, or tags. In that case, we can always resort to looking it up in the dictionary. This can be triggered by running the `<C-x><C-k>` command (see :h compl-dictionary 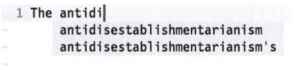).

To enable this feature, we need to supply Vim with a suitable word list. The easiest way to do this is by running :set spell to enable Vim's spell checker (see Chapter 20, *Find and Fix Typos with Vim's Spell Checker*, on page 295, for more details). All of the words in the spelling dictionary become available through the `<C-x><C-k>` command.

If you don't want to enable Vim's spell checker, you can also use the 'dictionary' option to specify one or more files containing word lists (see :h 'dictionary').

Dictionary autocompletion is perhaps most useful when you want to complete a word that is long or difficult to spell. Here's an example:

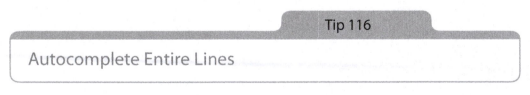

There's one other form of autocompletion that uses the spelling dictionary. We'll find out how to use it in Tip 123, *Fix Spelling Errors from Insert Mode*, on page 299.

Tip 116

Autocomplete Entire Lines

In all of the examples so far, we've looked at completing words, but Vim can also autocomplete entire lines.

Line-wise autocompletion is triggered by running `<C-x><C-l>` (see
:h compl-whole-line ⓘ). Suppose that we started off with this snippet:

`auto_complete/bg-colors.css`
```
.top {
  background-color: #ef66ef; }
.bottom {
```

We want to duplicate the second line and place it at the end of the file. Here's
how this can be done using whole-line autocompletion:

Keystrokes	Buffer Contents

{start}	`.top {`
	`  background-color: #ef66ef; }`
	`.bottom {`

oba	`.top {`
	`  background-color: #ef66ef; }`
	`.bottom {`
	`ba`

`<C-x><C-l><Esc>`	`.top {`
	`  background-color: #ef66ef; }`
	`.bottom {`
	`  background-color: #ef66ef; }`

The same files that provide the source for generic keyword autocompletion
(see Tip 114, *Understand the Source of Keywords*, on page 285) are also used
to generate a list of suggestions for line-wise autocompletion. Also, note that
Vim ignores any indentation at the start of the line.

The beauty of line-wise autocompletion is that we don't have to know the
location of the line we're duplicating. We need to know only that it exists.
After typing out the first few characters, we hit `<C-x><C-l>`, and bang! Vim fills
out the rest for us.

We've seen two other methods for duplicating a line by means of a register
(*Duplicating Lines*, on page 147) or an Ex command (*Duplicate Lines with the
':t' Command*, on page 61). Each has its strengths and its weaknesses. Try
to identify the scenarios where each of these techniques shines, and use them
accordingly.

Tip 117

Autocomplete Sequences of Words

When we use autocomplete to expand a word, Vim remembers the context from which that word was taken. If we invoke autocomplete a second time, Vim will insert the word that followed the original completion. We can repeat this again and again to fill in entire sequences of words. This can often produce results faster than using copy and paste to duplicate phrases.

Suppose that we're working on this document:

auto_complete/help-refs.xml
```
Here's the "hyperlink" for the Vim tutor:
<vimref href="http://vimhelp.appspot.com/usr_01.txt.html#tutor">tutor</vimref>.

For more information on autocompletion see:
<vimr
```

The <vimref> tag is a custom element that I use throughout the XML manuscript for this book to mark up links to Vim's :help pages. We want to insert a <vimref> tag on the last line of this document for the :h ins-completion ⓘ entry in Vim's documentation. The tag will look just like the existing <vimref> entry, except that instead of usr_01 we want insert, and instead of tutor we want ins-completion.

We can get the result we want quickly by duplicating the existing <vimref> tag and altering the parts that need to change. We could move our cursor to the existing <vimref> tag, yank it, then move back to where we want to insert a new tag and paste the text that we yanked. That wouldn't be too much hassle in this case, because the document we are working on is so short. But if we were working on a document containing thousands of words, finding an instance of <vimref> to yank could mean moving the cursor a long way from where we want it.

Alternatively, we could use Vim's autocompletion to insert a copy of the <vimref> tag right where we want it:

Keystrokes	Buffer Contents
{start}	<vimr
a <C-x><C-p>	<vimref
<C-x><C-p>	<vimref>.

Keystrokes	Buffer Contents
`<C-p>`	`<vimref href█`
`<C-x><C-p>`	`<vimref href="http█`
`<C-x><C-p>`	`<vimref href="http://vimhelp█`

We start by pressing `a` to switch into Insert mode. Now we can use `<C-x><C-p>` to autocomplete the partial word vimr to vimref. (We could just as well use `<C-x><C-n>` throughout this example.)

It gets interesting when we use `<C-x><C-p>` a second time. Vim remembers the context from where in the document it found the completion for vimref. When we invoke the autocomplete command again, Vim completes the next word that followed vimref. In this case there are two possible options, because the word vimref appears as an opening tag and a closing tag. Vim pops up the completion menu, prompting us to choose which context we want to use for our completion. Pressing `<C-p>` a second time gets us the result we want.

Now we can continue pressing `<C-x><C-p>` again and again. Each time we invoke this command, Vim inserts the next word that it finds in the context where the original autocomplete match came from. It doesn't take long to fill out the rest of the XML tag. After we've done this, we can edit the tag by hand, changing usr_01 to insert, and tutor to ins-completion.

Vim's autocompletion doesn't only let us insert sequences of words. It also works for sequences of lines. If we repeatedly use the `<C-x><C-l>` command (which we met in Tip 116, *Autocomplete Entire Lines*, on page 288), it lets us insert a sequence of consecutive lines from elsewhere in our document.

Being able to autocomplete sequences of words and lines can often let us duplicate text more quickly than using copy and paste. When your coworkers see you using this technique, they'll stop you to ask how you did it!

Tip 118

Autocomplete Filenames

When we work at the command line, we can hit the `<Tab>` key to autocomplete paths for directories and files. With filename autocompletion, we can do the same from within Vim.

Filename autocompletion is triggered by the `<C-x><C-f>` command (see `:h compl-filename` ⓘ).

Vim always maintains a reference to the *current working directory*, just like the shell. We can find out what this is at any given time by running the :pwd command (*print working directory*), and we can change our working directory at any time using the :cd {path} command (*change directory*). It's important to understand that Vim's filename autocompletion always expands paths relative to the working directory, not relative to the file that is currently being edited.

Suppose that we were working on a small web application comprised of the following files:

```
webapp/
  public/
    index.html
    js/
      application.js
```

Now let's say that we were editing the index.html file:

```
auto_complete/webapp/public/index.html
<!DOCTYPE html>
<html>
  <head>
    <title>Practical Vim - the app</title>
    <script src="" type="text/javascript"></script>
  </head>
  <body></body>
</html>
```

We want to fill out the src="" attribute to refer to the `application.js` file. But there's a complication if we want to use filename autocompletion:

⇒ **:pwd**
❮ webapp

If we were to invoke filename autocompletion now, it would complete the path relative to the webapp directory, giving us src="public/js/application.js". But we actually want it to reference src="js/application.js". If we want to use filename autocompletion, we'll first have to change to the public directory:

⇒ **:cd public**

Now we can invoke filename autocompletion, and it will work relative to the webapp/public directory:

Keystrokes	Buffer Contents
i	<script src="▊"/>
js/ap	<script src="js/ap▊"/>
<C-x><C-f>	<script src="js/application.js▊"/>

Having inserted the filepath, we can revert back to our original working directory:

⇒ `:cd -`

Just like in the shell, `cd -` switches to the previous working directory (see :h :cd-ⓘ).

In the documentation for filename autocompletion, it states that "the 'path' option is not used (yet)." Perhaps in future versions of Vim it won't be necessary to change directories to use this feature for our hypothetical web app scenario.

Tip 119

Autocomplete with Context Awareness

Omni-completion is Vim's answer to intellisense. It provides a list of suggestions that's tailored for the context of the cursor position. In this tip, we'll look at how it works in the context of a CSS file.

Omni-completion is triggered with the `<C-x><C-o>` command (see :h compl-omniⓘ). The functionality is implemented as a file-type plugin, so to activate it we have to source these lines of configuration:

essential.vim
```
set nocompatible
filetype plugin on
```

We also have to install a plugin that implements omni-completion for the language that we're working with. Vim ships with support for about a dozen languages, including HTML, CSS, JavaScript, PHP, and SQL. You can find the full list by looking up :h compl-omni-filetypesⓘ.

Here's the results of triggering omni-completion in a CSS file in two slightly different contexts.

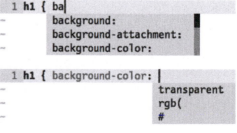

Given "ba" as a fragment of a CSS property, it shows a list of completions, including background, background-attachment, and a few others. In this example, background-color is selected. The second time that omni-completion is triggered, no fragment of text is provided, but Vim can tell from the context that a color is expected, so it offers three suggestions: #, rgb(, and transparent.

The relatively static nature of CSS makes it well suited to omni-completion, but if you try out the feature with a programming language, your mileage may vary. If you're unsatisfied with the support for a particular language, shop around for an alternative plugin or write your own. To figure out how to write omni-completion plugins, start with :h complete-functions ⓘ.

Find and Fix Typos with Vim's Spell Checker

Vim's spell checker makes it easy to find and correct spelling mistakes. In Tip 120, *Spell Check Your Work*, on page 295, we'll find out how to operate the spell checker from Normal mode, and in Tip 123, *Fix Spelling Errors from Insert Mode*, on page 299, we'll learn that it can also be operated from Insert mode.

Vim usually ships with a spell file for the English language only, but it's easy to install others. Also, as we'll see in Tip 121, *Use Alternate Spelling Dictionaries*, on page 297, we can switch between American and British English (beside others). And if a word is incorrectly marked as misspelled, adding it to a spell file is a simple matter, as we'll see in Tip 122, *Add Words to the Spell File*, on page 298.

Tip 120

Spell Check Your Work

With the spell checker enabled, Vim flags words that are not in its spell file. We can quickly jump between spelling mistakes and have Vim suggest corrections.

Take this excerpt of text:

spell_check/yoru-moustache.txt
```
Yoru mum has a moustache.
```

The first word has clearly been misspelled. We can make Vim highlight it as such by enabling the built-in spell checker:

⇒ `:set spell`

The word "Yoru" should now be flagged with the SpellBad syntax highlighting. Typically, that means the word will be underlined with a red dashed line, but how it looks will depend on which color scheme you use.

By default, Vim checks spellings against a dictionary of English words. We'll see how to customize this in Tip 121, *Use Alternate Spelling Dictionaries*, on page 297, but for now we'll make do with the defaults.

Operate Vim's Spell Checker

We can jump backward and forward between flagged words with the `[s` and `]s` commands, respectively (see :h]s ⓘ). With our cursor positioned on a misspelled word, we can ask Vim for a list of suggested corrections by invoking the `z=` command (see :h z= ⓘ). This figure shows two screenshots taken before and after triggering the `z=` command:

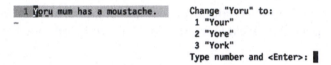

We can replace the misspelled word with "Your" by pressing `1<CR>`. If the list doesn't contain what we're looking for, we can dismiss it by pressing `<Esc>`.

We can skip the prompt altogether by prefixing the `z=` command with a count, which instructs Vim to use the numbered suggestion. If we're confident that the first suggestion will be correct, we can run `1z=` to fix it in one go.

When writing, I prefer to separate the composition and spell-checking processes into separate tasks. I'll often disable the spell checker while I write to avoid being nagged each time I make a mistake. Then I'll make a final pass through the document with the spell checker enabled, fixing the typos it flags.

Here are the essential Normal mode spell checker commands.

Command	Effect
`]s`	Jump to next spelling error
`[s`	Jump to previous spelling error
`z=`	Suggest corrections for current word
`zg`	Add current word to spell file
`zw`	Remove current word from spell file
`zug`	Revert `zg` or `zw` command for current word

We'll meet the `zg`, `zw`, and `zug` commands in Tip 122, *Add Words to the Spell File*, on page 298.

Tip 121

Use Alternate Spelling Dictionaries

Out of the box, Vim's spell checker supports regional variations of English. Find out how to specify the region and how to obtain spelling dictionaries for other languages.

When we enable Vim's spell checker, it compares words against an English dictionary by default. We can change this by tweaking the 'spelllang' option (see :h 'spelllang' ⓘ). This isn't a global setting; 'spelllang' is always local to the buffer. That means it's possible to work simultaneously on two or more documents and use a different spell file for each—handy if you're bilingual.

Specify a Regional Variant of a Language

Vim's spell file supports several regional variations of English. The default spelllang=en setting will permit a word whose spelling is acceptable in any English-speaking region. No matter whether we write "moustache" (using the British spelling) or "mustache" (the American way), Vim's spell checker will let it pass.

We can tell Vim to permit only American spellings:

```
⇒ :set spell
⇒ :set spelllang=en_us
```

With this setting, "moustache" would be flagged as a misspelling, but "mustache" would be permitted. Other supported regions include en_au, en_ca, en_gb, and en_nz. See :h spell-remarks ⓘ for more details.

Obtain Spell Files for Other Languages

Vim ships with a spell file for the English language, but spell files are available for dozens of other languages at this URL: http://ftp.vim.org/vim/runtime/spell/.

If we try to enable a spell file that isn't available on our system, Vim offers to fetch and install it for us:

```
⇒ :set spell
⇒ :set spelllang=fr
‹ Cannot find spell file for "fr" in utf-8
  Do you want me to try downloading it?
  (Y)es, [N]o:
⇒ Y
‹ Downloading fr.utf-8.spl
```

```
In which directory do you want to write the file:
1. /Users/drew/.vim/spell
2. /Applications/MacVim.app/Contents/Resources/vim/runtime/spell
[C]ancel, (1), (2):
```

This functionality is provided by a plugin called spellfile.vim, which ships with Vim (see :h spellfile.vim ⓘ). To make it work, you need to have these two lines in your vimrc (at the very least):

```
set nocompatible
plugin on
```

Tip 122

Add Words to the Spell File

Vim's spelling dictionaries are not comprehensive, but we can augment them by adding words to a spell file.

Sometimes Vim will incorrectly mark something as misspelled because the word doesn't appear in the dictionary. We can teach Vim to recognize words with the `zg` command (:h zg ⓘ), which adds the word under the cursor to a spell file.

Vim also provides a complementary `zw` command, which marks the word under the cursor as a misspelled word. In effect, this command allows us to remove words from the spell file. If we were to trigger the `zg` or `zw` command unintentionally, we could end up adding or removing words from our spell file by accident. Vim provides a dedicated undo command for just such an occasion, `zug`, which reverts the `zg` or `zw` command for the word under the cursor.

Vim records words added to the dictionary in a spell file so that they persist from one session to another. The name of the spell file is derived from the language and file encoding.

For example, if we were working with a UTF-8 encoded file and the spell checker was using an English dictionary, any words added with the `zg` command would be recorded in a file called ~/.vim/spell/en.utf-8.add.

Create a Spell File for Specialist Jargon

With the 'spellfile' option, we can specify the path of the file where Vim tracks words added or removed using the `zg` and `zw` commands (see :h 'spellfile' ⓘ).

Vim allows us to specify more than one spell file simultaneously, which means we can maintain multiple word lists.

This book contains many strings of text that don't count as words in English, including Vim commands (such as `ciw`) and settings (such as 'spelllang'). I don't want Vim to keep flagging these as misspelled, but neither do I want to tell Vim to consider them as valid English words. As a compromise, I maintain a separate word list of Vim terminology. I can load this as a spell file any time that I'm writing about Vim.

When I'm ready to check the spelling in a chapter of this book, I source a file containing these lines of configuration:

```
spell_check/spellfile.vim
setlocal spelllang=en_us
setlocal spellfile=~/.vim/spell/en.utf-8.add
setlocal spellfile+=~/books/practical_vim/jargon.utf-8.add
```

~/.vim/spell/en.utf-8.add is the default path, where Vim saves words added with the `zg` command. The ~/books/practical_vim/jargon.utf-8.add path points to a file within the repository for my book, where I keep a list of Vim terminology.

For each word that the spell checker flags incorrectly, I now have a choice. I could press `2zg` to add it to my list of Vim terminology, or `1zg` to add it to the default word list.

Tip 123

Fix Spelling Errors from Insert Mode

Vim's spelling autocompletion allows us to fix typos without even having to leave Insert mode.

Picture this: we've just typed a line of text, and then we realize that there's a spelling mistake a few words back. What can we do?

Preparation

This technique depends on having the spell checker enabled:

⇨ `:set spell`

The Usual Way: Switch to Normal Mode

To fix the mistake, we could switch to Normal mode, use the `[s` command to jump back to the spelling mistake, and then use `1z=` to fix it. Having made the correction, we could then switch back to Insert mode with the `A` command, continuing where we left off.

The Fast Way: Use Spelling Autocompletion

Alternatively, we could fix the error from Insert mode using the `<C-x>s` command, which triggers a special form of autocompletion (see :h compl-spelling ⓘ). We could just as well use `<C-x><C-s>`, which is slightly easier to type. In this figure, we see screenshots taken before and after triggering the `<C-x>s` command. Note that we're in Insert mode throughout:

```
 1 Yoru mum has a moustache.|

-- INSERT --

 1 Your| mum has a moustache.
~    Your
~    Yore
~    York
```

The autocomplete word list contains the same suggestions as we saw in Tip 120, *Spell Check Your Work*, on page 295, when we used the `z=` command.

When we trigger an autocomplete command, Vim usually offers suggestions on how to complete the word at the current cursor position. But in the case of `<C-x>s`, Vim scans backward from the cursor position, stopping when it finds a misspelled word. It then builds a word list from suggested corrections and presents them in an autocomplete pop-up menu. We can choose a result using any of the techniques described in Tip 113, *Work with the Autocomplete Pop-Up Menu*, on page 283.

The `<C-x>s` command really comes into its own when a line contains more than one misspelled word. Using the same example as in the previous figure, if we were to run :set spelllang=en_us, then the word "moustache" would also be marked as misspelled. Starting off in Insert mode with our cursor at the end of the line, we could fix both mistakes just by typing `<C-x>s` twice. Try it yourself. It's neat!

Now What?

Congratulations—you've reached the end of *Practical Vim*! Now what?

Keep Practicing!

Keep working at it. With practice, things that once seemed tricky will become second nature. Make it your goal to operate Vim without having to think about what you're doing. When you reach that level, you'll be able to edit text at the speed of thought.

Practical Vim doesn't intend to provide a linear reading experience, so you won't have taken everything in on your first pass. Some of the tips are basic, while others speak to the advanced user. I expect that you'll be able to pick up this book again and learn something new.

Make Vim Your Own

We've been working with stock Vim pretty much as it runs out of the box. The factory settings have served as a useful baseline, giving us a common feature set to work with, but I don't mean to suggest that you stick with them. Vim has some unfortunate default settings. If you want to know why something behaves a certain way, the answer often seems to be, "Because that's how vi did it!"

But you don't need to put up with those defaults. You can customize Vim to make it behave the way you want. If you save your preferences in a vimrc file, you can make it so that Vim is always configured in a way that suits your workflow. Appendix 1, *Customize Vim to Suit Your Preferences*, on page 303, provides a basic primer to get you started.

Know the Saw, Then Sharpen It

In Bram Moolenaar's classic essay "Seven Habits of Effective Text Editing," he advises that you invest time *sharpening the saw*.[1] Building your vimrc file is one way to do that, but it's vital that you understand Vim's baseline functionality before you build on top of it. First learn to use the saw. Then sharpen it.

I've seen people customizing Vim in ways that blunt the saw. I've even seen people sharpening the wrong edge! Don't worry; because you've read *Practical Vim*, you're not going to make those same mistakes. You already know Vim's core functionality.

Build your vimrc from scratch. As a starting point, you could use the essential.vim file that's distributed with this book's source code. Many Vim users publish their vimrc files on the Internet, and they can be a great source for inspiration. Copy the parts that solve your problems, but leave behind what you don't need. You should own your vimrc. That means understanding what's in it.

I've resisted the temptation to share the best bits from my vimrc (had I done so, this book would be double the length), but I've dropped hints in the occasional sidebar. You can find my vimrc file on github, along with many of my dotfiles.[2] I've also documented some of my customizations at Vimcasts.org, where I also recommend some of my favorite plugins.[3]

Vim has an unusual license: it's distributed as charityware (:h license ⓘ). That means that you can use it freely, but you are encouraged to make a donation to the ICCF Holland foundation,[4] which helps needy children in Uganda. Please show your thanks to Vim's authors by pledging something toward this worthy cause.

⇒ :x

---

1. http://www.moolenaar.net/habits.html
2. http://github.com/nelstrom/dotfiles
3. http://vimcasts.org/
4. http://iccf-holland.org/

Customize Vim to Suit Your Preferences

The focus of this book is on mastering the core functionality of Vim, but some default settings may not be to your taste. Vim is highly configurable; we can make tweaks to suit our preferences.

Change Vim's Settings on the Fly

Vim has hundreds of options that let us customize its behavior (see :h option-list ⓘ for the full list). We can use the :set command to change them.

Let's take the 'ignorecase' setting as an example (as discussed in Tip 73, *Tune the Case Sensitivity of Search Patterns*, on page 186). This is a boolean option: it can either be on or off. We can enable it by running this:

⇒ `:set ignorecase`

To turn this feature off, we prefix the name of the setting with the word "no":

⇒ `:set noignorecase`

If we append a trailing bang symbol after a boolean option, we can toggle the setting:

⇒ `:set ignorecase!`

If we append a trailing question mark, we can find out what the option is currently set to:

⇒ `:set ignorecase?`
‹ `ignorecase`

We can also append a trailing & symbol to reset any option to its default value:

⇒ `:set ignorecase&`
⇒ `:set ignorecase?`
‹ `noignorecase`

Some of Vim's settings expect a value either as a string or as a number. For example, the 'tabstop' setting specifies the number of columns that a tab character should represent (:h 'tabstop' ⓘ). We can set the value like this:

⇒ `:set tabstop=2`

We can make multiple assignments with a single set statement:

⇒ `:set ts=2 sts=2 sw=2 et`

The 'softtabstop', 'shiftwidth', and 'expandtab' settings also influence Vim's treatment of indentation. To find out more, watch the Vimcasts episode about tabs and spaces.[1]

Most of Vim's options also have a shorthand version. The 'ignorecase' setting can be abbreviated to ic, so we could toggle this feature by running :se ic! or disable it with :se noic. I tend to use shorthand option names for convenience when customizing Vim on the fly, but I prefer to use the longhand names in my vimrc for the sake of readability.

Vim's settings usually apply globally, but some options are scoped to a window or buffer. For example, when we run :setlocal tabstop=4, it applies to the active buffer only. That means we can open several different files and customize the 'tabstop' setting for each one individually. If we wanted to apply the same value to all existing buffers, we could run the following:

⇒ `:bufdo setlocal tabstop=4`

The 'number' option can be configured on a per window basis. When we run :setlocal number, it enables line numbering for the active window. If we wanted to enable line numbering for every window, we could run this:

⇒ `:windo setlocal number`

The :setlocal command scopes the change to the current window or buffer (unless the option can only be set globally). If we were to run :set number, it would enable line numbering for the current window as well as set a new global default. Existing windows would retain their local settings, but new windows would adopt the new global setting.

Save Your Configuration in a vimrc File

Changing Vim's settings on the fly is all very well, but if you have customizations that you are particularly fond of, wouldn't it be handy if they persisted between editing sessions?

---

1. http://vimcasts.org/e/2

We can save our customizations by writing them to a file. Then we can use the :source {file} command to apply the settings from the specified {file} to our current editing session (:h :source ⓘ). When sourcing a file, Vim executes each line as an Ex command, just as though it had been entered in Command-Line mode.

Suppose that we often work on files indented with two spaces. We could create a file with the appropriate settings and save it to disk:

customizations/two-space-indent.vim

```
" Use two spaces for indentation
set tabstop=2
set softtabstop=2
set shiftwidth=2
set expandtab
```

Whenever we want to apply those settings to the current buffer, we run this command:

⇒ `:source two-space-indent.vim`

When changing settings on the fly, we start by typing a colon to switch to Command-Line mode. The leading colon isn't necessary when saving settings to a file because the :source command assumes that each line of the file is to be executed as an Ex command.

When Vim starts up, it checks for the existence of a file called vimrc. If the file is found, then Vim automatically sources the contents of that file on launch. Using this mechanism, we can save our favorite customizations to the vimrc file, and they will be applied every time we start Vim.

Vim looks for a vimrc in several places (see :h vimrc ⓘ). On Unix systems, Vim expects to find a file called ~/.vimrc. On Windows, the expected filename is $HOME/_vimrc. No matter which system you're running, you can open the file from inside Vim by running this command:

⇒ `:edit $MYVIMRC`

$MYVIMRC is an environment variable in Vim, which expands to the path of the vimrc file. After saving changes to the vimrc file, we can load the new configuration into our Vim session by running this:

⇒ `:source $MYVIMRC`

If the vimrc file is the active buffer, then this can be shortened to :so %.

Apply Customizations to Certain Types of Files

Our preferences may vary from one type of file to another. For example, suppose that we work with a house style that advises two spaces for indentation in Ruby and four-column-wide tabs for JavaScript. We could apply these settings by putting the following lines in our vimrc:

customizations/filetype-indentation.vim
```
if has("autocmd")
  filetype on
  autocmd FileType ruby setlocal ts=2 sts=2 sw=2 et
  autocmd FileType javascript setlocal ts=4 sts=4 sw=4 noet
endif
```

The autocmd declaration tells Vim to listen for an event and to execute the specified commands whenever that event fires (:h :autocmd ⓘ). In this case we're listening for the FileType event, which is triggered when Vim detects the type of the current file.

We can have more than one autocommand listening for the same event. Suppose that we want to use nodelint as the compiler for JavaScript files. We could add this line to the example above:

```
autocmd FileType javascript compiler nodelint
```

Both autocommands would be executed each time the FileType event was triggered on a JavaScript file.

Putting autocommands in the vimrc file works fine if you only have to make one or two customizations for a file type. But if we wanted to apply lots of settings to a particular kind of file, then it starts to look messy. The ftplugin is an alternative mechanism for applying customizations to file types. Instead of declaring our JavaScript preferences in the vimrc using autocommands, we could place them in a file called ~/.vim/after/ftplugin/javascript.vim:

customizations/ftplugin/javascript.vim
```
setlocal ts=4 sts=4 sw=4 noet
compiler nodelint
```

This file is just like a regular vimrc, except that the settings will only be applied to JavaScript files. We could also create a ftplugin/ruby.vim file for Ruby customizations and another for each file type that we work with regularly. For more details, look up :h ftplugin-name ⓘ.

For the ftplugin mechanism to work, we must ensure that both file-type detection and plugins are enabled. Check that this line is present in your vimrc file:

```
filetype plugin on
```

Index

Command Line for the Win!

Learn the joys of tmux for a more productive command line, and build better command line apps yourself.

tmux

Your mouse is slowing you down. The time you spend context switching between your editor and your consoles eats away at your productivity. Take control of your environment with tmux, a terminal multiplexer that you can tailor to your workflow. Learn how to customize, script, and leverage tmux's unique abilities and keep your fingers on your keyboard's home row.

Brian P. Hogan
(88 pages) ISBN: 9781934356968. $16.25
https://pragprog.com/book/bhtmux

Build Awesome Command-Line Applications in Ruby 2

Speak directly to your system. With its simple commands, flags, and parameters, a well-formed command-line application is the quickest way to automate a backup, a build, or a deployment and simplify your life. With this book, you'll learn specific ways to write command-line applications that are easy to use, deploy, and maintain, using a set of clear best practices and the Ruby programming language. This book is designed to make *any* programmer or system administrator more productive in their job. This is updated for Ruby 2.

David Copeland
(224 pages) ISBN: 9781937785758. $30
https://pragprog.com/book/dccar2

Practice Makes Perfect

Want to be better programmer? Practice! And rediscover the joy of pure mathematics to expand your brain.

Exercises for Programmers

When you write software, you need to be at the top of your game. Great programmers practice to keep their skills sharp. Get sharp and stay sharp with more than fifty practice exercises rooted in real-world scenarios. If you're a new programmer, these challenges will help you learn what you need to break into the field, and if you're a seasoned pro, you can use these exercises to learn that hot new language for your next gig.

Brian P. Hogan
(118 pages) ISBN: 9781680501223. $24
https://pragprog.com/book/bhwb

Good Math

Mathematics is beautiful—and it can be fun and exciting as well as practical. *Good Math* is your guide to some of the most intriguing topics from two thousand years of mathematics: from Egyptian fractions to Turing machines; from the real meaning of numbers to proof trees, group symmetry, and mechanical computation. If you've ever wondered what lay beyond the proofs you struggled to complete in high school geometry, or what limits the capabilities of the computer on your desk, this is the book for you.

Mark C. Chu-Carroll
(282 pages) ISBN: 9781937785338. $34
https://pragprog.com/book/mcmath

Seven in Seven

From Web Frameworks to Concurrency Models, see what the rest of the world is doing with this introduction to seven different approaches.

Seven Web Frameworks in Seven Weeks

Whether you need a new tool or just inspiration, *Seven Web Frameworks in Seven Weeks* explores modern options, giving you a taste of each with ideas that will help you create better apps. You'll see frameworks that leverage modern programming languages, employ unique architectures, live client-side instead of server-side, or embrace type systems. You'll see everything from familiar Ruby and JavaScript to the more exotic Erlang, Haskell, and Clojure.

Jack Moffitt, Fred Daoud
(302 pages) ISBN: 9781937785635. $38
https://pragprog.com/book/7web

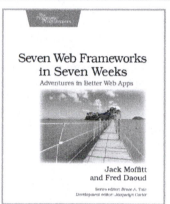

Seven Concurrency Models in Seven Weeks

Your software needs to leverage multiple cores, handle thousands of users and terabytes of data, and continue working in the face of both hardware and software failure. Concurrency and parallelism are the keys, and *Seven Concurrency Models in Seven Weeks* equips you for this new world. See how emerging technologies such as actors and functional programming address issues with traditional threads and locks development. Learn how to exploit the parallelism in your computer's GPU and leverage clusters of machines with MapReduce and Stream Processing. And do it all with the confidence that comes from using tools that help you write crystal clear, high-quality code.

Paul Butcher
(296 pages) ISBN: 9781937785659. $38
https://pragprog.com/book/pb7con

Put the "Fun" in Functional

Elixir puts the "fun" back into functional programming, on top of the robust, battle-tested, industrial-strength environment of Erlang.

Programming Elixir

You want to explore functional programming, but are put off by the academic feel (tell me about monads just one more time). You know you need concurrent applications, but also know these are almost impossible to get right. Meet Elixir, a functional, concurrent language built on the rock-solid Erlang VM. Elixir's pragmatic syntax and built-in support for metaprogramming will make you productive and keep you interested for the long haul. This book is *the* introduction to Elixir for experienced programmers.

Maybe you need something that's closer to Ruby, but with a battle-proven environment that's unrivaled for massive scalability, concurrency, distribution, and fault tolerance. Maybe the time is right for the Next Big Thing. Maybe it's *Elixir*.

Dave Thomas
(340 pages) ISBN: 9781937785581. $36
https://pragprog.com/book/elixir

Metaprogramming Elixir

Write code that writes code with Elixir macros. Macros make metaprogramming possible and define the language itself. In this book, you'll learn how to use macros to extend the language with fast, maintainable code and share functionality in ways you never thought possible. You'll discover how to extend Elixir with your own first-class features, optimize performance, and create domain-specific languages.

Chris McCord
(128 pages) ISBN: 9781680500417. $17
https://pragprog.com/book/cmelixir

Past and Present

To see where we're going, remember how we got here, and learn how to take a healthier approach to programming.

Fire in the Valley

In the 1970s, while their contemporaries were protesting the computer as a tool of dehumanization and oppression, a motley collection of college dropouts, hippies, and electronics fanatics were engaged in something much more subversive. Obsessed with the idea of getting computer power into their own hands, they launched from their garages a hobbyist movement that grew into an industry, and ultimately a social and technological revolution. What they did was invent the personal computer: not just a new device, but a watershed in the relationship between man and machine. This is their story.

Michael Swaine and Paul Freiberger
(424 pages) ISBN: 9781937785765. $34
https://pragprog.com/book/fsfire

The Healthy Programmer

To keep doing what you love, you need to maintain your own systems, not just the ones you write code for. Regular exercise and proper nutrition help you learn, remember, concentrate, and be creative—skills critical to doing your job well. Learn how to change your work habits, master exercises that make working at a computer more comfortable, and develop a plan to keep fit, healthy, and sharp for years to come.

This book is intended only as an informative guide for those wishing to know more about health issues. In no way is this book intended to replace, countermand, or conflict with the advice given to you by your own healthcare provider including Physician, Nurse Practitioner, Physician Assistant, Registered Dietician, and other licensed professionals.

Joe Kutner
(254 pages) ISBN: 9781937785314. $36
https://pragprog.com/book/jkthp

The Pragmatic Bookshelf

The Pragmatic Bookshelf features books written by developers for developers. The titles continue the well-known Pragmatic Programmer style and continue to garner awards and rave reviews. As development gets more and more difficult, the Pragmatic Programmers will be there with more titles and products to help you stay on top of your game.

Visit Us Online

This Book's Home Page
https://pragprog.com/book/dnvim2
Source code from this book, errata, and other resources. Come give us feedback, too!

Register for Updates
https://pragprog.com/updates
Be notified when updates and new books become available.

Join the Community
https://pragprog.com/community
Read our weblogs, join our online discussions, participate in our mailing list, interact with our wiki, and benefit from the experience of other Pragmatic Programmers.

New and Noteworthy
https://pragprog.com/news
Check out the latest pragmatic developments, new titles and other offerings.

Save on the eBook

Save on the eBook versions of this title. Owning the paper version of this book entitles you to purchase the electronic versions at a terrific discount.

PDFs are great for carrying around on your laptop—they are hyperlinked, have color, and are fully searchable. Most titles are also available for the iPhone and iPod touch, Amazon Kindle, and other popular e-book readers.

Buy now at *https://pragprog.com/coupon*

Contact Us

Online Orders:	*https://pragprog.com/catalog*
Customer Service:	*support@pragprog.com*
International Rights:	*translations@pragprog.com*
Academic Use:	*academic@pragprog.com*
Write for Us:	*http://write-for-us.pragprog.com*
Or Call:	+1 800-699-7764

CPSIA information can be obtained at www.ICGtesting.com
Printed in the USA
BVOW07s0053151215

430254BV00002B/13/P

9 781680 501278